The Amazing Civil War

A Fascinating
Collection of
Little-Known Facts
of the Four-Year
Conflict that
Changed America

WEBB GARRISON

MJF Books
New York

Published by MJF Books
Fine Communications
Two Lincoln Square
60 West 66th Street
New York, NY 10023

The Amazing Civil War
Library of Congress Catalog Card Number 98-67587
ISBN 1-56731-304-3

Copyright © 1998 by Webb Garrison

This edition published by arrangement with Rutledge Hill Press.

Manufactured in the United States of America on acid-free paper

MJF Books and the MJF colophon are trademarks of Fine Creative Media, Inc.

10   9   8   7   6   5   4   3

Contents

Introduction

CARL SANDBURG'S monumental six-volume biography of Abraham Lincoln, published in 1939, still holds the record as the all-time most popular work about the wartime president. Sandburg's home in Flat Rock, North Carolina, now a national historic site, is only fifty miles from my home in Haywood County. It would be nice to say that the author of "Chicago" has been a lifelong inspiration to me, but that isn't the case. The reference to Sandburg here is pertinent because of the research methods he used.

Sandburg's *Lincoln*, which brought him a Pulitzer Prize in history, came together after years of hard work. An omnivorous reader, the native of Galesburg, Illinois, habitually stored information he found relevant and interesting, then retrieved it while working on his manuscript. Because he died in 1967, he used processes that today seem quaint. In fact, they are reminiscent of the time-gobbling techniques used during the production of the mammoth 127-volume *Official Records* of the Civil War, which some authorities estimate required more than a million hours of work.

Sandburg spent his last twenty-five years in the tranquil hills that abut the Great Smoky Mountains and transcribed most of his notes with pen and pencil. Some were done by typewriter. The rest were newspaper clippings. When some nugget of information caught his eye, another hand-copied text or an inch or two of newsprint went into a labeled cigar box. Long before his productive years ended, the poet had thousands of cigar boxes on his shelves containing items concerning the life and career of the president known as the Great Emancipator as well as other subjects that interested Sandburg.

This great bank of information took up hundreds of cubic feet. To retrieve any information Sandburg had to find the appropriate cigar box and riffle through its contents. The thousands of hours required to produce the six-volume study of Lincoln is anybody's guess. The total would be prodigious to say the least. Today's easy access to the most basic computer and its storage capacity would likely baffle Sandburg.

A few short years ago my interest in the Civil War came to focus on people and subjects other than the usual campaigns, battles, strategies, troop movements, and logistics. Only recently did I realize that I had accumulated a bank of data that is truly "different." Perusing just the first letter of the alphabet reveals subject headings like Abandoned, Acoustic Shadow, Adoption, Age, Alcohol, Amputation, Artillery, and Atrocity. I have chosen to treat just a few of these subject categories in the following pages. Each entry is annotated, and the source is easily found in the notes section at the back of the book.

To avoid confusion, unless otherwise designated, all military units cited are infantry regiments made up of volunteers. General officers on both sides are identified with the generic rank of general without designating whether brigade or divisional command is involved. In the case of well-known officers, such as Lee and Grant, the title may be omitted.

Special appreciation is due to Larry Stone of Rutledge Hill Press. His interest, understanding, and encouragement have paved the way for *The Amazing Civil War* to see the light of day.

Part 1

This Cruel War

A soldier of the Army of the Potomac, labeled a coward, is drummed from his regiment.

1

NEVER FLOGGED, NEVER TAUGHT

WHIPPED WITH WIRE

Scores of maxims stress the value, inevitability, and nature of punishment. In the military, punishment was usually meted out with a whip. From the "Never flogged, never taught" of classical Greece to Lord Byron's "Two dozen, and let you off easy," the whip runs through this mass of sayings. There is no evidence that any Civil War officer in the North or in the South had a culprit whipped with wire, but that is because no wire was available or no officer happened to think of it in the heat of the moment.

Flogging had been officially abolished in both the American army and navy before the Civil War. During the prewar years Capt. Charles Wilkes, later to play a role in the *Trent* Affair that almost brought about a simultaneous war with Britain during the Civil War, was publicly reprimanded for illegally punishing a seaman. Similarly, Capt. David G. Farragut, who won lasting fame during the war, was briefly the focus of national attention when a gagged seaman under his command died while being punished. To reinforce the ban on flogging, both the Federal and the Rebel Congresses passed special acts in August 1861 and April 1862, respectively, by which officers were forbidden to have soldiers disciplined with a whip.[1]

Since use of the whip by military men and the cat o'-nine-tails by naval officers was a long-established and deeply entrenched custom, the new and relatively humane standard was often ignored. According to the *Milwaukie* [sic.] *Wisconsin* newspaper of October 30, 1861, Pvt. James Cahel was tied to a gun at Charleston Harbor and received "one hundred and twenty-five lashes, well laid on." Capt. R. Barnwell Rhett Jr., son of the editor of the *Charleston Mercury,* was named as the officer who dictated this punishment.

Lt. Walter A. Montgomery of the Twelfth North Carolina was of the opinion that Gen. Richard Ewell "lost his head" at Spotsylvania, for there the Confederate officer personally flayed some of his men. No whip being at hand, he stripped the skin from their bare backs with his sword.[2]

On December 9, 1863, Federal Lt. Col. Augustus W. Benedict also lost his composure. Two men of his all-black Fourth Regiment of the Corps d'Afrique were caught trying to slip out of camp without permission. To show his men that such conduct would not be condoned, Benedict personally whipped the culprits with many of their comrades watching. Anger was so widespread that a full-fledged mutiny broke out that evening, and Benedict had to hide to save his life. After a court-martial hearing, he was forced to return to civilian life.[3]

Jacob Parrott, a member of the Thirty-third Ohio, was among the volunteers who followed James J. Andrews in the famous but failed 1862 raid upon the Western and Atlantic Railroad in Georgia. Captured in civilian clothes and hence treated as a spy, Parrot was given at least a hundred lashes while in jail. After being exchanged on March 17, 1863, the soldier whose back looked like that of a slave frequently depicted in abolitionist literature became one of the first men to receive the Medal of Honor.[4]

Confined to Richmond's Libby Prison, Capt. J. W. Chamberlain of the 123d Ohio was among those who heard a dreadful beating. During the night of July 24, 1863, he wrote: "Those of us on the second floor were aroused by the cries for mercy of a poor darky being whipped. As we afterward learned, a barrel was laid on the floor, [the black soldier] was stretched over it, and received on his bare back two hundred and fifty lashes by actual count . . . for attempting to escape." Although this account is by an officer who kept a meticulous diary, his report is suspect, as it is unlikely that any man could survive 250 lashes with a bullwhip.[5]

If humiliation rather than agony is the measure, the all-time record for getting a Civil War flogging probably belongs to Confederate congressman George G. Vest of Mississippi. He's the only man who reportedly was on the receiving end of punishment in which a woman wielded the whip.[6]

Work details were the most commonly inflicted punishment among those who fought during 1861–65. "Pick-and-shovel squadrons," such as those used by Sherman's subordinates during the March to the Sea, often worked under the supervision of armed guards. It was little if any more arduous to dig ditches or grub stumps than to go about ordinary drills and exercises, but such work hurt a fellow's pride and that was often punishment enough.[7]

Standing at attention on top of a barrel or riding some form of improvised "horse" or "mule" was equally humiliating and much more painful than digging trenches under guard. Yet the Federal deserter who was captured at Stoneham, Massachusetts, in January 1863 and forced to "ride a rail" for hours was lucky; many deserters were shot.[8]

Lt. George B. Peck of the Second Rhode Island became angry with a man who claimed to be too ill to stand guard but refused to attend sick call. After discussing the matter with a fellow officer, Peck ordered the offender to serve mounted punishment. He wrote: "The day was extremely severe. The 'horse's' back was higher than the top of the fence, so the poor unfortunate had the full benefit of a piercing northwest wind, rushing down the valley of Mill river, with fearful impetuosity. No stirrups were provided; the comforts of his situation may be imagined." The man was sentenced to "ride the horse" from 9 A.M. to 12 P.M. and from 2 to 5 P.M. each day "until he preferred other occupation." After twenty minutes the private begged to be taken down and next morning attended sick call.[9]

At the Federal guardhouse in Vicksburg, Mississippi, some offenders were made to "ride the sawbuck"—a plank about six inches wide. N. B. Stanfield of the First Kentucky Cavalry was just one of many prisoners at Camp Douglas in Chicago who had to sit astride a named "animal." Of the experience he later wrote, "They put those of us who had tried to escape to ourselves, and built a plank fence [inside of which was] a horse made of joists, with legs twelve feet high, which they called 'Morgan's horse.'" Men who were being punished had to sit on Morgan's horse for hours at a time in extreme cold.[10] The ankles of these "riders" were often bound, making it impossible for them to become more comfortable by stretching their legs. In many instances, a crudely lettered placard hung about a culprit's neck, naming him as a "THIEF," "COWARD," or other offender.[11]

At a Vicksburg, Mississippi, guard-house, Federals of the occupation force made wrongdoers "ride the sawbuck."

PICTORIAL HISTORY

Confinement of some sort, for short or long duration, was probably second in frequency to enforced labor. Some offenders who received court-martial sentences were sent to such prisons as the Dry Tortugas off the coast of Florida or the Federal "Rip-Raps" near Norfolk. Guardhouses, "camp jails," and brigs of ships were used much more frequently, however. Many men sent to these improvised prisons were given only bread and water; some spent weeks or even months in solitary confinement.

A harsh variant of imprisonment was confinement to a cage or a sweatbox. In the former, prisoners were in open view of their comrades and were subjected to constant taunts and jeers. The name of the latter stemmed from the use of a coffin as a miniature cell placed where an "inmate" could smell the food he could not get. Thrown inside it and pondering the possibility of execution, an offender often sweated so profusely that his condition became life-threatening.[12]

Four common forms of punishment forced an offender to remain immobile, sometimes for hours and occasionally for days. Although dreadfully uncomfortable, the least lethal were improvised stocks. Thomas Owens, a member of Joseph E. Johnston's forces that defended Georgia from Federals under Sherman, preserved an account from his experiences near Dalton, Georgia. He wrote: "Two posts were erected and planks fastened in mortises

Spread-eagled on a caisson wheel.

JOSH BILLINGS—HARDTACK AND COFFEE

from one to the other, one above the other, and at the joint a large hole cut for the neck and then smaller holes for the arms. The top plank would be raised and then let down, making a close yoke for the neck and arms; and the poor fellow would have to stand in this position for hours at a time."[13] The punishment of being tied to a tree for as short a time as an hour or as long a period as three days was less painful but equally humiliating.[14]

The editors of the *Richmond Examiner* revealed their horror at a far more dangerous kind of immobility on January 22, 1862. "Thumb torture" was described as being worse than the cat-o'-nine-tails: "The mode of punishment is to hang the soldier by straps on the thumb, so that his toes may scarcely touch the ground, and the weight of his body depend from the strained ligaments." A man undergoing this form of punishment was likely to begin screaming in less than an hour. His cries often led some of his comrades to risk harsh discipline by cutting him loose.[15]

A man's weight was a major factor in yet another form of immobility known as "the spread-eagle." Because he kicked an artillery horse at Fredericksburg, a soldier's upper arms were lashed to an upright wheel, where he remained for hours. At that, he was very lucky. Many a fellow subjected to this punishment had both his arms and his legs tied. The wheel typically used was a spare carried at the rear of a caisson, which was often driven over rough ground with the culprit moaning or crying. Aboard ship, rigging was widely substituted for the wheel used on land.[16] When no spare wheel was available, some officers forced culprits to stretch themselves out on the bare ground. With arms and legs firmly staked, a fellow was barely able to move his torso an inch or two in any direction. At Baton Rouge, Louisiana, on August 7, 1863, Lt. Col. Augustus Benedict directed that two of his men who had picked roasting ears from a cornfield should be spread-eagled in this fashion. Then their commander sent to the commissary for molasses, which was smeared on the faces, hands, and feet of the prisoners. On the second day of this punishment, numerous men of the regiment staged a mutiny that brought release of the culprits.[17]

Some men who had seen others spread-eagled and had firsthand memories of being "bucked and gagged" said that the latter punishment may have been the more severe. A man disciplined in this fashion was likely to have his hands and feet tied pretzel-like over a horizontal rod at a height permitting his toes barely to touch ground. His mouth was stuffed with rags to keep him quiet. During the Second Bull Run campaign, Confederate Gen. Charles S. Winder once had thirty men bucked and gagged as punishment for having "straggled on the march."

Both at sea and on land an offender could be put into leg irons. After having had a spar, stick, or musket thrust between his elbow and knee joints to prevent movement, the man was likely to have a stick pushed between his teeth and tied behind his head. Trussed in this fashion, he was "as secure as a trapped rat." At Memphis a Federal artilleryman who endured four hours of this punishment broke down and sobbed. When released, he could not walk, so his comrades carried him to his quarters.[18]

Although generally considered to be relatively low in pain, branding placed a permanent mark upon a man's body. Many a deserter had a red-hot iron applied to his thigh or back, which made him wear his D for the rest of his life. Compared with execution—the prescribed punishment for this offense—the man who was branded got off extremely lightly. Many a regimental blacksmith not only forged a D or two but also fashioned a T for theft and a C for cowardice. Some kept an iron W on hand for use upon fellows whom an officer considered to be worthless.[19]

Some considered being bucked and gagged as one of the severest punishments.

JOSH BILLINGS, HARDTACK ANC COFFEE

Humiliation with little or no physical pain was usually prescribed for minor offenses but was sometimes meted out to men with good records who committed serious one-time offenses. In both Federal and Confederate forces, many a private had half of his head shaved and was ordered back into the ranks to be derided by his comrades.[20]

When a thief was caught, he was likely forced to parade before his assembled regiment and carry the stolen article or a replica of it. One Confederate picket had fired at a slight rustle in some bushes and killed a dog. His commander made him march at the double quick around the entire camp while carrying the slain canine. Fellows who took one drink of beer too many were forced to strip and then climb inside a barrel for a stay of hours or days. This mild punishment was imposed so frequently that any ordinary barrel came to be called "a wooden overcoat."[21]

In at least one instance, a general who earlier had murdered another general became enraged when some of his men took dresses from the homes of enemy civilians. Humiliation was punishment enough, Jefferson C. Davis told his provost marshal. Thus the culprits were tied behind wagons after being forced to don their stolen finery and wear placards reading "STOLEN" that hung from their backs.[22]

After receiving a dishonorable discharge, a soldier would be "drummed out of camp." This ceremony required the culprit, stripped of his buttons and insignia, to march slowly from an assembled regiment or brigade escorted by former comrades in front and behind, carrying their arms reversed, as drummers tapped "The Rogue's March."[23]

Some sentences were so light they can only be called ridiculous. At Chattanooga, Gen. William S. Rosecrans humiliated a body of fifty men whom he judged to have surrendered too easily. After having been exchanged, each was forced to parade through the streets wearing a nightcap.[24]

If the sentence imposed by Rosecrans was laughable, that meted out to an early black Federal recruit was unbelievably harsh. Hilton Head, South Carolina, was the site of the first grand experiment with black soldiers by the U.S. government. Volunteers were recruited for pioneer black units with the promise that they would be treated and paid like white soldiers.

Sgt. William Walker of the Third South Carolina became a crusader when he discovered that he and his comrades were to receive only seven dollars per month in cash and a clothing allowance of three dollars per month. White soldiers were getting thirteen dollars a month in cash.

Walker was so angry over the inequities in pay that he was accused of using threatening language when addressing an officer. Since that was not a minor offense, a court-martial was convened and he went on trial for mutiny.

When he was convicted, he was reduced in rank to private and sent to Jacksonville, Florida, "to be shot to death with musketry." On February 29, 1864, Walker paid with his life for the offense of crusading for equality of pay among men fighting to preserve the Union. This sorry episode is not reported in the *Official Records*.[25]

No commissioned officer could be punished until after having been found guilty by a court-martial. Yet all of the punishments described above could be meted out to any private by any officer who cared to serve as prosecutor, judge, and jury.

2

CITIES UNDER THE GUN

CIVILIAN SURRENDERS

At his headquarters seven miles from the center of Atlanta, Gen. Henry W. Slocum was startled by a series of violent explosions during the evening of September 1, 1864, and had no idea what had happened within the besieged railroad center. Before daylight on the following morning, he dispatched Capt. Henry M. Scott and a small body of cavalry into the suburbs to investigate. Scott reported to his immediate superior, Gen. W. T. Ward: "Soon after passing through the works formerly occupied by our army a body of men was observed coming out of the city. Advancing rapidly toward them, I discovered that they were citizens bearing a flag of truce. Going forward, I asked them what proposition they had to make. One of them then made himself known as the mayor, and said he had come to surrender the city."[1]

The explosions, Mayor James Calhoun explained, were caused by the destruction of a trainload of munitions—twenty-eight cars in all—that had been fired by Confederate Gen. John Bell Hood's engineers as the Rebels were abandoning Atlanta. Because he was then about twenty miles south of the city, Union Gen. William T. Sherman, the architect of this Federal incursion into Georgia, knew nothing of the pullout by the Southern army he had pushed southward from Chattanooga during weeks of hard fighting.

Calhoun hastily wrote a note to the Federal commander, saying, "The fortunes of war have placed the city of Atlanta in your hands, and as Mayor of the city, I ask protection to non-combatants and private property." Scott, Capt. A. W. Tibbetts, and Lt. J. P. Thompson signed the document to attest to the authenticity of the surrender that involved an estimated twenty-five thousand residents and refugees.[2]

Although Gen. William T. Sherman is credited with the capture of Atlanta, it was Gen. Henry W. Slocum (right) who accepted the city's surrender from Mayor James Calhoun.

RICHARDSON ENGRAVING

Atlantans, including the horde of refugees who had crowded into the city in recent weeks, breathed easier when they learned of Calhoun's actions. Life under Yankee occupation would be better, they assured one another, than enduring the siege that had pounded the city mercilessly for the past forty-two days. Soon after Sherman arrived and chose a handsome residence as his head-quarters, Calhoun was informed that his request for protection of noncombatants would not be honored.

In Washington Gen. Henry W. Halleck received an outline of Sherman's plans just two days after the civilians surrendered the city. "I propose to remove all the inhabitants of Atlanta," wrote Sherman. "If the people raise a howl against my barbarity and cruelty, I will answer that war is war and not popularity seeking." To justify his actions to critics in the North, Sherman told newspaper correspondents that the deportation was necessary to transform Atlanta into a permanent Federal camp. Calhoun reluctantly told the residents that all of them must leave, and the forcible expulsion was soon completed.[3]

In Washington, Gen. Henry W. Halleck raised no objections to the forcible evacuation of captured Atlanta.

U.S. ARMY MILITARY HISTORY INSTITUTE

Collectively, civilian surrenders during the war involved eight or ten times as many persons as the April 15, 1865, capitulation of the Army of Northern Virginia at Appomattox. According to the *Boston Journal,* this series of dramatic events was probably launched at Biloxi, Mississippi, on the last day of 1861. Federal naval vessels left Ship Island around 7 A.M. Accompanied by Stephen A. Ryder, Comdr. Melancton Smith of the USS *Massachusetts* was the first officer to come ashore at Biloxi. Accosting two or three men near the lighthouse, Smith demanded to see the mayor.

A shotgun-toting band of around twenty-five citizens had as their leader an unidentified fellow "armed with a double-barreled gun, an old cavalry sword, and a silver-mounted Colt's revolver." While this group milled about, "some of the citizens went off in quest of the chief magistrate."

Soon the mayor of Biloxi, whose name was not recorded, pushed his way toward Smith and deposited his shotgun at the head of the pier. The Yankee officer demanded "the surrender of the town, with all the fortifications, battery, and vessels in the waters, and all military and warlike stores." Taken aback, the mayor, described as "an old man about sixty," requested but did not receive an armistice of twenty-four hours. Smith threatened, rather casually, that if naval guns should "open fire on the town, there would be great destruction of property and life," but the Federals wished to avoid this.

Having been told he had one hour to consult his constituents, the mayor hurried off. Returning with "Judge Holey, Dr. Framer and several [other] citizens," the mayor reportedly said to Smith, "Sir, I surrender you the town of Biloxi and the battery, owing to the utter impossibility of defending it." Smith responded that his chief goal in Biloxi was "to make good Union men of its citizens in spite of themselves." Snorting, the mayor muttered, "Old Abe Lincoln will never make a Union man of me; I'll pack myself and wife in a buggy and be off to New Orleans."

This exchange seems to have put an end to "surrender ceremonies for the town of Biloxi in the State of Mississippi." Prowling about the Rebel center, a Northern newspaper correspondent found many residents "to be in a very destitute condition, some wanting shoes, some clothing, and others bread."[4]

Ordered to Fredericksburg, Virginia, on April 16, 1862, Gen. Christopher C. Augur was given no further specific instructions. His chief mission, he was told, was to preserve three bridges leading into the city. To the surprise of the Federal commander, his substantial force met no resistance. Instead, on April 21 "the city council waited upon him, stating that the Confederate forces had evacuated"; hence there would be no resistance to the town's occupation by "the National troops." Although Fredericksburg is close to Richmond, in the Rebel capital on April 23 Robert E. Lee knew nothing of what seems to have been one of the most spineless surrenders in history.[5]

New Orleans was defended by two stout forts—Fort Jackson and Fort Saint Philip—on a narrow neck of land that projected into the Gulf of Mexico. Additional defensive works were erected at Quarantine Station and the Chalmette batteries closer to the city, and a small Confederate fleet lay in the harbor. Nevertheless, the Yankee assailants who undertook the task of capturing the Crescent City were more powerful, and after several days' bombarding the forts, a Federal fleet of seventeen vessels under David G. Farragut raced past Jackson and Saint Philip shortly after midnight on April 23. Less than two hours later, the Union flotilla was anchored at New Orleans and was master of the harbor.

Correctly believing that Federal forces now had nothing more to do than conduct a mop-up action against the outlying forts, Farragut ordered Capt. Theodorus Bailey of the USS *Cayuga* ashore to demand the surrender of the city. About noon on April 24, Bailey, accompanied by Lt. George H. Perkins, was conveyed ashore under a flag of truce.

Perkins preserved a vivid description of their reception by a mob of angry civilians. Many carried small Rebel flags, which they waved vigorously while shouting enthusiastically, "Three cheers for Jeff Davis and [P. G. T.] Beauregard and three groans for Lincoln." When their anger turned to rage, they began to threaten Bailey and Perkins directly and chanted, "Hang them! Hang them!" as the two naval officers maneuvered through the crowd toward the city hall.

At their destination Bailey and Perkins found Mayor John T. Monroe standing before a defiant city council, and he was flanked by Gen. Mansfield Lovell, commander of an estimated fifteen thousand Confederates. Monroe shook his head vigorously when the surrender demand was presented and referred the fate of the city to Lovell. After saying he would not defend the 168,000 residents of New Orleans because he did not want to see the city and its inhabitants shelled, Lovell suddenly claimed that he had no authority inside the corporate limits. In one of the strangest gestures of the war, he returned the city to Monroe's authority. Outside, the crowd of armed civilians was growing larger and more unruly. The Federal officers exited the building through a back door and returned to the pier where their small boat was waiting.

Meanwhile, after being pounded mercilessly by a fleet of nineteen mortar ships under David Dixon Porter, the two Confederate forts surrendered on Sunday, April 28, 1862. A few hours later Farragut sent a strongly worded letter to Monroe and demanded "the unqualified surrender of the city." When the mayor responded defiantly, Farragut vowed to shell the city once women and children were removed and "the fire of this fleet" could be directed against New Orleans rather than military targets.

The next day Farragut sent Lt. Col. John Broome and a body of U.S. Marines ashore. When they landed, Monroe meekly yielded to them but refused to take part in a formal surrender ceremony that he branded as "idle and unmeaning." He had already acknowledged to Farragut that "by the power of brute force and not by any choice or consent of its inhabitants, the city is yours." Five days later Gen. Benjamin F. Butler arrived at the head of a Federal force and established martial law. Within days, Butler's orders and actions led the citizens of New Orleans to nickname him "Beast."[6]

Few civilian officials matched Monroe's willingness to defy Federal authority. A strong Union force under Gen. John E. Wool marched against Norfolk on Saturday, May 10, 1862. The importance of the expedition is indicated by the fact that Wool was accompanied by Salmon P. Chase, secretary of the treasury. According to the *New York Times,* about two miles from their destination Wool and Chase were met by a flag of truce whose bearer said that his mission was "to treat for the surrender of the city." The newspaper reported:

> Mayor William W. Lamb said that he had come to surrender the city into the hands of the United States, and to ask protection for the persons and property of the citizens. . . .
>   A general conversation then took place between the officials on each side, in which their sentiments and opinions were freely exchanged. The party then broke up to go to the City Hall for the formal inauguration of the new military authorities. The Mayor invited Gen. Wood and Secretary Chase to ride with him in his carriage, and they proceeded together, followed by the General's body-guard and the troops.[7]

Norfolk was the home of the Gosport Navy Yard, the largest installation of its kind in the South. Lamb's surrender represented a military loss to the Confederacy that was more serious than that occasioned by any but the very largest battles.

At Natchez, Mississippi, a May 17 report to Confederate Gen. Thomas Jordan informed him that a small force within the city had realized that, after five days, they faced overwhelming odds in defending the city. As a result, wrote the group's leader, "I notified the city authorities of my inability, and turned the control of the city over to them." A formal demand for the surrender of Natchez was delivered to the mayor and the council on May 13. When they

J. C. BUTTRE ENGRAVING

Gen. John E. Wool commanded men in blue who drove the enemy from Norfolk and its all-important naval base.

yielded, Gen. C. G. Dahlgren and his men withdrew into the countryside and ordered that all cotton within ten miles of the city should be burned.[8]

Less than a month later, flotillas of naval vessels clashed in the Mississippi River not far from Memphis. After a two-hour fight, Flag Officer C. H. Davis dispatched a memorandum from the USS *Benton* to the mayor of Memphis, demanding the surrender of the city "to the authority of the United States." Mayor John Park lost no time in responding. Before night Davis was informed that "as the civil authorities have no means of defense, by the force of circumstances the city is in your hands." Copies of the "correspondence" between Davis and Park were sent to Secretary of the Navy Gideon Welles in Washington.[9]

With the war eighteen months old, Fredericksburg, Virginia, was the last important city to be surrendered during 1862. Three weeks before the December 11–15 battle, Gen. Edwin V. Sumner addressed the "Mayor and Common Council of

Norfolk's famous Gosport Navy Yard was abandoned, torched, and fell to secessionists on April 20, 1861, but the base and the city were surrendered to the Federals a little over a year later, on May 10, 1862.

Fredericksburg." His ultimatum informed the civilian officials: "By direction of General Burnside, I demand the surrender of the city into my hands . . . at or before 5 o'clock this afternoon. Failing an affirmative reply to this demand by the hour indicated, sixteen hours will be permitted to elapse for the removal from the city of women and children, the sick and wounded and aged, &c., which period having expired, I shall proceed to shell the town."

Distraught at the prospect of a bombardment, Mayor M. Slaughter protested that the lack of any rail transportation made the evacuation impossible. That evening Sumner canceled his deadline and told Slaughter that "a committee or representative from your town" must meet with Gen. Marsena Patrick before 9 A.M. on November 22 to finalize the surrender terms.[10]

Two days before the mayor of Atlanta surrendered, the nearby railroad town of Jonesboro had been the scene of heavy fighting. When it became apparent that William T. Sherman's troops would score yet another victory, Capt. W. L. Curry of the First Ohio Cavalry was so overjoyed that years later he wrote: "The sound of the guns and scream of the shell was sweet music to the ears of the skirmishers, and they moved forward with a shout, and the bang! bang! of their sharp-ringing carbines swell the chorus as the mayor and a few citizens appeared in the main street with a white flag to surrender the town."[11]

Nearly a year later, with Union leaders confident of ultimate victory, the gunboats *Pawnee, Ottawa, Winona, Wando, Potomska, Sonoma,* and *J. S. Chambers* provided cover for eight thousand troops under Gen. Jacob D. Cox as they advanced on Charleston, the most hated of Confederate cities. Knowing themselves to be outnumbered, Southern soldiers abandoned the ring of forts that was designed to protect the city and set out to join the forces of Robert E. Lee in Virginia. After nearly six hundred days of siege, the city where the war began was stripped of its defensive forces.

Months earlier Jefferson Davis had urged Mayor Charles Macbeth to organize local defense forces that would include all able-bodied civilians. If such defenders were found, they must have evaporated when Cox's Federal troops drew near. The fate of the defenseless port city was in the hands of the civilian leaders and some anxious Federal commanders.

Soon after daylight on February 17, 1865, a naval detachment led by chief scout John L. Gifford ventured out to Fort Sumter and found the installation deserted. Gifford had been back in his boat only a few minutes before he was hailed from Mount Pleasant, a town lying just across the Cooper River from Charleston and close to the fort. Intendant Henry S. Tarr had already secured the signatures of five town wardens to a memorandum stating that Mount Pleasant acknowledged the authority of the United States and asked that "persons and property" should be respected.

Adm. John A. Dahlgren wrote to Adm. David D. Porter that "the navy's occupation [of Charleston] has given this pride of rebeldom to the Union flag." That jubilant message was less than accurate, however. Around 9:00 A.M., Mayor Macbeth formally surrendered the city to Union Gen. Alexander Schimmelfennig.[12]

Gen. Jacob D. Cox, one of
Sherman's subordinates, forced
Mayor Charles Macbeth to
surrender the city of Charleston.

BATTLES AND LEADERS

A few days after Charleston's surrender, a small Union naval squadron reached Georgetown, South Carolina. There, Ens. Allen K. Noyes "led a party ashore and took control, while a small party climbed to the city hall dome and ran up the Stars and Stripes." The formal surrender of the city was made by a document from the pen of intendant R. O. Bush and four of his wardens.[13]

Once Grant and Lee had come to terms at Appomattox, the fall of the Confederate capital was inevitable. Jubilant regiments of men in blue pushed into the burning city after its evacuation by Jefferson Davis and his aides. Delight that Richmond had fallen was overwhelming among Federals, but Mayor Joseph Mayo and his colleagues found it difficult to hold their emotions in check. A few days later Washington ordered the arrest of all city officials who had not signed an oath of allegiance to the United States.

With soldiers of the army of occupation holding dress parades among the ashes of Richmond, Confederates held only a few scattered sites deep inside the Cotton Belt. Early in April, the village of Cahawba, Alabama, was formally surrendered—apparently for the second time—to Gen. James H. Wilson by its "Intendent & Town Council."[14]

The last major city to surrender was Mobile, Alabama. Fearful of dire consequences if he did not act, on April 12 Mayor R. H. Slough led an impromptu ceremony. Flying a white flag and accompanied by several citizens, Slough walked out to meet the enemy. After having surrendered the big port to Gen. Gordon Granger, he reputedly said: "Our city has been evacuated by the military authorities, and the municipal government is now under my control. Your demand [for immediate and unconditional capitulation] has been granted, and I trust, for the sake of humanity, that all the safeguards we can extend to our people may be secured to them."[15]

According to the *New York Tribune,* if a single civilian surrender took place in a Northern city, official records concerning it were nonexistent. "Such unseemly conduct on the part of elected officials was limited to cities inhabited by the enemy," an editorial informed readers.

That writer, however, did not have access to the memoirs of Col. A. K. McClure of Chambersburg, Pennsylvania. According to him, a band of Rebels rode into the town under a white flag in October 1862. After a parley with their leader, McClure and a hastily formed committee of citizens took the only course of action they deemed feasible: "The committee went through the form of a grave but brief consultation, somewhat expedited, perhaps, by the rain, and we then solemnly and formally surrendered the town. . . . So rebel rule began at Chambersburgh."[16]

Both Hagerstown and Frederick, Maryland, fell to Confederates under Jubal Early nearly two years later. In exchange for promises that these prosperous towns would not be destroyed, their respective mayors persuaded their constituents to pay ransoms of twenty thousand dollars and two hundred thousand dollars, respectively.[17]

3

HENRY WILSON

THE STORY BEHIND THE OFFICIAL RECORD

NOT MUCH happened on January 20, 1864, and it was judged a quiet day on all military fronts. The most important military foray of the day was launched from the waters of the Gulf of Mexico. At the mouth of Mobile Bay, scouting parties dispatched from Federal warships assessed the strength of Confederate Forts Gaines and Morgan. Both of these installations would have to be subdued before an assault upon the port of Mobile could be attempted.

In North Carolina Gen. Innis Palmer left his Plymouth head-quarters and launched a nine-day raid against nearby Confederate sites. When he returned to Plymouth, he reported capturing or destroying 150,000 pounds of Rebel supplies.

Hundreds of miles to the west, the only significant Confederate action was staged in Tennessee by about a hundred men of Capt. Joe Carter's cavalry and some other units. Two members of the band of raiders were conspicuously attired; both wore the full uniform of a Federal trooper. Successfully disguised, the pair of riders went to the home of a Union sympathizer, S. P. Tipton, at Altamont and shot him dead. Proceeding to Tracy City, the raiders subdued its defenders and then mortally wounded Capt. Andrew Upson of the Twentieth Connecticut. Upson had thrown down his weapon in surrender before he was shot.[1]

A skirmish at tiny Island No. 76 in the Mississippi River was hardly significant enough to go on record. That verdict was also applied to an action in Richmond, where Nathaniel H. Harris and Clement H. Stevens were made brigadier generals.[2]

In Washington the big news of the day was created when President Lincoln exercised his power to overturn punishments decreed by military tribunals. The executions of James Lane of the

Deserters who took to the fields and woods could expect no mercy unless a relative or friend reached Abraham Lincoln and begged for mercy.

Seventy-first New York, Henry C. Fuller of the 118th New York, John Sedgwick of the Seventy-first Pennsylvania, and Albert A. Lacy of the Fourth Rhode Island were commuted to imprisonment. The execution of Henry Wooding of the Eighth Connecticut was also suspended, but he was given a dishonorable discharge. Full pardons were extended to Charles M. Shelton of the Second Connecticut and Thomas J. Kellinger of the 145th New York. Regarding W. D. Walker of the Third Missouri, a Confederate imprisoned at Point Lookout, Maryland, Lincoln ordered his release contingent on Walker's taking an oath of loyalty.[3]

Except for other lawmakers, most of whom showed little interest in a bill to which they gave perfunctory assent, few persons in the capital or outside it gave even passing notice to a bill drafted by Sen. Henry Wilson of Massachusetts. With most of their attention focused on distant battlefields, none of Wilson's colleagues objected that day to a joint resolution that called for "the collection and subsequent publication of military reports and correspon-

Sen. Henry Wilson was among the most powerful men in Washington during the Civil War.

dence." Wilson himself did not then realize that the brief bill he had framed would lead to the most massive publication project in the history of the nation.

Veteran congressional watchers should have realized that anything in which Wilson was involved might some day be newsworthy. Known to many Massachusetts voters as "the Natick cobbler," the man whom the legislature sent to the Senate in 1855 was earlier known to a few as Jeremiah Jones Colbath of New Hampshire.

After having settled in the Bay State, Colbath made shoes and spent his spare time poring over any books he could find. Inspired by one of them, he did not bother with legal technicalities when he decided to change his name to Henry Wilson and throw his hat into the political arena as a Whig.

When Wilson aka Colbath went to Washington as a freshman senator, he quickly attracted attention by his unyielding opposition to slavery. With his seat in the Senate barely warm, he made a passionate speech advocating repeal of the Fugitive Slave Law and proposing the emancipation of slaves in the District of Columbia. Neither of these proposals was enacted at that time, but they made their author—now a Republican—a celebrity in a city filled with celebrities. Soon the New Hampshire native was rewarded by appointment to the prestigious Committee on Military Affairs, of which he served as chairman throughout the Civil War.

Only a few months after reaching the capital, Wilson sharply criticized Congressman Preston S. Brooks of South Carolina for his famous—or rather infamous—attack on Sen. Charles Sumner of Massachusetts on the floor of the U.S. Senate. Brooks responded by challenging Wilson to a duel, an invitation that the former shoemaker wisely declined.

Less than ninety days after having delivered his inaugural address, Lincoln acted in what was later called the "presidential exercise of war powers." Relying upon a flimsy precedent, the president asked for five times as many volunteers as there were regular soldiers in the U.S. Army. Without congressional authorization, he enlarged both the army and the navy and proclaimed a blockade that ignored international law. On April 27, 1861, he suspended the writ of habeas corpus "at any point on or in the vicinity of the military line between the City of Philadelphia and the City of Washington." All of these and other less significant actions were charitably characterized as "extralegal in nature."

When Congress assembled on July 4, 1861, in response to Lincoln's call, Wilson knew that the chief executive might soon face awkward political difficulties for these actions beyond the bounds of the Constitution. Hence on the first day of the special session, the Bay State senator introduced legislation that gave post facto legitimacy to the president's exercise of "war powers." Even in a body dominated by Republicans, this measure troubled many lawmakers, and it was tabled and not scheduled for debate.

One of the last bills to be introduced during the special session was meant to boost the pay of "privates and volunteers in the service of the United States." Even the rawest of first-term lawmakers knew that it would be political suicide to voice any objection to this measure. With the August 7 adjournment date only hours away, Wilson managed to attach to the soldiers' pay bill a rider stipulating that the actions of the sitting president concerning all branches of the Federal armed forces "are hereby approved and in all respects legalized and made valid . . . as if they had been issued and done under the previous express authority and direction of the Congress." With the Wilson rider attached, the measure passed the Senate by a vote of thirty-seven to five and the House of Representatives by a margin of seventy-four to nineteen.

To the astonishment of official Washington, P. G. T. Beauregard led his Confederates to a smashing victory at Bull Run.

TO THE HERO OF SHILOH & CHARLESTON

BEAUREGARD'S CHARLESTON

QUICKSTEP

Only days prior to this legislative victory, Wilson had been among those from Washington who eagerly ventured into the Manassas region to watch the Federal volunteers defeat the Southerners led by P. G. T. Beauregard. When the Northerners were routed at Bull Run, several dignitaries from the Federal capital were captured on the battlefield. Wilson, however, was not among that group. He found a scruffy mule and made his way to safety.

In the years following Wilson wielded the power of his chairmanship. He largely framed the Enrollment Act that was passed on March 3, 1863. The measure was designed to end the chaos and graft in recruiting volunteers and set a precedent for the mobilization of U.S. military manpower for the Spanish-American War, World Wars I and II, Korea, and Vietnam.

Wilson's 1864 measure concerning the collection and publication of military records had no impact until the war's end. In the month after Lee's surrender at Appomattox, Gen. Henry W. Halleck

Atlanta, whose fall helped Lincoln to win a second term in 1864, is the subject of five entire volumes of the *Official Records*.

visited occupied Richmond to gather Confederate documents. Although huge quantities had been burned, Halleck managed to find enough to fill ninety boxes, which he took to Washington to augment War Department records that were piled helter-skelter in a four-story warehouse.

Surprisingly, within seven months of the surrender, thousands of reports, letters, dispatches, and telegrams had been sorted and arranged for publication. When this first large section of what became *The War of the Rebellion: Official Records of the Union and Confederate Armies* (*OR*) was ready for the printer, there was no money available to publish it. During an entire decade in which more and more military documents were processed by clerks, Congress dawdled. By the time an initial appropriation for publication was made, a staff under the direction of Col. E. D. Townsend had processed enough material to fill tens of thousands of printed pages.

On March 4, 1873, Wilson was sworn into office as Ulysses S. Grant's vice president. In that office he used his influence to accelerate the lagging project he had launched a dozen years earlier. With the leadership of the gigantic project turned over to Capt.

Robert N. Scott, forty-seven volumes were set in type by the end of 1877.

Today that accomplishment may not sound impressive, but at the time, barely a generation after hostilities had ceased, it was almost unbelievable. Clerks had deciphered hundreds of styles of handwriting, ranging from formal reports written from luxurious headquarters in splendid copperplate to crudely scrawled battle-field memoranda. Working without the new device beginning to be offered to the business world as "the type-writer," detailed indexes were generated for the forty-seven volumes. In 1880 Congress authorized an edition of ten thousand copies of each existing volume. These began coming from the press five years before the Linotype machine was first put into commercial use in New York.

Pouring from the U.S. Government Printing Office in a steady stream, 127 immense black-bound volumes were created, containing practically all military material from 1861 to 1865 that was then known to exist. Five volumes were devoted to the Atlanta campaign while both Vicksburg and Gettysburg filled three volumes, and an October 2, 1862, skirmish near Columbia, Missouri, merited half a page. In 1901, this project—considered to be finished at the time—climaxed with a 1,248-page general index that was accompanied by an official atlas of the Civil War.

Including the atlas, the *Official Records* runs to just under 140,000 pages that cost taxpayers the staggering total of $2.8 million—equivalent to perhaps forty times that sum in today's dollars. Entire sets were sent free of charge to most public libraries that simply requested it. The fact that a set required twenty-one feet of shelf space meant that many libraries—some of them relatively large—had to decline the free offer.

Many users found it inconvenient that the 127 volumes were divided into four separately numbered series and that numerous numbered volumes were divided into two to five parts. This cumbersome system has been largely overcome by the current practice of citing serial numbers, such as 79, in lieu of Series 1, Vol. 39, part 3. Material originally designed for use in Series 1, Vol. 54, parts 1 and 2, went elsewhere. As a result, serial numbers 112 and 113 were never produced.

The index alone (serial 130) is a monument to years of hard work. In an era when indexes were prepared from handwritten entries on index cards, *OR* 130 was packed with more than 146,000 listings. Most of them are personal and geographical names and listings of military units from each of the thirty-four states that existed when the conflict began and from war-born West Virginia. Each entry in the index refers to the volume or volumes in which references are to be found. The index of a typical nine-hundred-page volume runs to about one hundred pages.

Indexes of individual volumes include thousands of full names of persons whose surnames only appear in the text. By the time the general index was ready, compilers had discovered approximately eighteen hundred errors in volumes whose serial numbers ran from 1 through 129. Indexes of individual volumes refer users to such errors by the use of a plus symbol at the end of an affected entry. Clumsy as this system appears to current users, it was the product of tens of thousands of hours of diligent work.

To some who had worked full time for years on the gargantuan project, it must have seemed that the record was as complete as it could be when serial 130 came off the press in 1901. At least a decade earlier, however, U.S. Navy officials complained that naval activity had been ignored in the compilation of the massive record of the war. In response, Congress authorized publication of *The Official Records of the Union and Confederate Navies in the War of the Rebellion* (*NOR*) on July 31, 1894. Since masses of source material had already been sorted and made ready for printers, the first volume came off the press before the end of the year. It launched a second spree of publication that stretched for more than thirty years, during which thirty thousand printed pages and another comprehensive index were produced.

The final *NOR* volume came off the press in 1917. By that time, researchers had uncovered significant caches of Confederate material not known when the *OR* was completed. Authorization to publish a second series under *NOR* came while Josephus Daniels was serving as secretary of the navy.

During a period of five years, three large volumes of Confederate material were issued, two of which were almost entirely devoted to naval matters. The third volume was 1,336 pages long and filled with such things as proclamations and appointments of Confederate president Jefferson Davis and Confederate State Department correspondence with diplomatic agents. Since the *OR* was completed in 1901, it offers no hint that immense quantities of material dealing with Confederate actions on land are included in NOR. The index volume, last of the series and comparatively small at 458 pages, was issued in 1927.

Together, the *OR* and the *NOR* constitute by far the largest project that the U.S. Government Printing Office had undertaken up to that point. Part of the amazement that every user finds here stems from the fact that when a search is made for information about a given person or place, relevant passages are virtually guaranteed to yield gems of information that were not sought specifically.

Tom Broadfoot of Wilmington, North Carolina, issued from the publishing house that bears his name a modern reprint of the entire *OR* slightly more than a century after the war ended. In the process, he realized that substantial primary materials about actions on land were not known when the massive set was produced. As a result, in 1994 he launched a multivolume *Supplement to the Official Records of the Union and Confederate Armies* (SOR). The diaries, letters, newspaper reports, and other source material offered here add substantially to the government-published set.

Logically, the accumulation and publication of enough supplementary material to fill about 10,000 pages in addition to the existing 170,000 pages issued in Washington should end the saga of the *OR*. That it does not is due to the way in which we have come to consider desktop computers as indispensable as telephones. In recent years at least three publishers set out to make the OR available on compact disk. In addition to accelerating the speed with which searches can be performed, a CD-ROM is not limited to the personal, geographical, and unit names that dominate the indexes of the printed version of the *OR*.

During four years in which Americans fought Americans with ever-increasing fury, their experiences—almost wholly confined to battlefields—generated a publishing program like no other. Using methods and equipment that today seem primitive, hundreds of people put together an estimated one million words that keep every minor clash and major struggle alive for future generations.

4

SOUTHERN YANKEES

TRANSPLANTS BY CHOICE

Robert E. Lee never hesitated when confronted by conflicting loyalties: he threw his lot in with his native Virginia. Numerous less notable figures in both the North and the South regarded their native states as paramount and the federal union as subordinate. Yet many a man whose birth was registered north of the Mason-Dixon Line weighed his alternatives and decided to fight for his adopted rather than his native state.

Confederate Gen. John C. Pemberton of Pennsylvania, whose defense of Vicksburg, Mississippi, ended only by starvation after forty-seven days of siege, was not in a class by himself. Although his story as a transplanted Yankee is dramatic, half a hundred men from a dozen states other than Pennsylvania became Rebel leaders. California, Illinois, Iowa, and the District of Columbia each contributed Confederates of distinction.

California rancher-miner Archibald C. Godwin left his holdings in 1861 to come to Richmond, Virginia, and was named provost marshal of the city. In that capacity he was in charge of several prisons, of which Libby is probably the best known. Godwin was later sent to oversee the prison at Salisbury, North Carolina, but in July 1862 he raised the Fifty-seventh North Carolina and became its colonel. Two years of almost constant fighting followed, with Fredericksburg, Chancellorsville, and Gettysburg prominent on the list of his battles. Godwin was captured soon after Gettysburg and spent months as a prisoner of war. Awarded a general's stars as soon as he was freed, Godwin wore them only a few weeks before he was killed at the battle of Third Winchester. Had a

Federal bullet not dropped the former Californian in battle, Godwin might have gone on trial after the war with Henry Wirz, commandant at Andersonville Prison. Accused of having been unduly harsh toward captives, Godwin was on a list of "suspected war criminals" until Washington learned that he died in action on September 19, 1864.[1]

James Lusk Alcorn was born in Illinois while it was still a territory, and while he was a child his family moved to Kentucky, the state of Lincoln's birth. Like the future president, Alcorn read law and was active in the Whig Party. Soon after Lincoln's single term in Congress, Alcorn tried but failed to win a seat from Mississippi. Although openly opposed to secession, he was sent to the convention at which Mississippi withdrew from the Union. There a majority of delegates voted for a measure that made the newcomer a brigadier general of state militia. He served only a few months before being assimilated into Confederate ranks. After brief field service, Alcorn was captured in Arkansas but never exchanged. In the years following the war he resumed planting cotton and reputedly became wealthy.[2]

Iowa's most notable contribution to the Confederacy was Leonard F. Ross, regionally famous for having killed Comanche chieftain Peta Necona. Drifting into Texas, he joined the Texas Rangers for a time before enlisting in the Sixth Texas Cavalry as a private. It took Ross about a year to become a colonel, but six months later he was wearing stars. At Corinth he led an attack by dismounted cavalry and later took part in an attempt to relieve Vicksburg. As a brigadier, the Iowa native fought through the Atlanta, Franklin, and Nashville campaigns before joining forces led by Nathan Bedford Forrest.[3]

Although Washington, D.C., was essentially a southern city, it was never held by Southern forces. When Mansfield Lovell was born there in 1822, the capital was still a small town whose chief distinction was its deep mud holes. Lovell was the ninth-ranked graduate in the West Point class of 1842 and served in the Mexican War, after which he resigned and settled in New York City. He was a deputy street commissioner there when he resigned to don a gray uniform with two stars on its shoulder straps.

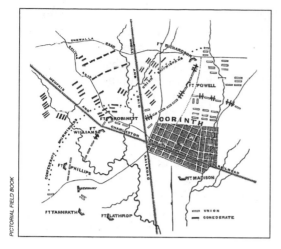

Corinth, Mississippi, was a railroad center of sufficient importance to make it a military prize.

PICTORIAL FIELD BOOK

Outranking Pennsylvanian Johnson K. Duncan, the native of the nation's capital was in command in April 1862 when New Orleans fell to the enemy. Lovell later led a division at Corinth and headed a corps that tried to halt Grant's drive toward Vicksburg. In April 1863 a court of inquiry was convened at his request and absolved him of blame for the loss of New Orleans—but he received no other active assignment. Sent to Joseph E. Johnston's army without a command, he was among those who surrendered to Sherman in North Carolina.[4]

A quartet of Northern states gave nearly a dozen soldiers to the Southern cause. Gov. Oliver Morton of Indiana repeatedly said that the state included thousands of Copperheads, yet only two Hoosiers gained prominence in the ranks of Confederate fighting men. Francis Asbury Shoup of Laurel graduated from West Point in 1855, ranking fifteenth of thirty-four cadets, and was soon en route to Key West as a brevet second lieutenant. After a year at the southernmost post, Shoup was sent to Charleston's Fort Moultrie. Soon after his transfer, the Seminole chieftain Osceola was captured and sent to Moultrie as a prisoner. Stricken with malaria during his time in Florida, Shoup recuperated at home in Indiana then resigned to practice law. Drawn to the South he had come to love, he was admitted to the bar in Saint Augustine, and when the war began he offered his services to the Florida governor.

Shoup became a major of Confederate artillery in October 1861 and within a year was a brigadier general. His guns played a prominent role at Shiloh and at Prairie Grove, but in 1863 he was trapped inside Vicksburg during the long siege. When the river city surrendered, the Rebel from Indiana was paroled and waited to be exchanged. Restored to command he became the chief artillerist for the Army of Tennessee during the Atlanta campaign.[5]

West Pointer William S. Gilham of Indiana was commandant of cadets at the Virginia Military Institute in 1861. Later colonel of the Twenty-first Virginia, he led a brigade at Cheat Mountain. When relieved of brigade command, Gilham returned to VMI as a full-time instructor. The performance of his students in the battle of New Market in May 1864 was among the most memorable incidents of the war.[6]

Danville Leadbetter of Leeds, Maine, ranked third out of forty-nine graduating cadets at West Point in 1836. He left the army in 1852 and became chief engineer for the state of Alabama. When the war began, Leadbetter entered Confederate service as a colonel and won a star without being in combat. Following the collapse of the Confederacy, he escaped to Mexico and later went to Canada.[7]

Zebulon York left Maine for Louisiana and became owner of a half-dozen plantations that were worked by seventeen hundred slaves. He entered Confederate service as a major, but in spite of his wealth, York did not become a brigadier until May 1864. The transplanted Yankee was under fire many times and lost an arm at the battle of Third Winchester. Late in the war he drew an assignment that sent him to North Carolina, where he persuaded a few foreign-born prisoners of war to join Confederate ranks.[8]

New Hampshire did not produce a single Confederate general, but one of her sons has a prominent place in the annals of the war. The town in which J. D. Edwards was born and reared is not known, but at about age thirty he opened a photography shop in New Orleans. He was skilled in the new art, and his battlefield prints were so good that some were pirated by *Harper's Weekly* in the North. After having produced numerous views that no other photographer captured, Edwards dropped out of sight late in 1862. It was speculated that he had run out of supplies and was no longer able to use his camera, and some believe he may have begun a second career as a Confederate spy.[9]

Rhode Island produced three Confederates of great diversity. Only one of them, Lunsford L. Lomax, became a general officer. After leaving West Point in 1856 as twenty-first in his class of forty-nine, he fought Indians in the West until he resigned after Fort Sumter's fall. His leadership of the Eleventh Virginia Cavalry at Gettysburg brought him stars, and he wore them at Culpeper Court House and through the battle of the Wilderness.

In 1864 Lomax became a major general. After the fall of Richmond, he managed to join Gen. Joseph E. Johnston in North Carolina just in time to take part in the surrender. In postwar years, the Rhode Islander was head of what is now Virginia Polytechnic Institute before becoming an early commissioner of Gettysburg National Park.[10]

Richmond postal clerk John McAnerny Jr. came to the Confederate capital from Rhode Island by way of New Orleans. His only military service was as an officer in a local defense unit made up of postal workers. In this role, the native Yankee had an hour of glory. On the evening of March 2, 1864, he helped to set up an ambush that was designed to trap a party of Federal raiders. When the trap was sprung, Union Col. Ulrich Dahlgren was among the dead and papers found on his body proved to be among the most controversial documents of the war. According to Dahlgren's papers, the raid on Richmond had as its goal the kidnapping or assassination of President Jefferson Davis and other prominent Confederate leaders.[11]

Although he was a native of Rhode Island, Lloyd J. Beall received an appointment to West Point from Maryland. After fourteen years in the U.S. Army, he resigned to become a Confederate colonel. Transferred to the fledgling navy one month later, he was named colonel and commandant of the Confederate Marine Corps, which was barely as large as a regiment in size. Nevertheless, Beall's marines won distinction in battles ranging from Virginia to Texas.[12]

New Jersey, Connecticut, Massachusetts, and Ohio produced a total of about a dozen notable Confederates. Julius A. de Lagnel, who grew up near Newark, developed a love for Virginia during fourteen years in the U.S. Army. As a Southern officer, he directed artillery at Rich Mountain before being captured and held prisoner for nearly a year. Made a major after being exchanged, he was offered a two-level jump in rank. De Lagnel's April 15, 1862, decision not to take the promotion made him one of a handful of officers known to have turned down Confederate stars. Soon afterward he was sent to Richmond, where he served for nearly three years as assistant to the chief of the Ordnance Bureau, Josiah Gorgas. De Lagnel eventually accepted a promotion to lieutenant colonel.[13]

Samuel G. French of Gloucester City, New Jersey, was seven places ahead of U. S. Grant when they were both graduated from West Point in 1843. French took off his uniform thirteen years later and became a Mississippi planter. When the war broke out, the Garden State native entered Confederate service as a brigadier general. His superior handling of the rear guard after Second Bull Run brought him a promotion to major general. French was assigned to Joseph E. Johnston's Army of Tennessee in May 1864 and saw the most combat of his career for the next six months in the defense of Atlanta. He led the attacking Confederate force at Allatoona but broke off the fighting prematurely, which generated controversy. French claimed the Northerners were about to be reinforced and also noted that his orders were to demonstrate only against the Federals, not attack. When Johnston was relieved of command, French briefly ascended to temporary corps command, but permanent corps command was given to Benjamin Cheatham. Prior to the Franklin and Nashville campaign, French was given medical leave for an eye infection. When he was able to return to command, he was assigned to the garrison at Mobile and stubbornly defended the Alabama harbor until April 12, 1865, several days after Lee had surrendered at Appomattox. After the war, French resumed planting in Mississippi and wrote a memoir of his adventures.[14]

During a military career that began in 1815, professional soldier Samuel Cooper never engaged in a serious quarrel. Born in Hackensack, after forty-six years in the military he became the highest-ranking Confederate general. He moved from being adjutant general in the U.S. Army to the same position in the Confederate army. His close friendship with Jefferson Davis began when Davis was U.S. secretary of war. Cooper was married to a Virginian and had a home in the Old Dominion. He is rated by many as one of the most valuable general officers of the eleven-state nation to which he gave his latter years. Cooper's meticulous record-keeping is credited with providing the bulk of the Confederate sections of the *Official Record*.[15]

Connecticut owes her claim to Confederate fame to Clement H. Stevens, who with his family left Norwich at age fifteen. When South Carolina seceded, the son of a naval officer was managing the construction of a railroad in the state. That background may have inspired him in 1861 to design an iron-plated battery, the world's first armored fortification, on Morris Island facing Fort Sumter. Entering Confederate service as an aide to Gen. Barnard Bee, he was a brigadier by January 1864. This Rebel from the Nutmeg State wore his stars only six months before being killed at Peachtree Creek in Georgia.[16]

Ohio sent an estimated 360,000 men against the South, yet it produced three Confederate generals and the most infamous of all guerrilla fighters. Bushrod Johnson of Belmont City had George H. Thomas and William T. Sherman as classmates at West Point, where he graduated twenty-third in a class of forty-two in 1840. After seven years in uniform, he turned back to the classroom and taught in Kentucky and Tennessee. Johnson entered the war as a Confederate colonel and won a promotion early in 1862. Wounded at Shiloh, he recovered in time to play a key role at Chickamauga. After his division was assimilated by the Army of Northern Virginia, the Rebel from the Buckeye State was promoted again. Hence he was "the highest-ranking Yankee Quaker to surrender at Appomattox."[17]

Three years behind Johnson at West Point, where he was seventh in a class of thirty-nine, Roswell S. Ripley of Worthington, Ohio, served in the artillery. After marrying a Charleston woman, he resigned from the army and settled in South Carolina. During the bombardment of Fort Sumter, the Ohio native was a militia major in command of thirty guns at Fort Moultrie. He became a brigadier four months after Sumter's surrender.

Quarrelsome and contentious, Ripley joined the Army of Northern Virginia during the spring of 1862. His brigade suffered heavy casualties at Mechanicsville, Malvern Hill, and Gaines's Mill, and he was seriously wounded at Antietam. Gov. Francis Pickens then called him back to South Carolina to command the state's First Artillery District.[18]

The hamlet of McConnelsville, Ohio, saw Otho F. Strahl grow to maturity and pass the bar. He then went south and practiced law in a succession of small Tennessee towns. When the war broke out, without military training or experience, Strahl became captain of the Fourth Tennessee in May 1861 but saw no combat until he and his men fought at Shiloh in April 1862. Made a brigadier more than a year later, he was cited for gallantry in 1863 at Chickamauga. Yet when his men gave way at Missionary Ridge during the battle of Chattanooga, his superiors considered calling a court of inquiry. Strahl redeemed himself during the Atlanta campaign, then returned to Tennessee with John Bell Hood in November 1864. During the furious fighting at Franklin, he was one of six Confederate generals to die on the field there.[19]

Canal Dover, Ohio, has no shrine to the memory of William Clarke Quantrill, aka Quantrell. This Buckeye went west in early manhood and for a time was a schoolteacher barely earning enough to keep body and soul together. He decided gambling might ease his financial troubles, but when that failed, he turned outlaw. Said to have served the Confederacy briefly as a captain, Quantrill became a guerrilla leader in 1862. Some authorities claim that he recruited the James and Younger brothers as "partisan rangers." Ostensibly fighting for secession and the South, Quantrill was notorious in both the North and the South for atrocities that climaxed with the three-hour sacking of Lawrence, Kansas, on August 21, 1863. His men looted and burned the town, killing more than 150 townspeople. When he staged a raid into Kentucky in May 1865, Federal soldiers fatally wounded him, and he died on June 6 in Louisville.[20]

Although home to the seaports from which Yankee ships sailed to Africa and brought tens of thousands of slaves to America, Massachusetts became the center of abolitionist sentiment. Despite this cultural factor, the Bay State produced at least four Confederate general officers and a civilian Rebel of significance. Daniel Ruggles, in the bottom third of his class at West Point in 1833, served in the U.S. Army for eighteen years before

LIBRARY OF CONGRESS

Four of the Younger brothers, later notorious outlaws, were among William Clarke Quantrill's band at the time Lawrence, Kansas, was sacked.

becoming a lieutenant colonel in gray. Like Ripley of Ohio, he had married a southern belle—Richardetta Hooe of Virginia's King George County.[21]

Edward A. Perry of Richmond, Massachusetts, traveled south after a year at Yale College. He moved to Alabama before settling in Pensacola, Florida, and opening a law practice. There Perry became an ardent proponent of states' rights. Elected captain of Company A, Second Florida Infantry, in May 1862, he was made a brigadier just three months later. Unscathed at Seven Pines and during the Seven Days' battles, Perry was badly wounded at White Oak Swamp. He returned to duty in time to see action at Chancellorsville and Gettysburg, but his brigade sustained heavy losses at the later. In the Wilderness he was again badly wounded, and after several months' convalescence he served the remainder of the war in reserve in Alabama. Twenty years after the war he was elected governor of Florida on the Democratic ticket.[22]

Claudius W. Sears grew up in the village of Peru, Massachusetts. He graduated from West Point in 1841, forty-first in his class of fifty-two, and resigned from the army after a year to become a teacher in the South. Sears taught in Holly Springs, Mississippi, before becoming a professor of mathematics and engineering at the New Orleans college that became Tulane University. In 1861 he entered Confederate service as an enlisted man in the Seventeenth Mississippi and was elected captain of his company. In December 1862 he was made colonel of the Forty-sixth Mississippi and within two weeks opposed William T. Sherman's assault on Chickasaw Bluffs near Vicksburg. During the Vicksburg campaign he served along the Yazoo River, fought at Port Gibson, Champion's Hill, and during the forty-seven-day siege of the river town. Sears was captured in the surrender on July 4, 1863, and paroled but not exchanged for several months. He returned to active service in the spring of 1864 and was given the rank of brigadier general with five regiments and a battalion of Mississippi infantry. Sears earned a reputation as an aggressive battalion commander during the Atlanta campaign, but illness in September forced him to relinquish command briefly. He ended his years of combat with John Bell Hood's Tennessee campaign. Sears performed brilliantly at Franklin, where his men temporarily seized the main Union line, but in the battle of Nashville he lost a leg and was captured. He was not paroled until June 23, 1865. After the war he occupied the chair of mathematics at the University of Mississippi until 1889.[23]

Albert G. Blanchard of Charlestown, Massachusetts, was a West Point classmate of Robert E. Lee and Joseph E. Johnston. Graduating at the bottom of their twenty-six-member class, he was dispatched to the western frontier, where he spent eleven undistinguished years. Having established himself in New Orleans by 1861, the New Englander offered his services to the state and was made colonel of the First Louisiana. Four months later he was a brigadier, but his stars never shone brightly. After serving as a recruitment and training officer, Blanchard briefly led troops under Edmund Kirby Smith before being relieved of his command and never getting another one.[24]

After six years in early manhood teaching and studying in his native state, Albert Pike joined expeditions of hunters and trappers in the Far West. After two years Pike returned to teaching in Arkansas. A poet of considerable talent, a lawyer, planter, and newspaper publisher, this three-hundred-pound Massachusetts native recruited and led American Indians who fought for the Confederacy. On March 27, 1862, the *New York Tribune* said the newly commissioned Confederate brigadier general "led the Aboriginal Corps of Tomahawkers and Scalpers at the battle of Pea Ridge." There were stories about atrocities on the part of the Native Americans who fought under Pike, who led more of these warriors into battle than any other general officer of the South or of the North. To avoid arrest and court-martial he disappeared and later resigned from the army.[25]

Newburyport native Caleb Huse remained in the U.S. Army barely a year after his graduation from West Point. In February 1861, while teaching at the University of Alabama, he was ordered to return to uniform. He did so but donned gray instead of blue and resumed his martial career as a captain in Confederate service. Because of his background in science, administration, and ordnance, he was appointed European purchasing agent for the Confederate army. Huse was responsible for muskets, rifles, pistols, and shipments of medicine and other scarce commodities being sent to the Confederacy. It has been said of him that "his success as a purchasing agent made the Civil War last for four years instead of two."[26]

New Yorkers in general and citizens of its largest city in particular harbored what Washington denounced as "secessh sentiments." As a result, as many men flocked to the Stars and Bars from the Empire State as from any three other Northern states. Several of them had significant military careers, but one man created the most repercussions, almost bringing Great Britain into the war as an ally of the Confederacy.

Manhattan-born William W. Allen launched his military career as a first lieutenant in the First Alabama Cavalry and ended it as a major general. Unscathed at Shiloh and Corinth as a colonel, he was wounded at Perryville and Murfreesboro. Returning to combat, he led a brigade under Joseph Wheeler. Allen was among the handful of general officers who nipped at Sherman's heels as he marched through Georgia and the Carolinas. Allen surrendered with Joseph E. Johnston in April 1865 at Durham Station.[27]

William H. Parker of New York City chose to make a career on the sea and graduated from Annapolis first in the class of 1848. Switching allegiance in 1861, as a lieutenant commander he spent two years on warships before becoming superintendent of the Confederate naval academy. Parker's most notable exploit was as a guardian of Confederate gold and records that went south into oblivion after the fall of Richmond.[28]

Although born in New York City, Franklin Gardner received his appointment to West Point from Iowa. Wearing a captain's bars after eighteen years in the U.S. Army, he resigned and was given command of a Confederate cavalry brigade two ranks higher than he had been. One year after Fort Sumter he became a brigadier general. The transplanted New Yorker commanded departments and divisions before being sent to Port Hudson, Mississippi. Although the defensive works of this river town were strong, the fall of Vicksburg doomed its neighbor. Gardner and seven thousand men surrendered on July 8, 1863. Unlike the Vicksburg garrison, he went to prison and stayed there for more than a year. Meanwhile, the Confederate Senate confirmed Gardner as a major general while he was a prisoner. Back in uniform, he returned to district command for the duration of the war.[29]

Manhattan merchant David B. Bridgford, who came to the metropolis from England, was sure that right lay on the side of the South when the war began. He hurried to Virginia, won a captain's commission, and served in obscurity until he became provost marshal of the Army of Northern Virginia. After Appomattox, he returned to New York but stayed there only briefly before helping to raise volunteers who sailed to Cuba to take part in one of the island's revolutions.[30]

Archibald Gracie Jr. resigned from the U.S. Army in 1856 to enter his family's extensive mercantile business. His father later said that the biggest mistake he ever made was "sending the boy to my Mobile branch as its manager." Archibald fell in love with the South and defied his family by accepting a commission as a captain in the Third Alabama. Having been educated at Heidelberg, Germany, and West Point, he required only a few months to win his stars. He saw action in Virginia, Kentucky, and Tennessee.

Capt. Charles Wilkes was central to the international incident known as "the *Trent* Affair."

HARPER'S WEEKLY

Fighting in the trenches near Petersburg, the wealthy aristocrat was killed by a Federal shell.[31]

After being financially ruined by the War of 1812, businessman John Slidell moved to New Orleans. Describing himself as "thoroughly southern in every respect," he wanted to fight in 1861 but at age sixty-eight was far too old. Jefferson Davis valued his experience too highly to ignore him, however, so Slidell was appointed to represent the Confederacy in France, sailing for his assignment on the British mail steamer *Trent*. When forcibly removed from that ship by Capt. Charles Wilkes of the USS *San Jacinto*, Slidell and a companion, James M. Mason, became central figures in an international dispute. Angry that Americans had stopped the *Trent* on the high seas, British leaders dispatched troops to Canada and prepared once more to wage war in North America. Lincoln and his cabinet members soon decided to release the Confederate diplomats, so tempers quickly cooled. Slidell once more set out for France and this time reached his destination, where he lobbied throughout the war but was unable to negotiate a formal alliance. He did, however, persuade the house of Erlanger to make a huge loan to Richmond.[32]

Reared in Albany, William Steele married into a Texas family while stationed in the West after his 1840 graduation from West Point. His Confederate career began in 1861 when he became colonel of the Seventh Texas Cavalry. Soon made a brigadier, he fought in the Trans-Mississippi region until he was sent to the Indian Territory (now Oklahoma) in 1863. In March 1864 he was given command of the Galveston defenses. He joined the Red River campaign, during which he was commended for his actions at Pleasant Hill on April 9, 1864, when he replaced Brig. Gen. Thomas Green as commander of a cavalry division.[33]

Marriage to a Georgia girl made a Rebel of Martin L. Smith, who grew up in Danbury, New York. He graduated sixth in the West Point class of 1842 and was sent to Florida to survey the Georgia-Florida coastline. Smith saw action in the Mexican War and returned to Texas and Georgia afterward. Possibly awarded a leave of absence, Smith moved to Florida and became chief engineer for a regional railroad. When war broke out, he resigned his commission to take another as a major of engineering for the Confederacy. By late 1862 Smith was a major general in gray having supervised the construction of defensive works around New Orleans and Vicksburg. Sent to Vicksburg to oversee preparations for its defense, he was another Northern-born officer who surrendered with Pemberton. After he was paroled, Smith served for a time as chief engineer of the Army of Northern Virginia. Later sent to the Army of Tennessee, he constructed many of Mobile's defenses. After the fall of Mobile, Smith surrendered at Athens, Georgia, in May 1865. He returned to civil engineering in postwar Savannah but died suddenly in 1866.[34]

Schenectady's Daniel M. Frost stayed in uniform for nine years after his 1844 graduation from West Point and was brevetted for gallantry during the Mexican War. Settling in Saint Louis, he entered the lumber business, served in the state legislature, and was made a member of the board of visitors at West Point. When the war began, Frost was a leader in the secessionist plan to seize the U.S. arsenal at Saint Louis. That scheme failed when Frost and

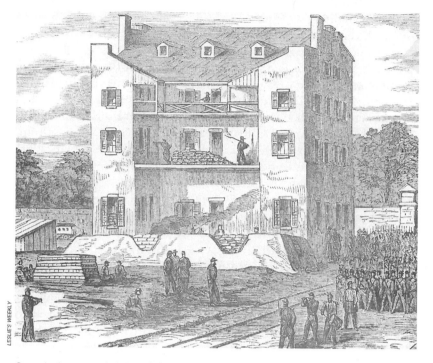

Secessionists correctly believed the Saint Louis arsenal held huge quantities of weapons and ammunition.

others were arrested by soldiers under Capt. Nathaniel Lyon, an action that precipitated a major riot.

After leading a militia brigade at the battle of Pea Ridge, Frost was made a Confederate general. Throughout 1863 he served in several campaigns without distinction. According to Rebel records, he was eventually relieved of command. Recent evidence suggests that the New Yorker who made a very poor Rebel was not relieved but deserted to join his wife in Canada after she was forced to leave their home because of the family's Southern sympathies. The Frosts returned to Saint Louis in 1865 and continued to farm their land until 1900.[35]

Walter H. Stevens, reared in the hamlet of Penn Yan, was an 1848 graduate of West Point whose years of service with the Corps of Engineers were focused on projects in Texas and Louisiana. He

married a southerner and became an avowed southerner in sentiment. After thirteen years in uniform, when the war broke out,
Stevens tried to resign and was refused; however, he was dismissed
from the army on a technicality. This Rebel from New York served
in the engineers for most of his Confederate career, acting as chief
engineer for P. G. T. Beauregard at First Manassas and in the same
capacity for Joseph E. Johnston for the Army of Virginia up until
Johnston's wounding and Robert E. Lee's elevation to command
of the Army of Northern Virginia. Lee charged Stevens with devel-
oping the defensive works of Richmond, and for two years Stevens
expanded and refined the earthworks that ringed the Confederate
capital. In the summer of 1864 Lee appointed Stevens chief engineer of his army and promoted him to brigadier general in August
of that year. In this capacity he engineered the defensive works
around Petersburg, which thwarted the Union Army of the
Potomac for nearly ten months. When the city fell, Stevens
retreated into Richmond. Some evidence supports the story that
this Yankee in gray was the last uniformed man to leave the
Confederate capital. Unwilling to take an oath of allegiance after
his surrender at Appomattox, Stevens fled to Mexico where he
became engineer and superintendent of the imperial railway.[36]

Born in Ithaca, William Miller was brought to Louisiana in infancy
and as a young adult migrated to Pensacola. He volunteered
during the Mexican War and served under Zachary Taylor in
northern Mexico. When the shooting started in Charleston, the
forty-one-year-old lawyer could not wait to get into the fight.
Following Braxton Bragg, Miller led a six-company battalion
through much of Kentucky. His moment of greatest distinction
came later, however. At Stones River his two Florida regiments
staged "a magnificent charge" whose only flaw was that it failed.
Miller was wounded in the action and absented himself to
Pensacola to recuperate. The New York native was made a
brigadier in August 1864 and placed in command of the Florida
reserves, but he saw no more combat. After the war he returned to
his law practice, managed a sawmill, and served three terms in the
Florida legislature.[37]

Before the war William O. Williams of New York was a private in
the U.S. Second Cavalry and alleged to be a distant relative of
Mary Lee, whose husband, Robert E. Lee, commanded the

At Corinth, Mississippi, transplanted Yankee William O. Wilson, aka Lawrence W. Orton, was wearing gray when other Northerners entered the town.

Second. When war broke out Williams transferred his allegiance to Virginia and joined the staff of Confederate Gen. Leonidas Polk. After directing artillery at Shiloh and Corinth, Williams was made a colonel, but his commission bore the name Lawrence W. Orton. Two months later Williams and a comrade posed as Federal inspectors and ventured behind enemy lines. When suspicions were raised, their identities were discovered and both were hanged following a drumhead trial. The New Yorker and his companion are believed to have been headed to Canada, where they could have taken ship to go on an arms-purchasing expedition.[38]

A fellow who never rose above the rank of major is a long way from the least among these New Yorkers who fought in gray. Born near Windsor in the Empire State, before the war Jedediah Hotchkiss took a walking tour of the Shenandoah Valley at age nineteen. He fell in love with the beautiful region and settled there as a schoolteacher. Within months of his becoming a Virginian by choice, Hotchkiss began studying cartography. Self-taught in this art of mapmaking, when the war broke out he closed his school for boys and volunteered as a mapmaker in western Virginia. When Thomas J. "Stonewall" Jackson learned of Hotchkiss's skill in 1862, he added the Yankee to his staff. This was no minor matter as events turned out. Hotchkiss is credited with significantly contributing to Jackson's smashing successes in the Shenandoah. After Jackson's death in 1863, Hotchkiss worked for several Rebel leaders. U. S. Grant once tried to purchase some of the New Yorker's maps, and many of them went into *The Official Military Atlas of the Civil War*. No other mapmaker in blue or in gray produced an equal volume of distinguished work.[39]

With bitterly divided Kentucky, Missouri, Maryland, and Delaware not included, more than a dozen states outside the Confederacy saw some of their sons throw in their lot with the secessionists. New York, Pennsylvania, and Massachusetts gave the South more general officers than other Northern states, but notable Rebels had birthplaces that ranged from Maine to Iowa. When southerners who went North are added to this impressive list, doubts are raised about the longstanding view that the Civil War was strictly a regional struggle. If scores of men with trans-planted loyalties became general officers and a few became in-fluential civilians, tens of thousands of obscure privates and noncommissioned officers must have chosen not to support the prevailing views in the regions where they were reared. There are no reliable records concerning the number of men who fought against their own region or their collective impact upon the long-drawn struggle. Yet the recognition that many participants chose sides on the basis of individual loyalties and passions reveals the Civil War to have been much more complex in nature than is sometimes assumed.

Part 2

Money Makes the Mare Go

Aging Julia Ward Howe never forgot that her "Battle Hymn of the Republic" brought her just four dollars when first published.

5

HARD MONEY

AND SOFT

BETWEEN THE spring of 1861 and the fall of 1862 the cost of bread in Charleston skyrocketed to twenty-five cents for a half-pound loaf. This highly inflated price was established by the city's bakers, who met and debated how to make even token profits when flour was costing them sixty-five dollars a barrel.[1]

Real Money

In 1861 the value of farms, improvements, and machinery in the seceded states, calculated in hard money—gold and silver coin or certificates redeemable in coin—ran to about $1.9 billion. This region, whose wealth was derived largely from cotton and tobacco, was labeled agrarian, in contrast to the industrial North. Farms, improvements, and machinery in the North, including the Border States, were worth much more. Calculated in hard money these assets of these states that did not secede were estimated to be worth $5 billion.

This factor gave the North 2.63 times the economic strength of the Cotton Belt, measured in terms of land and its accessories alone. Disparities in the value of livestock were less striking. The horses, cattle, oxen, mules, sheep, and swine of the North were valued at only 1.83 times those of the South—$716 million against $391 million.

Many a Southern fighting man went to war confident that the Yankees could never match the horsepower of the seceded states. This unfounded belief may have helped to create the wartime situation in which the Rebels were required to furnish their own mounts, while the Federals had them provided by the government.

Although Confederates believed themselves to be better horsemen than the Federals, the animals of the North were worth nearly twice as much as those of the South.

Had the men in gray looked at data from the U.S. Census of 1860, they might have altered their views. Horses owned in the seceded states were valued at only $1 million in hard money, against $4 million in the states that did not secede.[2]

Whether viewed from a Northern or Southern perspective, the industrial power of the seceded states was far less than that of the North. No reliable data concerning industrial output were accumulated by census takers prior to 1880, but the results of some private surveys are available. The industrial strength (including railroads) of the Confederacy is believed to have been less than one-fifth that of the Union.

Without recording the amounts of their annual profits, industrial plants were counted in 1861. Virginia had the most in the South—4,890 firms against 23,236 in New York. The total number of industrial plants in the South was a trifle over 18,000, while the North included more than 110,000.

During the fiscal year that ended on May 31, 1860, U.S. capital invested in large and small factories was reported to be about $1 billion in hard money. Surprisingly, capital investment in factories and plants was often exceeded by the value of goods produced in a twelve-month period. In this category Virginia again led the South by turning out finished goods with an estimated market value of just over $51 million in the last prewar fiscal year. Pennsylvania topped that output by a wide margin, as did New York and Massachusetts. It is estimated that manufactured goods worth $1.9 billion came from American industries during 1859–60. Of this total, all states that later seceded produced substantially less than 10 percent.[3]

During the years of conflict, it cost approximately $2.50 to alter an old-fashioned musket and convert it into a percussion-type weapon.

Iron foundries could and did make a profit by producing and selling three-inch Parrott guns for less than $200 each. After surveying masses of data, Civil War historian Bruce Catton concluded that upon the outbreak of the conflict, "the North possessed all the requirements of a potentially great manufacturing nation," but the South was barely over the threshold of the Industrial Age.[4]

Calculated in specie—or hard money—the national debt in 1860 was just under $65 million. This meant that every man, woman, and child in the thirty-four states that made up the Union was obligated to the tune of $2.06. By war's end, individual indebtedness for the central government's expenditures had multiplied thirty-six times and stood at $75.01—for a total of more than $2 billion for the reunited nation.[5]

Much of the cost of the war to the two governments was indirect, and immense sums were expended by both Northern and Southern states. Strictly military expenditures on the part of the Washington government ran to an estimated $3 billion. The Confederacy, whose economic clout was far less powerful, spent almost two-thirds of this amount for its army and naval operations.

With the direct military cost to the central governments exceeding $5 billion, each inhabitant in both the victorious North and the decimated South lost approximately $160 through taxation, assessment, seizure, and national debt. That was enough money for every man, woman, and child in the nation to hire a full-time laborer for seven months.[6]

Since he was late in hiring a rig, William H. Russell of the London *Times* had to pay $1,000 to get transportation to Manassas Gap, Virginia, in time to witness the battle of July 21, 1861.

NEW YORK ILLUSTRATED NEWS

When the Confederate capital was evacuated, a hasty check showed that the treasury held both coins and bullion. The loss of records makes it impossible to know the precise amount, but it is believed to have been in the range of $300,000 to $350,000. When Davis fled south, wagonloads of specie went with him.

Davis was adamant that the last gold should be used to pay soldiers, but since the sum available was inadequate, this order was never carried out. Instead, the Confederate treasure rolled out of Richmond, and six wagonloads of it are believed to have reached Washington, Georgia, where it vanished. Since then many treasure seekers have hunted for it in vain.[7]

William H. Russell, a war correspondent for the London *Times,* did not learn until July 20, 1861, that a major battle was in the offing. Eager to see the action near Manassas, Virginia, Russell was so desperate for transportation that he rented a buggy and horses for a fee of $1,000.[8]

W. R. Shoemaker made an inventory of "the property belonging to the United States" at the remote post of Santa Fe, New Mexico, and reported it to be worth "$271,147.55 at Eastern cost." All of this, along with a great deal more, was soon confiscated by Rebel raiding parties.[9]

One of the few U.S. Army officers who escaped from the West with money on his person was Lt. Kenner Garrard. Somehow he got past Rebel scrutiny with about $20,000—half of the hard money then held by soldiers in blue whose Texas fortresses were surrendered at one time.[10]

Upon the collapse of the Confederacy, P. G. T. Beauregard, his officers, and men were owed a huge sum in back pay. The general and each member of his staff accepted one silver dollar as "mustering out pay"—perhaps the last hard money still circulating in the South.[11]

Soft Stuff

By early winter 1861 it was clear to U.S. Secretary of the Treasury Salmon P. Chase that the Union was out of money— gold and silver, that is. Not enough coins were in circulation to permit ordinary commercial transactions. In this crisis, Chase pushed lawmakers very hard and as a result a Legal Tender Act was passed on February 25, 1862. It provided for the use of paper currency as a substitute for gold. A bill of this sort was actually a note of indebtedness on the part of the government, but it paid no interest.

This new and controversial type of money was printed in green on one side, and soon the nickname "greenbacks" was in general use. Many opponents of "this desperate fiscal measure," especially farmers and laborers, felt that "the sorry business was devised to fatten the purses of Eastern financial tycoons" at the expense of hard-working citizens. A grass-roots challenge of the constitutionality of paper money as "legal tender for all debts, public and private" was not successful, despite the fact that minstrel Dan Bryant issued a comic song demanding "How Are Your Green-backs?"

Just five months after paper money was first authorized, the supply was exhausted. Congress passed the second Legal Tender Act on July 11, increasing the amount in circulation so that within weeks the value of a paper dollar had dropped to 91¢ in specie. About the time of the December 1862 battle of Fredericksburg, economists estimated that $135 in greenbacks could be bought with just $100 in gold. By then it was realized that a man with $15,000 in gold could buy greenbacks with it, then use the

Minstrels based in New York City
ridiculed the new paper money
known as "greenbacks."

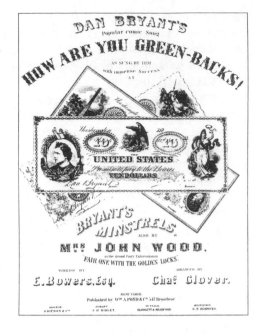

currency to purchase $20,000 in U.S. gold bonds that paid 6 percent interest. At the bottom of the fall of the greenback, a $10 bill was worth just $3 in gold.

Although they clearly helped to ease a fiscal crisis, greenbacks were of trifling importance in war finances: a total worth only $450 million was issued. When the war was over, Congress abandoned the use of greenbacks with little opposition. By this time, however, ordinary citizens had found the new kind of money to be so convenient that few of them were willing to return to gold and silver coins exclusively. Instead of retiring the greenbacks in circulation, the U.S. Mint purchased new printing presses and launched the production of paper money in ever-growing volume.[12]

Imprudent investments financially ruined Ulysses S. Grant soon after he left the Executive Mansion. Mark Twain came to his rescue by encouraging him to write his *Memoirs,* and his publisher undertook a rash new enterprise—door-to-door selling. The venture was so successful that after Grant died of cancer, his widow received royalties of nearly $450,000.[13]

At the outbreak of the conflict, secessionist leaders—first in Montgomery and then in Richmond—were confronted by a critical shortage of gold and silver. This led them very early to turn to the use of currency. The first issue of about $1 million came from the presses of the National Bank Note Company—not in New Orleans or Mobile but in New York City. By 1862 international merchant-banker George A. Trenholm of Charleston estimated that the Confederate economy required only about $120 million. Already Confederate currency in circulation amounted to at least $250 million, however.

To overcome problems created by shortages of small coins, nearly every seceded state, as well as many banks and mercantile establishments, issued paper money of less than one dollar in denomination. Such fractional currency, sometimes called "paper coins," was backed only by the integrity and resources of the agency or business that issued them.

Confederate paper money that came largely from presses in Richmond and Columbia, South Carolina, was quite different from state and private issues. All of it was supposed to be redeemable in gold six months after having been issued, or "two years after the ratification of a treaty of peace between the Confederate States and the United States."

Depreciation of all currency issued by Richmond or within the borders of the Confederacy began almost as soon as the first of it entered circulation, and a never-ending inflationary spiral began. Eventually the cost of a dozen eggs passed $10. Late in the war anyone lucky enough to have hoarded a single gold dollar could exchange it for $70 in Confederate currency.

The collapse of the Confederacy rendered all of the South's paper money worthless, of course. By 1865 a Confederate bill with face value of $1,000 was contemptuously called a "shin-plaster," meaning it was worthless except to bandage an injured leg.[14]

One Southern expedition went into the record as "the Greenback Raid." On October 13, 1864, eighty-four partisan rangers under John S. Mosby tore up track to wreck a passenger train with Union personnel aboard. When their scheme succeeded, Confederates fanned out through cars that lay on their sides, hoping to find a Union general. No man of this rank was aboard, but the rangers discovered two army paymasters and took $173,000 in greenbacks

Jay Cooke of Ohio was the champion bond salesman of the Union and amassed a fortune in the process of "largely financing the Union war effort."

from them. Mosby saw to it that $2,100 was counted out to each of his "stockholders" but kept nothing for himself.[15]

After spending months in Richmond's Libby Prison, Capt. George N. Bliss of the First Rhode Island Cavalry learned that a timid fellow prisoner had managed to hide a gold piece worth $2.50. Concealing the treasure on his person, Bliss dickered with a guard and eventually was handed $75 in Confederate currency in exchange for the tiny coin.[16]

In addition to currency, government bonds played a major role during 1861–65. Ohio-born Jay Cooke established a special agency for the sale of these financial instruments and was so successful that he is sometimes credited with having largely financed the Union war effort.

On a good day Cooke and his agents could dispose of nearly $10 million in bonds. During six months beginning in February 1865, their sales passed $853 million. No other fiscal agent in the North or South came close to challenging Cooke as the top sales-man of government bonds—for which he received commissions that made him wealthy.[17]

Nearly all currency issued by Richmond included the portrait of an official of the central government, but states and business establishments selected their own designs. A $50-note issued in 1863 by the state of Louisiana is in a class by itself. It has the distinction of being the only currency circulated in North America that was adorned with the portrait of a man who was simultaneously a general and a bishop—Leonidas Polk.[18]

Cotton broker Zachariah C. Deas of Mobile, Alabama, desperately wanted to get into the conflict, but not as a buck private in the rear rank. With the help of Robert B. Armistead he recruited enough men to form a regiment of which he naturally was elected colonel. Once his unit was full, the brand-new officer, whose wealth came from cotton, used $28,000 in Confederate notes to purchase an Enfield rifle for each of his officers and men.[19]

Abraham Lincoln never abandoned one of his pet notions. To him it seemed not only logical but also wise to send freed slaves into colonies established for them in Central America and other overseas points. He persuaded a majority of lawmakers to agree upon a measure he proposed, and Congress appropriated $600,000 for overseas colonization of former slaves.[20]

Big Bucks and Small Potatoes

During the Confederate invasion of Kentucky in the summer of 1862, Gen. Henry Heth conceived a grandiose plan to make the biggest monetary haul of the war. His target was Cincinnati. If Heth could seize the city, he could offer the citizens two choices: see the town sacked or pay a ransom of $15 million. Before he could implement his plan, however, Federal troops under Gen. Lew Wallace occupied the town and closed the opportunity.[21]

Less familiar than Sherman's devastating March to the Sea is Gen. David Hunter's systematic destruction in the Shenandoah Valley in 1864. In the single Virginia county of Rockbridge, burned-out civilians estimated that their losses exceeded $2 million.[22]

Both Confederate privateers and Federal warships called any ship that was captured "a prize of war." After adjudication in a prize court, the officers and men divided among themselves the proceeds of the sale of the enemy vessel and its cargo. The total value of prizes taken by Union sailors was estimated to be $31 million, with the English blockade-runner *Memphis* topping the list at $510,000.[23]

Not far from Valley Forge, the Phoenix Iron Company of Pennsylvania concentrated upon production of a single weapon: the three-inch rifle. Its first powerful guns were sold to the government for just $300 each, but the price kept rising until it reached $450. A postwar accounting showed that after April 1861 this relatively obscure manufacturer received from the federal government $347,374.80.[24]

Stonewall Jackson's foray into the Shenandoah Valley resulted in the capture of a significant number of men in blue. When he seized and destroyed a supply depot belonging to the enemy, the former VMI professor did not calculate its worth, but he carefully tabulated the value of the supplies he captured and turned over to Confederate forces. According to his records, the goods were worth exactly $125,185.[25]

Consul S. C. Hawley, stationed at Nassau, probably saw as many blockade-runners come and go as did any other U.S. official. Upon arrival at his post, he recorded that he thought that blockade-running was "an unprofitable business." Once he began keeping records, however, he changed his mind. A single unidentified blockade-runner, whose initial expenses were $115,000, brought in a full load of cotton. From this one voyage, Hawley calculated, the owners of the vessel recovered all expenses and made a net profit of $119,000.[26]

Initially threatened with the gallows after the war, Jefferson Davis was offered conditional freedom after months in prison. He could go free, Federal authorities told him, once he posted bond in the amount of $100,000.

That sum was stipulated because it was known to be far beyond the means of the former Confederate president. Strangely in the eyes of many, three prominent Yankees stepped up and signed Davis's bail bond. Publisher Horace Greeley, Gerrit Smith (a former financial supporter of John Brown), and Cornelius Vanderbilt saw to it that Jefferson Davis was freed.[27]

In his prison cell, the former president of the Confederacy learned that he could go free if he could post a bond of $100,000.

R. R. Goode, chief surgeon of Confederate cavalryman John Hunt Morgan, pulled off what may have been the biggest one-man bank robbery of the war. In Mount Sterling, Kentucky, Goode found and captured at his home cashier William Mitchel of the Farmer's Bank of Kentucky. Forced to go to the bank at gunpoint and there to open the vault, Mitchel delivered to Goode at least $60,000, a sum equivalent to about $1 million today.[28]

Compared with the Goode heist, the formation of a new state from territory that had seceded from the Old Dominion involved comparatively little money. Leaders who fashioned West Virginia got the new government into motion with the help of a $10,000 loan split between two banks.[29]

Although the financial misdeeds of many a military officer were known to his immediate subordinates, only a few were caught with their hands in the cookie jar. Col. Frederick D'Utassy, who claimed to be a count, was at the top of the roster of known thieves in blue uniforms. Hauled before a court-martial on nineteen specifications, the officer of the Thirty-ninth New York, or Garibaldi Guard, was convicted of forging vouchers valued at $3,265.40.[30]

After the Federal draft was established, the demand for substitutes was so great that in big cities a crimp (a person who tricks or coerces another into serving in the army or navy) who provided them could make a fortune in a matter of months. When this corrupt system was investigated, one noncommissioned Federal officer testified that he had been offered $1,500 to desert and reenlist under another name. At a time when a British sergeant was paid $1 a day, this did not seem adequate compensation to the officers, so the crimp added 160 acres of land as a bonus.[31]

After the war, many people filed claims against the federal government. Some wanted compensation for services they said they had performed, and others itemized losses they said they had incurred. Samuel Ruth of Richmond, whose assertion that he was a Union spy has considerable supporting evidence, was believed by friends to have rendered services worth at least $40,000. When his claim was finally settled, he accepted $500 as payment in full.[32]

In Franklin, Tennessee, F. B. Carter kept meticulous records of property losses he suffered during the Federal occupation of the town. Items he listed ranged from 10,018 pounds of seed cotton at 25¢ per pound to three bushels of corn worth $2. His total claim amounted to $20,061.10, but his heirs finally received $335—in 1886.[33]

Union spy Pauline Cushman's career got off to a fast start when she hoodwinked a group of Confederate sympathizers in New Orleans. During the occupation of the city, they offered the aspiring actress $300 to go on stage and offer a toast to the Confederacy. She made the toast, collected her pay, and used it to secure necessities with which to go under cover and feed information to the North.[34]

When soldiers of the army of occupation decided to transform Port Royal, South Carolina, into a naval repair center and supply depot, they were in dire need of experienced workmen. Men recruited in New York and promised pay of $2.50 to $4 a day were transported to the Southern port aboard the ship *Relief*, which was chartered at the rate of $250 a day.[35]

Hundreds of ships ranging from fast steamers to little sailboats were seized as prizes by enemy naval forces. At the bottom of the list of valuable captures was the sloop *Alligator*. After she was captured and sold at auction, this prize enabled officers and crew of the gunboat *Tahoma* to split among themselves a total of $50.[36]

To deceive Rebel gunners stationed on the banks of the Mississippi River, David D. Porter rigged up a fake ironclad and sent it downriver at night. His dummy, which drew the fire of one battery after another, was put together at a cost of $8.63—a trifle more than the cost of a single shell thrown at it.[37]

The most enduring Civil War musical composition, Julia Ward Howe's "The Battle Hymn of the Republic" brought her payment of $4 when it was first published in the February 1862 issue of the *Atlantic Monthly.*[38]

Accompanied by David Herold, fugitive John Wilkes Booth stopped at the farm of Dr. Richard H. Stewart and was given a warm welcome, including bed and what the host considered to be an ample meal. Stewart, who didn't know the identity of his unexpected guests, later received from Booth "payment in full" in the sum of $2.50.[39]

In 1863 the commercial steamer *Commander* was chartered to take workmen to the South. Owners of the vessel charged no transportation fee but collected 75¢ per day per man for room and board.[40]

Unlike their enemies, Federal officers did not furnish their own mounts. Because the horse a man rode was owned by the government, he was charged 40¢ per day for use of the animal.[41]

As Union Gen. Philip Sheridan rode toward Winchester, Virginia, in September 1864, local citizen Charlotte Hellman saw him approaching along a toll road. She hastily lowered a wooden crossbar and demanded and received from the rider the customary toll of 25¢ before raising the crossbar to let him pass.[42]

6

GRAFT AND CORRUPTION

THE AGE OF SHODDY

THE FOLLOWING telegram was directed to a member of Lincoln's cabinet and delivered to the Washington office of Quartermaster General Montgomery C. Meigs:

Saint Louis, July 28, 1861

Hon. Montgomery Meigs:
  Maj. McKinstry has made a requisition for funds. Will you see that it is sent on immediately? It ought to be multiplied by three to meet urgent demands of service here. Condition of this State critical and precarious, demanding utmost promptitude.

J. C. Frémont
Major General, Commanding

Meigs passed the communication along to Secretary of War Simon Cameron, noting: "[Frémont] says that to save Missouri, now in a critical condition, the public service urgently demands three times the amount of Major McKinstry's [the quartermaster] last requisition. That requisition was for $353,761. Will you request the Secretary of the Treasury to make the needed remittance? I inclose a requisition."[1]

Maj. Justus McKinstry, a native of New York, spent twenty-two years in the U.S. Army before the Civil War. Except for brief combat in the Mexican War, the West Point graduate spent his entire prewar career in the quartermaster corps, apparently by choice. His long experience in this specialized branch of the military service made it natural for his superiors to choose him as chief

Maj. Justus McKinstry was skilled at collecting kickbacks from suppliers of essential military goods.

LIBRARY OF CONGRESS

supply officer at Saint Louis in the weeks following the December 1860 secession of South Carolina.

At the immense arsenal there, McKinstry soon told Chester Harding Jr. to buy everything he needed. Numerous other officers and agents seem to have had the same instructions. It was routine to issue requisitions for purchases such as 250,000 rations plus "4,000 shoes and clothing to match" and 8,000 bed-sacks for use at Cairo, Illinois. The establishment of two supply depots designed to hold everything needed by eighteen thousand men was "all in a day's work." So was the hasty creation of a camp from rough boards at a cost of fifteen thousand dollars—equivalent to far more than five hundred thousand dollars today.[2]

Most officers whose needed supplies did not reach them on time or were found to be substandard in quality seem to have been afraid to challenge. Only one written complaint concerning the major was voiced early in the conflict. "Requisitions were made upon Quartermaster McKinstry some days since for camp equipage, &c, but as yet I have received nothing," U. S. Grant wrote from Ironton on August 15.[3]

Nathaniel Lyon, promoted from captain to brigadier general shortly before the firing upon Fort Sumter, made no secret of his dislike for McKinstry but avoided mentioning it directly in his

LIBRARY OF CONGRESS

Nathaniel Lyon jumped in rank from captain to brigadier general soon after hostilities broke out between North and South.

official reports. A fallback of Federals at Wilson's Creek, wrote the Federal commander, was caused by a woeful shortage of essential supplies—but no one listened. The colleagues of the two men agreed that both of them were ambitious and jealous, so they paid little heed to Grant's and Lyon's complaints.

Failure to scrutinize and challenge the actions of the man responsible for purchasing and distributing nearly everything the fighting men needed was later seen to have been a colossal mistake. Since McKinstry had been given a free hand by his superiors, the veteran quartermaster filled his own pockets and those of his associates by paying high prices for goods of inferior quality and accepting what is now called kickbacks.

This quartermaster had no sensitivity for the men in the field. Had McKinstry been told that, with winter approaching, Federal soldiers needed stout tents, sturdy coats, and warm uniforms, he might have thought to himself, "Let 'em freeze!" In September 1861 Capt. Parmenas T. Turnley led a team of investigators, which reported that blankets purchased by McKinstry "were found to be made of cotton and to be rotten and worthless."[4]

Instead of being monitored, McKinstry recived nothing but praise from his commander. In gratitude for his performance, Frémont rewarded him, not once, but repeatedly. On August 14,

In Washington, Montgomery C. Meigs was in charge of purchasing for Federal military purposes.

NATIONAL ARCHIVES

1861 he declared martial law in Saint Louis and appointed McKinstry provost marshal with unlimited power of arrest. Two weeks later McKinstry was promoted to brigadier general of volunteers and turned his duties over to former subordinates. With Federal troops marching toward Springfield, the purchasing agent was elevated to the rank of acting major general on September 21.[5]

In Washington the prevailing crisis mood allowed officials to give a free hand to anyone needing money for supplies or weapons. Quartermaster General Meigs went on record as condoning the practice of paying beyond market prices. He wrote, "If General Frémont orders Captain Turnley [then a McKinstry aide] *to pay $1,000 for an ax, Captain Turnley will be supported by this Department in obeying.*"[6]

Washington's eagerness to bring the war to an early end, regardless of cost, helped to create the climate in which McKinstry became rich. At the same time, the high-flying ways of his commander made it difficult for anyone in the military Department of the West to raise questions. Frémont selected a Saint Louis musician as director of music for his staff, then put him on the payroll "with the rank and commission of *captain of engineers.*" An investigation of other Frémont appointments revealed that in a single list of forty-two officers whose rank ranged from second lieutenant to

Gen. John Charles Frémont encouraged McKinstry to spend with a free hand.

colonel, nineteen were listed as engineers who were entitled to pay at the cavalry rather than the infantry level.[7]

The McKinstry-Frémont bubble burst almost as soon as the former rode out of Saint Louis at the head of his brigade. Adj. Gen. Lorenzo Thomas then arrived from Washington heading a select body of men empowered to make an investigation. Maj. Robert Allen, an experienced quartermaster, wrote an October 11 report in which he said in part: "Accounts involving hundreds of thousands of dollars have been presented to me within the few days I have been here, informal, irregular, and not authorized by law or regulations. Some three days ago I telegraphed the Quartermaster General, M. C. Meigs, a message; and I give an extract from memory: 'If the reckless expenditures in this department are not arrested by a stronger arm than mine, the Quartermaster's Department [of the entire U.S. Army] will be wrecked in Missouri alone.' "[8]

On the day the Allen report was submitted, Assistant Quartermaster Turnley reported to Thomas that work under McKinstry left his health so broken that he was no longer able to stand on his feet. "I left my public accounts open, in an incomplete and exposed condition, on my office table in Saint Louis, besides a vast deal of property not turned over," he confessed.[9]

Ten days later Thomas reported to Secretary of War Cameron that he had gone to the arsenal where he had quizzed an unidentified captain who was in charge of manufacturing ammunition. This officer told him that "he heard that some person had a contract for making the carriages" of numerous heavy guns designed for gunboats and mortar boats.

Armed with documents, chief paymaster Col. T. P. Andrews called upon Thomas and talked freely. Andrews had been required to handle both payments and transfers of money "contrary to law and regulations," he said. When he once ventured to object to making a payment that he considered to be improper, "he was threatened with confinement by a file of soldiers." To support this incredible allegation, he showed Thomas an irregular order for the transfer of one hundred thousand dollars to the quartermaster's department.[10]

A stunning picture of gross mismanagement of funds soon emerged. Against regulations, Capt. Leonidas Haskel of Frémont's staff had served as a contractor who furnished hay, forage, and mules to the army, all of them being sold to the army at prices well above the market. "In a country of abundant supply," Frémont purchased "500 half barrels to carry water." With the only available ice having been harvested in winter and kept in special ice houses until sold, Frémont bought 500 tons of it.

At Paducah, Kentucky, the general ignored the presence of an Ohio River ferry and threw a pontoon bridge across the stream. In Saint Louis he paid rent of six thousand dollars per year for his headquarters, the Brant House. A hasty audit indicated that the quartermaster's department in Saint Louis was $4.5 million in debt—despite an ever-increasing flow of ever-larger remittances from Washington.[11]

Without having led his men into combat of any significance, McKinstry was placed under arrest on November 13, 1861, and confined in the arsenal he earlier had commanded. More than a year later he became the only general officer on either side to be cashiered "for neglect and violation of duty, to the prejudice of good order and military discipline."[12]

McKinstry's case is so unusual that in 1960 historian Allan Nevins expressed doubts that he had been treated fairly, having been dismissed from the service by President Lincoln early in 1863. Apparently relying upon a single pamphlet, Nevins branded the handling of the quartermaster as a case of arbitrary confinement—having failed carefully to examine records that came to light long after the shooting stopped. A quite different verdict was expressed by another analyst, who said that McKinstry was "chiefly celebrated for having been one of the most thoroughgoing rogues ever to wear a United States uniform."[13]

The war years made many unscrupulous manufacturers and merchants rich at the expense of the Union military. Many profited from clothing made of shoddy. This form of cloth, earlier produced in England by tearing rags to shreds to recycle their fibers, was prone to rip at the slightest touch and to come apart during a rain shower.

Huge quantities of shoddy were manufactured and foisted upon military units. General in Chief Henry W. Halleck raged in April 1864 about "shoddy contractors who infest every department of the government and abuse everybody who will not grind their axes." In 1865 the *London Daily Telegraph* denounced "the codfish, shoddy, and petroleum aristocracy." Five years later a commentator on Wall Street made a sardonic suggestion that it should be the site for "a marble palace that would make all Shoddydom red with envy."[14]

Clothing and blankets were among items needed so badly that graft was practically invited. So much shoddy was produced and sold that its name became synonymous with anything of inferior quality. Merchants of shoddy also provided substandard tents, flags, food, horses, mules, forage, and other essentials to Union forces. At the May 1863 battle of Chancellorsville, Capt. Henry N. Blake of the Eleventh Massachusetts reported: A man who was loading his musket threw away the cartridge, with a fearful oath about government contractors; and I noticed that the paper was filled with fine grains of dry earth instead of gunpowder."[15]

Clearly, McKinstry was not the only military officer who lined his pockets at the expense of the safety and comfort of fighting men. He simply happened briefly to hold rank that made him the highest uniformed villain to be caught.

7

THE OVERLOOKED BLOCKADE

INLAND RIVER TRADERS

PETER HAYS, in command of the *Satellite,* certified that the statement below (abbreviated here) was "true in every particular."

Potomac Flotilla—Certificate of Capture
Name and character of prize: One yawl boat, laden with Goods, and three men, giving their names as William Bagby, of King and Queen County, Va.; James J. Leatch of Hanover County, Va.; free negro, James R. Ashton, Westmoreland County, Va.
By whom and by what vessel capture made: Volunteer Lieutenant P. Hays, steamer *Satellite.*
When capture made: November 2, 1862, 8 P.M.
The cargo, if any, on board: One barrel of whiskey, 1 barrel sugar, 4 sacks salt, 1 keg carbonate soda, 1 box shoes; 1 box shoes, dry goods, crockery, etc.; 1 bag containing 7 hats, 1 piece gingham, 1 pieces calico, 2 pounds coffee, 6 pounds soap, remnant of cloth, 1 bag containing 7 pair shoes, 1 bag skeleton skirts, 1 bag shot, 5 tin pans, 1 box soap, 1 box candles, 11 corn brooms, 1 pound powder, 1 jug molasses, 1 keg nails.
Remarks: Eleven corn brooms, 2 pounds powder, 1 jug molasses, kept for ship's use. The goods were taken in the boat; The prisoners were found in the woods guarding the boat; the captain of the boat made his escape. The prisoners state that they left Virginia for Maryland Thursday night, October 30.[1]

This document was one of scores generated during a period of about six months, beginning in late summer 1862. Although widely overlooked, the war on the water was not confined to the open seas. Inland rivers offered tempting opportunities for men

Salmon P. Chase, U.S. secretary of the treasury, knew that Federal revenues were not being collected at any ports in the seceded states. That fact led to the president's ordering a blockade of all Southern ports.

eager to make a profit from trading with the enemy in spite of prohibitions and risks.

President Lincoln's papers reveal that he was preparing to use force against secessionists at least a month before Fort Sumter. On March 18, 1861, he sent a memo to Attorney General Edward Bates asking for a written opinion on a controversial matter. Speaking of himself in third-person style, he inquired whether "the Executive has power to collect duties on ship-board, off-shore, in cases where their collection in the ordinary way is, by any cause, rendered impracticable."

At the same time he posed to Secretary of the Treasury Salmon P. Chase a question to which he already knew the answer: Are there "any goods, wares and merchandise, subject by law to the payment of duties, now being imported into the United States without such duties being paid?"[2]

With the collection of revenue listed as a major consideration for taking decisive action, on April 19 the president proclaimed a blockade of ports in seven seceded states. Only eight days later, the blockade was extended to two Cotton Belt states that had not yet seceded—Virginia and North Carolina.[3]

Although no presidential proclamation was issued to cover importation and trade on inland waters, for practical purposes a naval blockade of some rivers was soon under way. Since much of the Mississippi River and some of its major tributaries were still open, military action directed against men seeking to make a profit by selling goods to the enemy was for a period concentrated upon the rivers of Virginia.

Almost all smugglers, usually natives of the region in which they operated, used small boats and refused to risk the transportation of valuable cargoes. Before going into action, however, they learned all they could about the Federal Potomac Flotilla. Some of them went so far as to establish signal systems employing lanterns of various colors. Despite the fact that scores of these traders in contraband goods were imprisoned for short or long periods, others were always ready to take their place. Both Confederates and Unionists alike risked their freedom for these potential profits. A look at these seizures gives special insight into early Confederate desperation for goods and the Federal use of massive force to try to thwart the traders.[4]

One August night in 1862 the flotilla seized a small vessel carrying wheat, salt, cigars, quinine, morphine, opium, tea, coffee, and various medicines.[5] One October evening, one of the Federal schooners found assorted merchandise hidden on a creek bank in Maryland.[6] Other seizures that fall included skirts, coffee, shoes, candles, cloth, boots, felt hats, coffee, soap, liquor, and men en route to join the Confederate army.[7]

Search and seizure required immense quantities of paperwork, with naval officers having to file a detailed certificate of capture even if they found only an empty canoe floating downstream. A report often followed the certificate. When merchandise was enumerated, it had to be sent to a special court for sale. By standard, Federal officials were authorized to seize and sell vessels known or believed to transport contraband merchandise. All such seizures and transactions were reported to the secretary of the navy, Gideon Welles. Some vessels disposed of through prize courts were as large as forty tons. Nothing, however, stopped the forbidden traffic.

On the Mississippi River huge quantities of cotton went from the Confederates to their enemies. Repeatedly banned by both

U.S. Secretary of the Navy Gideon Welles received reports on all captures made by Federal sailors on the high seas and the inland waterways.

Washington and Richmond, this trade involved hundreds of men and large sums of money. Sometimes the authorities winked at exchanging bales of cotton for bundles of greenbacks, and in the cash-hungry South and the fiber-hungry North a few transactions had the sanction of the opposing governments. A decidedly uncharacteristic stance was taken by Gen. William T. Sherman just two weeks after the fall of Vicksburg. In a communication directed to U. S. Grant, he proposed establishing "a kind of trading depot" at the Big Black River railroad bridge to allow Mississippi civilians to "exchange their cotton, corn, and produce for provisions, clothing, and family supplies."[8] Apparently, no action was taken on Sherman's proposal.

Even after the entire Mississippi River came under the control of Federal gunboats, James A. Seddon, U.S. secretary of war, urged in August 1863 that "the use of the Mississippi River for trade should, *if possible,* be debarred to the enemy (italics added)." Although river traders diminished in number after that summer, their influence continued to be significant.[9]

On May 1, 1865, Gen. N. J. T. Dana sent urgent messages to army and navy commanders of the Natchez district. From Gen. George Thomas, Dana had learned that the fleeing president of the

Gen. George H. Thomas relayed the news to his colleagues that Jefferson Davis and his party would use riverboats to cross the Mississippi en route to Texas.

NICOLAY & HAY, *LINCOLN*

Confederacy was headed toward Texas "with his co-conspirators and their plunder." Hence it was imperative, said Dana, to keep a watchful eye upon "cotton-boats which Jeff. might seize and attempt to run out [into the gulf of Mexico] with a guard of his cavalry dismounted."[10]

Davis and a few aides were captured in Georgia without having made any attempt to take to water by means of a trader's vessel. Yet the presence of these vessels on Southern waterways after the fall of Richmond clearly shows that the overwhelming numbers of Federal ships and men failed to curtail this traffic whose motive was money.

8

HIRELINGS IN UNIFORM

THE ORIGINAL DOUGH BOYS

WHEN PRESIDENT LINCOLN called for seventy-five thousand ninety-day volunteers in April 1861, the pay of a Federal enlisted man was eleven dollars per month plus food. The president's plans for a short and nearly bloodless war soon went awry, creating pressing new demands for volunteers. To encourage men to enlist, a bounty of one hundred dollars, amounting to almost a full year's pay, was offered.

Bounties

Cities and states eager to provide large numbers of men immediately began adding their own financial inducements. In Buffalo, New York, the common council appropriated enough money to pay a $75 bounty to each resident who enlisted. A recruitment poster designed to fill the ranks of the Twelfth Massachusetts Battery offered prospective fighting men "$138 before you leave the state, $75 at the end of the war."

At Troy, New York, the board of supervisors of Rensselaer County voted to appropriate seventy-five thousand dollars as bounty money for volunteers. Officials of Baltimore, Maryland, appropriated four hundred thousand for the same purpose.[1]

In the financially pinched Confederacy, the national bounty was just half that paid in the North. Secretary of War Judah P. Benjamin notified Gov. John Letcher of Virginia that all men responding to the call of President Davis "will receive $50 when their regiment or company is mustered into Confederate service, and will also be allowed transportation from home to the place of rendezvous." Leaders of partisan rangers and other

In the financially pinched Confederacy, Judah P. Benjamin could offer bounties of only token amounts.

semimilitary bodies offered the same bounty. By May 1862, however, a Confederate volunteer was promised one hundred dollars from Richmond.[2]

A man who offered his services to Lincoln but preferred a special branch got short shrift at first. The bounty for enlisting in the U.S. Navy in August 1861 was only thirty dollars, and a volunteer for the U.S. Marine Corps received just fifty dollars. That was five times the amount then given to a man who signed up for the fledgling Confederate Marine Corps at a recruiting station in Montgomery, New Orleans, Memphis, or Mobile.[3]

Increasing demands for manpower and growing resistance to voluntary service caused bounties to rise continually. Boston raised its bounty to $200, and so many men responded that drafting was temporarily suspended. In New York City in 1864 a first-time recruit received $302 from Washington, $75 from Albany, and $300 from the city. A special veteran's bonus, paid to men with two or more years of service, brought the total enlistment bounty for men in this category to $777. Late in 1864 a man with two years of military experience could get a bounty of $1,000 upon enlisting in what organizers hoped would become the Veterans Legion. A recruitment poster for a Philadelphia unit proclaimed that bounties and a year's pay would amount to $1,131. Manpower was abundant in many cities, but that was not the case in rural and frontier districts, some of which offered a bounty of $1,500 to men who would enter the army at $16 per month.[4]

Men needed for the U.S. Navy appeared to be abundant when the blockade of Southern ports was proclaimed in 1861, but problems soon emerged and grew. After enrollment quotas were assigned, men who chose the navy over the army were not credited to their states. This paradoxical situation led many officials to persuade or force seamen to go into the army. Growing in size and hence in manpower needs more rapidly than the army, the navy became so desperate that the fifty-dollar bounty paid for enlistment in 1861 soared to one thousand dollars less than four years later.[5]

Estimates of Northern expenditures for bounties vary widely, from $585 million to $750 million. Incredible as it may sound, the larger figure is considered extremely conservative since combined state and local payments were often much greater than those from Federal sources.[6]

Bounty payments fostered the rise of special brokers and spawned hundreds of abuses. On September 5, 1864, Lorenzo Thomas lodged a formal complaint with Edwin M. Stanton, the secretary of war, claiming that recruitment "agents from the Northern States offering large bounties" caused men of "one of the colored regiments" then at Natchez, Mississippi, to desert and secure civilian clothing in order to reenlist to collect bounties.[7]

Most bounty brokers had small operations, but in New York City Theodore Allen is believed to have netted at least one hundred thousand dollars from federal, state, and municipal bounty payments. There is no evidence that Allen swindled the men he recruited out of part or all of their bounty money. Gen. Francis B. Spinola, however, was involved in just such a scheme. Spinola was relieved of duty before the scandals broke and was convicted by a court-martial.[8]

On the positive side, the payment of bounties helped to fill ranks that otherwise would have been empty and partly reduced the anger caused by the first wartime draft. On the negative side, the availability of bounty money encouraged desertion. Many a man in blue deserted at least once in order to reenlist at another recruitment center under a new name and draw a bounty larger than he had earlier received.

A special class of semiprofessional bounty jumpers developed by the end of 1863. These fellows made brief careers out of

Then prominent only in and around Buffalo, New York, Grover Cleveland secured a Polish immigrant to enlist in the army as his substitute.

NATIONAL ARCHIVES

enlisting, drawing their bounties, deserting, enlisting, and so on, as many as three and four times. In the Department of the Great Lakes, Gen. H. B. Carrington became so furious at bounty jumping by Canadians who had crossed the border for the sake of money that he had several repeat offenders executed.[9]

Undoubtedly the champion bounty jumper of the Civil War was John O'Connor, who was tried by a court-martial at Albany, New York, in March 1865. O'Connor confessed to having deserted and reenlisted thirty-two times before he was recognized at a recruitment station. His brief hitches of service lasted hours instead of days.[10]

Substitutes and Commutation

Grover Cleveland, the twenty-second president of the United States, is frequently listed as the most prominent Northerner who avoided Civil War military service by hiring a substitute to fight for him. For the bargain price of $150 Cleveland managed to avoid the risks of combat by putting thirty-two-year-old Polish immigrant George Benninsky into uniform.[11]

Cleveland was not, however, the best-known man of his time to purchase the service of a military substitute. On September 30, 1864,

HARPER'S HISTORY

Visibly worn from the cares of his office, Abraham Lincoln paid an exceptionally high price to John S. Staples to be his substitute.

John S. Staples of Stroudsburg, Pennsylvania, agreed to become a substitute for a civilian who was exempt from conscription. Recruited by James B. Fry, provost marshal of the District of Columbia, Staples, a carpenter working in the capital, consented to become "a representative recruit" for President Lincoln. Although the *Collected Works* of the wartime commander in chief make no mention of Staples, it is well established that the carpenter donned a uniform as a substitute for the president who did not have to enlist. A few months earlier most persons who hired recruits paid them three hundred dollars or less, but Lincoln paid the native of the Buckeye State five hundred dollars in greenbacks to represent him in uniform.[12]

Vice president Hannibal Hamlin did not follow the example of his chief; he served for two months as a private soldier. Yet when Lincoln's personal secretary, John G. Nicolay, was drafted in 1864, he obtained the services of Hiram Child. A black from North Carolina, Nicolay's substitute died in battle, while Lincoln's substitute survived the war and was given a number of posthumous honors.[13]

The first battles of the most costly of all U.S. wars were fought by volunteers on both sides. When the war dragged into its

Vice President Hannibal Hamlin of Maine did not hire a substitute and served two months in the army.

thirteenth month, on April 16, 1862, the Confederate Congress passed America's first conscription act. Northerners were drafted the following year.

Especially in the North, conscription proved to be a cumbersome and costly failure. Four separate enrollments took place under the act of 1863. Collectively, they put only 160,000 men into uniform. Of these, about three-fourths fought because they had accepted money to serve as substitutes for more prosperous men.[14]

In the North anyone whose name was drawn in a draft lottery could legally avoid donning a blue uniform by paying the Federal government a three-hundred-dollar commutation fee. At the U.S. Treasury Department, Salmon P. Chase and his aides calculated that men who paid commutation fees put more than $26 million into Federal coffers. After draft quotas went into effect, every commutation fee paid went into the record as reducing a state's quota by one man. Yet the man who paid his three hundred dollars was shielded only for the moment. At the next draft, he was again in the eligible pool.[15]

Every man who enlisted in the Federal forces, however—whether eagerly, reluctantly, or as "a hireling in blue"—received a bounty of one hundred dollars. This sum, combined with the substitute's fee, was attractive to many poor farmers and unemployed urban dwellers. As a result, at first Northern substitutes were plentiful.[16]

The Confederate conscription act of 1862 provided for the hiring of substitutes, but the manpower pinch in the South operated to prevent the substitute's fee from becoming standardized. Any man who was hired to fight for another haggled to get the best price he could.

When the struggle was only six months old, the *Richmond Dispatch* began running columns of ads listing potential substitutes:

> A resident of Maryland, who has lately run the block-ade, wishes to become a substitute for any man who is willing to pay him his price. For particulars inquire at C. A. Brockmeyer's segar-store, No. 21 Main street.

> WANTED—A substitute for the war; one of good character, not subject to military draft. A liberal price will be paid if accepted. Apply at my office.—Edw. D. Eacho, 14th St., near Exchange Hotel.

> WANTED—A substitute on board Confederate States steamer Patrick Henry, as wardroom steward. Apply at the *Dispatch* office.[17]

Depreciation of Confederate currency, combined with soaring inflation, soon raised the cost of hiring a substitute in the South to fifteen hundred dollars and later to five thousand dollars. After that peak was reached, the secretary of war called for the repeal of the substitute system.

As substitutes came under closer scrutiny, the first response of the Bureau of Conscription in Richmond was considered by many citizens to be unduly harsh: "Hereafter any one furnishing a substitute will become liable in his own person whenever the services of the substitute are lost to the government from any cause other than the casualties of war." In December 1863 the Confederate Congress repealed the substitution provision, putting an end to what many had earlier denounced as "a sorry business."[18]

In the North draft riots in New York and other cities made substitutes more desirable than ever. With the conscription law branded "an atrocity," brokerage offices sprang up in many urban centers. James A. Garfield explained this new form of business in some detail: "A substitute broker pays bounties and gathers men in gangs for sale, and when the committees of any town are hard pressed to fill their quotas they send to him and buy his ware at exorbitant rates. He gets men for comparatively a small bounty and sells them at enormous prices to the districts that are otherwise unable to meet their quotas."[19]

Numerous brokers hired crimps who were paid twenty-five dollars or more per head for the men they persuaded to enlist or whom they dragged half-drunk to the recruiter. Initially crimps found Canada a fertile field. A sergeant in her majesty's service who was paid $365 a year could receive up to $1,500 up front upon slipping across the border and entering the Federal ranks. In addition to that, he received 160 acres of land when the struggle ended. According to Alan Nevins, thousands of substitutes "pocketed their payments, deserted, and sold themselves over again."[20]

As was the case with bounty payments, substitute inducements fostered the rise of unscrupulous brokers. When the supply of Canadian soldiers and able-bodied men willing to fight for the Union began to dwindle, substitute brokers turned to men past the age limit, young boys, cripples, blacks, and foreigners, hundreds of whom became victims of kidnap gangs. A few large-scale brokers sent agents to England and Europe. One of them recruited future newspaper magnate Joseph Pulitzer in Hamburg, Germany.

In the Federal capital, the asking price from a broker rose to nine hundred dollars per man. Provost Marshal Gen. James B. Fry put a stop to the use of blacks as substitutes, however. During the summer of 1863 he ruled that under the Enrollment Act, "Men of African descent can only be accepted as substitutes for each other."[21]

The relative failure of inducing men to fight by bribing them with bounties and other fees generated one of the most corrupt enterprises of the war. Twenty-four bounty-induced enlistees went into the Thirteenth Massachusetts during the winter of 1863–64; twenty-three deserted. In units where substitutes were numerous, they sometimes formed gangs whose goal was to "go through" every new man. While some engaged his attention, others would appropriate whatever he had that they desired. When one Connecticut substitute, a member of such a gang, was arrested and searched, $60 in greenbacks, a receipt for $480, a pocket knife, two diaries, and a discharge paper were found.[22]

A total of about 115,000 substitutes of all ages, physical conditions, and national backgrounds went into the ranks of blue. With few exceptions they proved to be less than acceptable soldiers. Men whose motivation was personal gain, who had to be financially swayed to carry a weapon, lacked the heart to fight and end a war that had as its ultimate goal freedom for an enslaved people.

Part 3

Stark Reality

Rivers gave both sides opportunities for long-deferred and eagerly anticipated baths. In this photograph, taken in May 1864, several Federals enjoy the comfort of the North Anna River.

9

OUT OF UNIFORM

SOLDIERS IN THE BUFF

CONFEDERATE CONGRESSMEN John W. C. Watson and John Perkins Jr. issued a report on March 3, 1865, on the condition and treatment of prisoners of war held by the South. It vehemently denied charges that Southerners were intentionally starving or treating captive Northerners cruelly. Watson and Perkins instead accused the Federal authorities of grossly misrepresenting the Southern treatment of escaped or paroled prisoners: "They have taken their own sick and enfeebled soldiers; have stripped them naked; have exposed them before a daguerreian apparatus [camera]; have pictured every shrunken limb and muscle— for the purpose of bringing a false and slanderous charge against the South."[1]

This allegation, like many Northern charges of Southern atrocities, was never substantiated. Dead and emaciated Union soldiers may have been photographed sans clothing to support stories of Confederate atrocities, but if so, they represent a small fraction of the foot soldiers in blue and in gray who for one reason or another were seen, sketched, or even photographed naked in the stark light of day. Some of these bodies were stripped by the enemy or even their own comrades; others shed their clothing more or less voluntarily.

If the accusations of Watson and Perkins are true, it is almost matched by an account of what was described in Northern newspapers as fiendishly deadly goings-on in South Carolina. Union Maj. Thomas B. Brooks, an aide to Gen. Quincy A. Gillmore, kept a journal of operations on Morris Island between July 12 and September 7, 1863. According to Brooks's journal, on August 26 a detachment of men in blue moved into a line of Rebel land mines (called torpedoes) and triggered one of the explosive devices, "throwing a corporal of the Third U.S. Colored Troops, of the fatigue detail, 25 yards, and depositing him, entirely naked, with his arm resting on the plunger of another torpedo." This bizarre battlefield death, wrote Brooks, "gave rise, on his being discovered next morning, to the absurd story that the enemy had tied him to a torpedo as a decoy."[2]

No Choice

Because clothing was scarce at times and shoes were always hard to get, it was common practice on both sides to strip the dead who were left on the fields of battle. In Newtonia, Missouri, late in 1862, Union Gen. Edwards Salomon requested permission from an unidentified Confederate counterpart to send clothing to captured officers. His request stemmed from the fact that following a deadly encounter, Federals "found our killed on the battle-field stripped naked."[3]

After the appalling loss of life in the December 13, 1862, battle of Fredericksburg, both sides agreed to a three-day truce to bury the dead. This long interval was necessary because three days would barely permit completion of the work of interment of the waves of Federal casualties shot down before the stone wall at Marye's Heights. One officer was horrified to watch the burial teams go about their business, noting, "Our men went to work robbing the dead without ceremony, and many were stripped of all their clothing—presenting a strange appearance lying on the field." Col. John R. Brooke of the Fifty-third Pennsylvania led a burial detail that took care of 918 bodies. "Nearly all the dead were stripped entirely naked by the enemy," Brooke reported.[4]

In September 1864, during Grant's Richmond campaign, Maj. Samuel Wetherill's Eleventh Pennsylvania Cavalry was attacked near Mount Sinai Church. His men held their ground until ordered to join forces with the Third New York Cavalry at a crossroads. As the body of men moved back toward the church, they found their dead comrades "to have been stripped" so that they "lay nearly naked where they fell."[5]

According to Union Gen. John W. Geary, Confederates desperate for shoes and clothing did not restrict their scavenging to the dead. Near Ringgold, Georgia, in December 1863, Geary reported that Southern indignities had "excited profound horror and indignation." He wrote: "Some of the men of this command, while lying helplessly wounded within the lines of the rebels, were stripped of their clothing, robbed of everything, and their naked bodies left exposed to the inclemencies of the weather until rescued by the advance of our column."[6]

After the 1864 battle of Cedar Creek, hundreds of dead and wounded lay on the ground during the night of October 19. The next morning, as his regiment fanned out over part of the battlefield, Lt. Col. John C. Bennett of the First Vermont Cavalry reported that his men found "the naked forms of their dead and wounded comrades—the former entirely and the latter partially stripped by our inhuman foe."[7]

In the West, where Native American tribes were often the enemy, Union soldiers became accustomed to finding their dead stripped of their clothing. Near Fort Crook, California, in August 1861, Lt. John Fielner's patrol discovered the stripped bodies of two civilians.[8] Like many Confederate units and an occasional body of Federals in the years ahead, these warriors considered the clothing of the dead legitimate spoils of war.

Conversely, outlaws and guerrillas who stripped the dead frequently acted out of pure malice. In Missouri, the civilian head of a mining company castigated "the tardiness and red tape that has characterized the military organization." This situation, he wrote, "has been appreciated by the bushwhackers." On August 23, 1864, a band of fifty-seven to eighty-four "mounted and well-armed men" entered Webster, Missouri, and cleared out the company store and most of the nearby houses. Adding insult to injury, they also stripped several men naked in the street. For the next three weeks, the townspeople complained, "The country seems to have been full of these roving bands."[9]

"Bloody Bill" Anderson and his gang stopped a train at Centralia, Missouri, in September 1864 and found among its passengers two dozen Union soldiers headed home on leave. Herded upon the station platform at gunpoint, the captives obeyed when told to strip and hand over their uniforms. Anderson, whose motive may have been eagerness to disguise his band, ordered the soldiers shot as soon as the last of them had undressed.[10]

At Warsaw, Missouri, after the surrender of all major Confederate forces, a band of irregulars captured James Taylor, a

"Bloody Bill" Anderson was photographed only after his death. At Centralia, Missouri, in September 1864 his band forced a group of captives to stand in the buff in public.

MISSOURI HISTORICAL SOCIETY

Unionist who had been a member of the state militia. According to an eyewitness, the bushwhackers stripped Taylor "naked in the presence of his wife, and cut his throat from ear to ear."[11]

The clothing of prisoners of war, living or dead, was envied by his captors and regarded as a legitimate prize of war. If not seized by guards, it was likely to be reduced to shreds during months of confinement. Prison officials on both sides seldom did anything to aid clothingless inmates because shirts and trousers were needed by fighting men.

D. C. Anderson and J. H. Brown, self-styled "investigators" for a Northern church board, visited Georgia's Andersonville prison in September 1864 and then submitted a horrified report directly to President Lincoln. They found the typical inmate "naked, without shelter by day and by night." One month later Union Judge Advocate General Joseph Holt reported having examined the Andersonville records and learned the names "of over 13,000 dead, buried naked, in one vast sepulcher."[12]

Union Gen. J. G. Foster, reporting to Gen. Henry W. Halleck about the same time, estimated that eighteen hundred captured Federal officers were imprisoned in Charleston. All of them were "destitute of clothing," he said, adding that among prisoners shipped by rail to the port city "one whole car-load was naked."[13]

Gen. Joseph Hayes managed to inspect Richmond's prisons in January 1865. Blankets were desperately needed, he wrote, and he had "instant need of at least 2,000 complete suits of clothing to clothe our men that are absolutely naked, or nearly so." This deplorable situation was not limited to men who were wearing blue when captured, however. Confederate records, scanty as they are, contain numerous comments about "naked prisoners in Federal cells and compounds."[14]

Nakedness was judged to add to the severity of punishment. So many men on both sides were "stripped naked and whipped upon the bare back" that officers seldom recorded these occurrences. Yet Confederate commissioners investigating the treatment of prisoners of war considered one form of chastisement "shameful and barbarous." According to them, imprisoned Confederates had been made "to sit down with their naked bodies in the snow for ten or fifteen minutes" at a time.[15]

There were many instances in which the turmoil of hand-to-hand conflict caused a soldier to lose most or all of his clothing. One such recorded loss took place at the September 1862 battle of Antietam. Pvt. Barney Rogers of the Sixty-first New York raced toward the Bloody Lane without a belt, having improvised one from a ragged strap. While crawling over a fence, the strap snapped and caused his trousers to fall down around his ankles, hobbling him. Sgt. Charles Fuller cut the impeding garment off with a pocket knife, evoking raucous laughter from Rogers's comrades when a lull in the fighting gave everyone a chance to gawk conspicuously at Rogers's "bare backside."[16]

Skinny Dipping

Rivers and creeks—clear or muddy, shallow or deep—offered perhaps the least heinous reason for causing men to shed their clothing. Armies moved across terrain regardless of the availability of roads or bridges. Faced with a river crossing, commanders had little choice but to cross the men as best they could. Water also gave the men an opportunity for long-deferred and eagerly anticipated baths, and Billy Yanks and Johnny Rebs willingly and eagerly took advantage of the occasion as often as possible. Charles W. Willis of the Eighth Illinois, stationed at Cairo, Illinois, during the early weeks of the war noted that the Ohio River was comfortably warm.[17]

Water crossings always made interesting reading in an officer's report, and frequently events contained an amusing element in the telling. For example, describing the exploits of a scouting party led by Col. James P. Brownlow of the First Tennessee Cavalry in July 1864, Gen. E. M. McCook wrote: "Brownlow performed one of his characteristic feats to-day. I had ordered a detachment to cross at a ford. It was deep, and he took them over naked, nothing but guns, cartridge-boxes and hats. They drove the enemy out of their rifle-pits, captured a non-commissioned officer and 3 men, and the 2 boats on the other side. They would have got more, but the rebels had the advantage in running through the bushes with clothes on. It was certainly one of the funniest sights of the war, and a very successful raid for naked men to make."[18]

Such orders were not that uncommon. Crossing the Potomac River into Maryland on September 5, 1862, Confederate Col. James A. Walker noticed that a Virginia unit just ahead of him was thoroughly wet. He halted his brigade long enough for his soldiers to remove their clothing, which they rolled around their cartridge and cap boxes. They then moved into the river "with their pants and shoes held above their heads." At White's Ford Gen. Joseph Kershaw's regiments did the same thing on the following day.[19]

Long before the war ended, this method of crossing deep water had become standard procedure. Dispatched to swing around Confederate forces in Georgia in July 1864, many troopers under Gen. James B. McPherson "swam the [Chattahoochee] river naked except for their cartridge belts."[20]

Maryland ladies who gathered on the bank of the Potomac to watch the Army of Northern Virginia launch its 1863 invasion of the North did not find the scene amusing. They were instead "shocked to see the long columns of Confederate soldiers wading the river" with their clothing and equipment held over their heads.[21]

Many a Yankee who waded or swam one or more rivers in the buff probably remembered the day his regiment was organized. Lengthy instructions for this exercise, issued in Washington on April 16, 1861, include this sentence: "The [physical] examination of a company naked, with the inconvenience generally felt at such places by the want of suitable buildings, requires two or three hours."[22]

Near Cedar Creek, a commander whom his men characterized as "easy-going" assented when captured Rebels begged permission to join bathers who had shed their blue uniforms. Watching Billy Yanks and Johnny Rebs splash in the river together, Capt. Theodore F. Allen of the Seventh Ohio Cavalry heard a Confederate officer muse, "It is difficult to tell 't'other from which.' "[23]

Sometimes bathing proved disastrous. Sixty Federals, members of the Sixth West Virginia Cavalry, snatched an opportunity to bathe in the South Branch River during the summer of 1864. Confederates led by Capt. John H. McNeil, probably numbering less than a hundred, slipped quietly upon their enemies and captured every man.[24]

Capt. H. C. Weaver of the Sixteenth Kentucky led one of the regiments that tried to stop John B. Morgan's famous 1863 cavalry raid into that state. According to Weaver, a band of retreating Confederates was heard approaching while "many of the infantry were bathing in the creek." His men "gathered their clothes and ran toward their guns as a preface to one of the most ludicrous spectacles of the war—half-nude soldiers fighting Morgan's men."[25]

During the same dramatic raid, many Confederates crossed the half-mile-wide Cumberland River in the buff. By the time they reached their destination, it was held by members of a Federal patrol. Bennet H. Young, who was among the raiders, said that soldiers "dashed upon the enemy" as they emerged from the river. Young noted, "The strange sight of naked men engaging in combat amazed the enemy. The Union pickets didn't know what to think of soldiers fighting as naked as jaybirds."[26]

These were not the only recorded instances of combat in the nude, however. Confederate Gen. Matt W. Ransom gave men of the Twenty-fourth North Carolina permission to bathe in a millpond on July 26, 1863. Most of them were still in the water when several hundred cavalrymen in blue converged upon the scene. Following orders to grab their weapons and man the trenches, Ransom's men had their fingers on their triggers when the enemy arrived. For five hours, the Union horsemen "tried to find a way around the entrenched nudists of Boone's Mill, but the swamp [behind them] was too vast."[27]

Fighting in Tennessee, Gen. Nathan Bedford Forrest and his rangers saw the Yankee steamer *Mazeppa* swing around a distant bend in a river. On the vessel the alert pilot realized that danger was ahead, so he ran his vessel aground. He and other members of

Some of William T. Sherman's soldiers managed to enjoy the Chattahoochee River after two months of hard fighting in northern Georgia.

the crew took to the woods as soon as the craft stopped—leaving it stranded in sight of enemies who had no way to reach it. In this strange situation, Confederate Capt. Frank Gravey stripped, "hung his pistol around his neck, and using a plank for flotation, swam to the beached steamer" and took possession of it.[28]

Confederate cavalry wizard Wade Hampton reportedly released a man in blue whom he captured bathing in the buff, but he kept the fellow's clothes. Incredulous at his good luck, the bather asked the name of his generous captor and blurted that he'd like to name a son for him as a token of gratitude. Years later, as a member of the U.S. Senate, the former general met a northerner who said he was the son whose name stemmed from release of his naked father.[29]

Another time Hampton almost succeeded in capturing Gen. Judson Kilpatrick, who was surprised by Rebels "while in the arms of his mistress." This time the Confederate commander did not get his man. Kilpatrick managed to make a hasty escape—reputedly clad only in his underwear.[30]

Renowned though he was for severity in dealing with the enemy, Gen. William T. Sherman did not mind being seen in daylight without his clothing. When many of his men stripped and plunged into the Chattahoochee River on July 9, 1864, "a jubilant Sherman" jumped into the water with them "to wash away two months of campaign grime." No artist was present that time, but a man from *Harper's Weekly* was on hand when other troops commanded by Sherman bathed at Cochran's Ford in the same river.[31]

Ulysses S. Grant never would have followed Sherman's example, regardless of how dirty he was. Described as careless to the point of being slouchy in dress, the Union's only lieutenant general scrupulously avoided being seen in the nude. Conversely, Gen. John A. Logan of Illinois, later commander of the Grand Army of the Republic and a serious candidate for the U.S. presidency, seems to have had few if any inhibitions. Newspaper correspondent Sylvanus Cadwallader once came upon "Black Jack" Logan during a period of relaxation and wrote that: "Wearing but his hat and boots, he sat at a table on which stood a bottle of whiskey and a tin cup." At intervals the general picked up a violin and played while some of the blacks who had flocked to his camp danced to his music. Appearances to the contrary, the correspondent asserted, Logan "was not intoxicated from the beginning to the end of the war." On this occasion, he seems simply to have reveled in the fun of fiddling in the buff.[32]

10

FEAR IN THE FIELD

COWARDS IN BLUE AND GRAY

GEN. DANIEL TYLER commanded the First Division, Army of Northeastern Virginia, at Centreville, Virginia, on the morning of July 18, 1861. As his men departed that village, they turned toward Manassas Junction and soon found themselves facing a Confederate force at Blackburn's Ford.

No man in blue on the field that morning had ever heard the whistle of an enemy's bullet hurled in his direction before that moment. With the exception of a few officers, all of Tyler's men were ninety-day volunteers whose terms of enlistment were due to expire soon. When the enemy lobbed a few shells into his line, the general ordered a withdrawal. Having stumbled upon the Rebel batteries, Tyler felt his mission had been accomplished.

As soon as the division began to pull back, something went very wrong. Companies A and I of the Twelfth New York had "stood their ground gallantly," but suddenly these soldiers were terrified. Some of them turned and ran until their officers were able to rally them a mile into the rear. These actions caused the New Yorkers to be the first Civil War soldiers branded as cowards. That charge, however, does not appear in Tyler's report of the "disorganization" produced by the Southern shelling.[1]

Traditionally, those who view the Civil War as a moonlight-and-magnolias affair tend to believe that every man who wore a uniform in the war was valiant and heroic—especially according to their descendants. While this perspective is not absolutely accurate, that belief comes very close to the truth. Only about one-tenth of 1 percent of those who wore blue or gray were labeled as cowards. Those who broke and ran under fire are generally

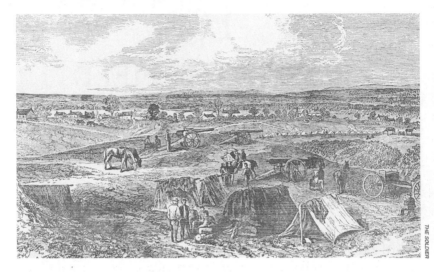

Federal volunteers who passed through the tiny village of Centreville, Virginia, later heavily fortified, had never heard the whine of an enemy's bullet.

unidentified. Only a handful of individuals, mostly officers, have been specified by name as lacking in courage.

There was a general rout of Union soldiers at the July 1861 battle of First Bull Run, but the literature about the first major encounter between the armed forces does not condemn those involved as lacking courage. Three months later at Ball's Bluff, Virginia, it was different story. The Federals moved on the bluffs without benefit of reconnaissance, and the Confederates caught them in the open and drove them into the river, maintaining a steady fire for "as long as the faintest ripple could be seen" on the water. Early in the action, London-born Col. Edward D. Baker, a sitting member of the U.S. Senate and a close friend of President Lincoln, was killed. Of the 1,700 men who began the assault, 49 were killed, 158 wounded, and 714 missing, of which as many as 100 had drowned—more than 50 percent casualties. The embarassment of the debacle led to the founding of the Joint Committee on the Conduct of the War, which held hearings on what went wrong at Ball's Bluff. Cowardice was listed as one of the chief causes. "When the day was hopelessly lost," a participant later said, "the [unidentified] colonel of the Twentieth

The death of Col. Edward Baker, a U.S. senator from Oregon, at Ball's Bluff, Virginia, triggered creation of the Joint Congressional Committee on the Conduct of the War.

sought refuge behind a tree." Along with his major and adjutant, the officer fled from the field, "leaving his men to follow as best they might."[2]

At Shiloh in April 1862, several incidents revealed more cowards among the ranks. Men of the Thirteenth Ohio Battery fled, leaving behind their guns, caissons, ammunition, and horses. Their commander, John B. Myers, was reputedly found "cowering under the banks of the Tennessee River."[3]

Some members of the Fifty-seventh Ohio had never fired a gun when they faced the enemy at Shiloh. After these green soldiers fell back from the line of battle, a junior officer found their colonel lying on the ground behind a tree. Efforts to persuade him to rally his men proved useless, for "our colonel was a coward," concluded E. C. Dawes, who later advanced to the rank of major.[4]

Following what initially seemed to be a Confederate victory that created chaos in Federal ranks, a newspaper correspondent found numerous skulkers lining the banks of the Tennessee River. "Agate," of the *Cincinnati Gazette,* told readers that the sight of these cowards made his cheeks tingle.[5]

Riding toward Pittsburg Landing, Gen. Ulysses S. Grant used a road described as "lined with fleeing and frightened men." After these cowards became battle-hardened, however, Gen. William T. Sherman said that they were among the best troops in his command.[6]

A few weeks after "Bloody Shiloh," in Virginia, George B. McClellan's Peninsula campaign began to unravel at the battle of Seven Pines (also known as Fair Oaks). This time the cowards wore gray. Confederate Gen. Daniel H. Hill reputedly found men of the Ninth Virginia huddled in a ditch and castigated them as "these cowardly Virginians."[7]

At Gaines's Mill in June 1862, Confederate Gen. William H. C. Whiting saw men "leaving the field in every direction and in great disorder." Some of these cowards, he reported, "were actually marching back from the fire."[8]

On the last day of the same month, men in blue were forced back from their position at White Oak Swamp (or Frayser's Farm). Thomas Livermore of the Eighteenth New Hampshire was aghast to see that members of an unidentified New York regiment "ran away when the first shell burst in front of them." Troops under Gen. John C. Caldwell stopped this flight with leveled bayonets. He and his men, Livermore later wrote, "were pleased to have rebuked this cowardice."[9]

Union Gen. Paul J. Semmes viewed the whole of the Seven Days' battles in retrospect. Well before the July 4 battle of Crew's Farm, he observed, "The coward and the skulker sought safety in inglorious flight from the bloody field under cover of the darkness."[10]

During the following month Gen. D. H. Hill "threw out skirmishers to stop stragglers." In a burst of anger he "tore off the bars of a lieutenant who was skulking to the rear."[11] Hill's actions at Cedar Run seem to have had little if any effect upon other cowards in gray. At Antietam (or Sharpsburg), the Confederate general raged at "the enormous straggling." In his official report of the battle, he pointed out, "The straggler is generally a thief and always a coward, lost to all sense of shame; he can only be kept in ranks by a strict and sanguinary discipline."[12]

During the last month of 1862, Col. Absalom B. Moore of the 104th Illinois reported to Gen. William S. Rosecrans that he had seen some men of the 106th Ohio stampede when ordered to charge the enemy. Moore asked "to have the conduct of every officer who ran like a coward from the field fully inquired into," but nothing came of his request.[13]

At Chancellorsville in May 1863, Regis de Trobriand felt the ground moving under his feet when he headed toward a point at which firing had nearly ceased. Puzzled, he investigated and found that "five or six poltroons" in blue had dug a hole in which to hide, "literally packed like sardines in a box."

In another part of the battlefield, members of the Eleventh Corps, comprised mostly of German immigrants, were later charged with fleeing from the enemy. Reports of their cowardice triggered a congressional investigation, but it went nowhere because Gens. Joseph Hooker and Oliver O. Howard—whose men were thus accused—were still in command.[14]

In July 1863 fighting near Charleston, the "poltroons" wore gray. Gen. William B. Taliaferro reported that members of the Thirty-first North Carolina behaved disgracefully. They created a hole in the line by "ingloriously deserting the ramparts," he said. As a result of their cowardice, the enemy pushed forward and occupied the Confederate work.[15]

Twenty-five years later the Gettysburg Battlefield Memorial Association fought with survivors of the Seventy-second Pennsylvania over the placement of a monument. In a case tried before the Pennsylvania Supreme Court, members of the Seventy-second were formally accused of cowardice. Veterans of the Zouave unit claimed to have been in the thick of the action at the western wall of the Bloody Angle. Not so, said the Memorial Association, which made the formal charges of cowardice based on evidence that the regiment faltered when it should have advanced.[16]

According to Capt. S. D. Duck of the Thirteenth Virginia, at Fisher's Hill members of a North Carolina brigade "broke without firing a gun or seeing a yankee." His account of this action concluded: "While the North Carolinians were breaking over us [Virginians] Gen. Jubal Early rode up and ordered our regiment to fire into them if they would not stop. His order was not obeyed."[17]

Two months later, far to the south at Bayou Bourbeau, Louisiana, according to Gen. Stephen G. Burbridge, men of the Sixty-seventh Indiana dawdled when they should have acted decisively. Eventually the outfit was surrendered en masse to Confederate cavalry. Hence Gen. Cadwallader C. Washburn charged the unit and its commander, Lt. Col. Theodore Buehler, with cowardice.[18]

Newspaper correspondent A. J. Daugherty was appalled by what he saw near Resaca, Georgia, on May 14, 1864. According to him, about one hundred of Sherman's demoralized men were driven from the field by officers. They huddled together near a battery for a time, reported Daugherty, then "gave way and ran" when the Rebels charged.[19]

One unit—the Twenty-second Virginia Battalion of the Army of Northern Virginia—was disbanded for cowardice. Although constituted of six companies on paper, the battalion had only 120 men fit for duty in October 1864 when Gen. Henry Heth notified Confederate Adjutant Gen. Samuel Cooper that "this Battalion on every battle field, from Gettysburg up to the present time, has behaved in a most disgraceful manner." Infamous as the only unit in gray or in blue in which every member was called a coward, the Twenty-second ceased to exist when its members were dispersed among other Virginia units.[20]

Troubles with command-grade officers began very early and continued until the end of the war. Confederate Thomas H. Bradley gained the dubious distinction as the first general officer to be dismissed from service. A general of Arkansas state forces who was branded in newspapers as cowardly and incompetent, Bradley was forced to take off his uniform in July 1861.[21]

Just three months later a Federal officer faced charges near Newport News, Virginia, when twelve members of a New York

Zouave regiment were captured by the enemy. Their commander was immediately charged with cowardice and placed under arrest.[22]

Before the year ended a group of U.S. congressmen asked the secretary of war to investigate the conduct of Maj. Isaac Lynde of the Seventh Infantry, U.S. Army. Because he surrendered Fort Fillmore, New Mexico, without firing a shot, they charged that he was a coward or a traitor—or both.[23]

Col. Jesse J. Appler of the Fifty-third Ohio lost his post during his first battle. At Shiloh he was alleged to have yelled to his men, "Retreat and save yourselves!" before leading the way to safety.[24]

In August 1862, Col. R. Mason of the Seventy-first Ohio was cashiered for cowardice at Clarksville, Tennessee.[25]

One month later Col. William H. Christian of the Twenty-sixth New York fled from the field, reputedly "ducking and dodging Confederate shells." His outraged men forced Christian to resign on September 19, 1862. In March 1865 an inept congressional body made him a brevet general, the only man forced from uniform for cowardice who attained that honorary rank.[26]

The colonel who led the Fiftieth Ohio at Perryville, Kentucky, was less fortunate. A fellow officer charged that during combat he found the colonel "lying on his face, crouching behind a stump." Facing a possible court-martial for cowardice, the officer resigned and nothing more was heard of him.[27]

Confederate Lt. T. B. Garrett was called a coward by the men who served under him. As a result, Col. S. W. Ferguson placed him under arrest in April 1863. What punishment he received, if any, was not recorded.[28]

At Battery Huger, Virginia, on April 19, 1863, numerous men of the Fifty-fifth North Carolina were captured, leading to recriminations by fellow Rebels from Alabama. In turn, Col. John K. Connally of the Fifty-ninth North Carolina charged that all but nine Alabamans under Capt. L. R. Terrill "deserted him" and ran for their lives when the bullets began to fly.

Gen. Evander Law investigated the growing quarrel and formally branded the Tar Heels as cowards. Enraged, Connally launched an investigation. When he discovered the names of the Alabamans who originated the charge of cowardice, he suggested a way to settle the issue. Officers of his regiment, he said, were willing to meet the Alabama officers in a mass duel.

Lt. Col. Maurice T. Smith of North Carolina opposed these proceedings on moral grounds, so the fight never took place. Two months later, on the first day at Gettysburg, Smith the peacemaker was killed in action.[29]

When Nathan Bedford Forrest accused a subordinate of cowardice, a fight actually erupted. Enraged that Forrest would not discuss the charge with him, Lt. Andrew W. Gould pulled out a pistol and shot his commander in the hip. Forrest, armed only with a penknife, used it so effectively that "the cowardly lieutenant was mortally wounded."[30]

Virginia native John R. Jones was furious when the Confederate Senate refused to confirm his promotion to general. The lawmakers were vindicated on May 2, 1863. During heavy fighting at Chancellorsville, Jones used an ulcerated leg as an excuse to stay out of the fight. His superiors did not buy that excuse, so they branded him as a coward and soon had him cashiered.[31]

Also at Chancellorsville, a recently confirmed general, Alfred Iverson, was hit in the groin by a nearly spent minié ball. He abandoned his men under fire and went to the rear. Subordinates, who disliked the haughty soldier from Georgia, called Iverson a coward. He had sufficient friends in high places to weather the storm, however, and soon led his brigade to Carlisle, Pennsylvania.[32]

Confederate Gen. George E. Pickett was not personally involved in the suicidal advance at the battle of Gettysburg known as Pickett's Charge. Some who actually took part in the fiasco branded Pickett as a coward. Generations later, there is still disagreement as to whether or not fear of his life kept Pickett out of the fray on that dreadful day.[33]

James S. Negley, a little-known Union general, was at Chickamauga in September 1863 when his division was swept back so rapidly that he was subject to court-martial on charges of cowardice and desertion. Officers who made up the court refused to convict Scott, but he never again received a field command.[34]

The case of a general in blue, John H. H. Ward, never went to trial. Accused of having run away from the fight in the Wilderness, he was relieved of command and arrested on May 12, 1864. Without benefit of a formal hearing, he was dismissed from the service two months later.[35]

In June 1864 fierce fighting erupted at Secessionville, South Carolina. This time, the culprit was an unidentified Confederate officer. Sgt. Samuel W. Dibble found him hiding and "drove him from behind a tree about four inches in diameter, which he supposed in his fright covered his whole body."[36]

Far to the north during the same month, many men of Union Gen. James H. Ledlie's division were slaughtered in the battle of the Crater at Petersburg. Ledlie was not injured. During the bloody fight, he was safely tucked into a bombproof, drinking rum with Gen. Edward Ferrero.

A court of inquiry issued harsh criticism of both cowardly generals, and Gen. George G. Meade soon read Ledlie out of the army. When he learned of the verdict, one subordinate said that his removal from command "was a heavy loss to Rebels."[37]

As a colonel of cavalry, George B. Hodge twice saw his nomination as general rejected by the Confederate Senate. With the fate of the seceded states virtually decided, he was formally charged with cowardice in January 1865. Less than sixty days later, Nathan Bedford Forrest relieved him of command and ordered him to Richmond for a new assignment that he never received.[38]

While the fighting was slowing grinding to a halt in 1865, Confederate Gen. W. H. C. Whiting charged Braxton Bragg with cowardice after the fall of North Carolina's Fort Fisher. Captured and imprisoned in the taking of the fort, Whiting brooded over his experience as commander of the defenses of Wilmington, North Carolina. On his deathbed in March 1865 he swore that Bragg displayed nothing but cowardice at Fort Fisher.[39]

Confederate Gen. Braxton Bragg
was accused of cowardice by a
fellow general who fought at
Wilmington, North Carolina.

U.S. ARMY MILITARY HISTORY INSTITUTE

Punishment meted out to a man who fled from the enemy with brass on his shoulders varied from dismissal to perfunctory reprimands, but a few were rewarded with promotions. Early in the struggle, Union Gen. E. D. Keyes warned that "to decorate a coward with shoulder-straps is to pave the road to a nation's ruin."[40]

One of his counterparts in gray, Gen. P. G. T. Beauregard, wanted all cowards to be "shot on the spot." Although there is no evidence that his views were adopted, men acting as file closers or field officers commonly ran beside charging units with drawn pistols, threatening to shoot any man who faltered.[41]

Self-humiliation was the only punishment inflicted on Prussian-born Alexander Schimmelfenning. He had immigrated in 1853. When the war started, he was made colonel of the Seventh Pennsylvania. Slightly more than a year later he was promoted to general and given command of a corps largely made up of German immigrants.

On the first day at Gettysburg, Schimmelfenning is believed to have been knocked unconscious during hand-to-hand fighting. When he regained his senses and found himself behind the Confederate lines, he reputedly spent the rest of the battle hiding in a pigsty. Humiliated, he requested a transfer and later took part in action near Charleston—still wearing the rank that he had taken into the pigsty.[42]

Proportionally, cowardly officers ranging from lieutenant to general were more numerous than enlisted men. Yet the total of officers and men who fled rather than fight was astonishingly small.

One estimate places the number of Union foot soldiers at 2.67 million. An additional 106,000 men are believed to have fought with the navy. Because Confederate records were lost or destroyed, estimates of the South's total enlistment vary from 600,000 to 1.4 million. If the conservative figure of 750,000 is accepted, more than 3.6 million men took part in the Civil War.[43]

Since no more than 3,000 to 4,000 men and officers were branded as cowards at some point during the war, the battlefield conduct of 999 out of every 1,000 fighting men ranged from acceptable to heroic.

11

WELL-KNOWN PERSONALITIES OF THE WAR

NAME THESE MEN

FEW PEOPLE in American history have been described in greater detail than the political and military leaders of the Civil War. They are sometimes so well known that their names come to mind after only a brief description highlights their distinctive traits. The names below match the descriptions that follow on the next few pages. How many can you identify? Eleven out of twenty one would be an excellent score. The answers are on page 131.

William Anderson
P. G. T. Beauregard
Benjamin F. Butler
Charles H. Davis
Jefferson Davis
Samuel F. Du Pont
Nathan Evans
Richard Ewell
David Farragut
Andrew Hull Foote
Nathan Bedford Forrest

Ulysses S. Grant
Benjamin Grierson
Henry W. Halleck
Henry Heth
Abraham Lincoln
George E. Pickett
Robert E. Rodes
John Sedgwick
Richard Taylor
Charles S. Winder

1. This youthful Confederate general was highly unpopular with his men because he was a strict disciplinarian. He first smelled Federal gunpowder at Fort Sumter. The historian Douglas Southall Freeman described him as having "thin, waving hair combed back from a wide and towering forehead. A curling beard seemed to lengthen his sensitive, intelligent face. Restless, alert

eyes, deep-set, reflected both daring and ill health. In the field he was flawlessly uniformed, even to immaculate gauntlets." His dashing appearance, however, meant nothing to Stonewall Jackson, who was angered to learn that thirty men had been bucked and gagged on orders from this comrade in arms, who was later killed at Cedar Mountain.[1]

2. A Confederate bushwhacker who wore a blue uniform coat, this horseman favored the slouch hat that was common at the time. About five feet ten inches tall, he was described as "slender, with thick brown hair that fell to his neck and a full beard and mustache. He had thin lips and cold expressionless eyes of a strange blue-gray color." At least one contemporary, awed by his prowess in hand-to-hand combat, said that in such a situation he raged like a wild beast and seemed to be "a man possessed of the devil." He was deservedly called Bloody Bill, and after his death his head was displayed on a telephone pole.[2]

3. A West Pointer who changed uniforms very early, this swarthy Confederate general has been described as having "bloodhound eyes." He had a prominent mustache but no beard, and he typically appeared in public with "his hair brushed forward at the temples." Tremendously popular in the South as the hero of Fort Sumter, he was a Creole who spoke French before he learned English.[3]

4. This army general in chief is rated more highly today than he was during the war. Despised by many Union subordinates, he had large, staring eyes under a bulbous brow that some observers called "fish eyes." When pondering a decision, he typically pursed his lips under his "hawk-beak nose." Described as "a man of icy reserve," he fancied himself a scholar, but his nickname of "Old Brains" was meant to be derogatory rather than complimentary. He brought discipline and efficiency to the army but was himself incompetent as a field commander.[4]

5. A contemporary said of this politician who became a Union major general despite his lack of military experience: "With his head set immediately on a stout, shapeless body, his very squinting eyes, and a set of legs and arms that look as if made for somebody else and hastily glued to him by mistake, he presents a combina-

tion of Victor Emmanuel, Aesop, and Richard III—which is very confusing to the mind." Another observer said that he looked like "a New York 'Blood-tub' or a 'plug-ugly.'" He was nicknamed Beast and Spoons. At Fort Monroe his treatment of escaped slaves helped to change Union policy toward African Americans.[5]

6. A musician who became an illustrious Federal cavalry leader, he was described as "a wiry, gangling man, his swarthy, scar-marked face surrounded by rich black hair and a beard worn in the down-spreading spade shape of the times." A reluctant horseman, he led his men on an eight-hundred-mile ride to try to divert as many Confederates as possible away from Grant's movements toward Vicksburg in 1863.[6]

7. This Confederate general, widely known as Shanks, was described as being "of medium height, slightly bald, with the fiercest of black mustachios, and small, restless eyes to match. His look was quick, cunning and contentious, as if he were always suspecting a Comanche ambush." At Ball's Bluff he won a spectacular victory and earned the thanks of the Confederate Congress; however, he later lost his command because of alcoholism and disobedience of orders.[7]

8. Called "more of a scholar than a sailor," this Union flag officer of the Mississippi flotilla was commander at the naval battle that resulted in the surrender of Memphis. He earlier had served as fleet officer at Port Royal. With "flowing brown mustache and gray rim whiskers," he headed the Naval Observatory after the war.[8]

9. He was adopted by Comdr. David Porter and went to sea in 1810 and served during the War of 1812. He was living in the South at the time the Civil War broke out and quickly moved his family north, but his loyalty was initially questioned. In April 1862 he captured New Orleans and then moved on to join Federal efforts at taking Vicksburg. During his greatest victory at Mobile in 1864 he shouted the famous battle cry, "Damn the torpedoes! Full speed ahead!" One historian described him this way: "His large brow, covered with curling black hair, his long face, keen hazel eyes, and tremendous jaw made him look the leader he was—'Old Heart of Oak'—but his face usually wore a genial smile."[9]

10. A Confederate general whose peers addressed him simply as "Dick," before the war he had fought against Mexicans and Indians then turned in his commission on May 7, 1861. After losing a leg at Groveton, he was strapped in his saddle so he could fight at Gettysburg. He was described as "bald, pop-eyed and long beaked, with a piping voice that seems to fit his appearance as a strange, unlovely bird" that some said was an eagle, but others saw as a woodcock. Nevertheless, he combined a fighting spirit with "a sharp tongue and an odd sense of humor."[10]

11. A Yankee who first saw this Rebel cavalry leader at night, by the dim glow of candles, was so fascinated by this charismatic leader and superb field commander with no military training that he penned a long account of his visual impressions: "His eyes appeared to be brown—pleasant looking and lit up occasionally by a gleam of soldierly bravery. His expression, both pleasant and striking, is given to his physiognomy by the slightest possible elevation of his eyebrows. The latter are black with a slight tinge of gray, and a black moustache and chin whiskers, both cut short, add to the military bearing of the man. His face is long, and cheekbones rather prominent, eyes large, though not noticeably so, and the head full above the eyes and ears. The contrast of the gray hair and the waxen face and black whiskers gives a very aristocratic appearance. His habitual expression seemed rather subdued and thoughtful, but when his face is lighted up by a smile, which ripples all over his features, the effect is really charming."[11]

12. This Rebel general failed to captivate a single Federal officer and his men viewed him with a unique blend of admiration and fear. At his first meeting with Thomas J. "Stonewall" Jackson, he saluted before announcing his name and rank. While waiting for a reply, he sized up his superior and of him said that he noticed "a pair of cavalry boots covering feet of a gigantic size, a mangy cap with visor drawn low, a heavy, dark beard, and weary eyes—eyes I afterward saw filled with intense but never brilliant light. A low, gentle voice inquired the road and distance marched that day." What gentle-sounding general was often greatly interested in how many miles had been covered during a march or ride?[12]

13. He graduated at the bottom of his class at West Point and was a close friend of James Longstreet. When Longstreet was wounded

during the storming of the palace at Chapultepec during the Mexican War, he turned and handed the American flag to this man, who carried it over the wall. When three of Longstreet's children died in a scarlet fever epidemic that raged through Richmond in 1862, the general and his wife were too grief-stricken to attend the children's funeral, and this man made the arrangements for the burial in a Richmond cemetery. Most critics contend that this man did not lead the famous charge that bears his name. Confederate Col. Gilbert Moxley Sorrel described him as "a singular figure, indeed [who was] a medium-sized, well-built man, straight, erect, and in a well-fitting uniform, an elegant riding whip in hand [and] wearing long ringlets that flowed loosely over his shoulders, trimmed, and highly perfumed. His beard likewise was curling and giving out the scents of Arab[y]."[13]

14. He was a graduate of the Virginia Military Institute and was in fact teaching there at the time the Civil War began. He was wounded at Seven Pines and Antietam. Subordinate to Stonewall Jackson, he led the famous flank attack on the Federal Eleventh Corps at Chancellorsville, after which he was promoted to major general. He was called "a martial figure" and described as "six feet tall, clear-eyed, thin, with a dropping tawny mustache." Who was this enigmatic figure who fought valiantly at Gettysburg, Spotsylvania, and Monocacy before being killed by a Federal shell at the battle of Third Winchester?[14]

15. This Federal admiral, a crusader for temperance and against the slave trade, led a Bible class for members of his crew on Sundays when not engaged in battle. A hero in the fight for control of the Mississippi River, he was seen as "a small man with burning eyes, a jutting gray chin-beard, and a long, naked upper lip." In February 1862 he worked in conjunction with Ulysses S. Grant to take Forts Henry and Donelson in Tennessee. He was removed from command due to ill health, promoted, and given a desk job in Washington. Unhappy away from the action, he requested a transfer and was given command of the South Atlantic Blockading Squadron, but he died en route to reporting for duty.[15]

16. During the battle of the Wilderness, Union Col. Horace Porter saw this general for the first time and said that he was surprised "to find in him a man of slim figure, slightly stooped, five feet eight

Col. Horace Porter wrote a terse but vivid description of this Union general after their first encounter during the battle of the Wilderness.

NICOLAY & HAY, *LINCOLN*

inches in height, weighing only a hundred and thirty-five pounds, and of a modesty of mien and gentleness of manner which seemed to fit him more for the court than for the camp." This man had expressive dark-gray eyes, a mouth "of the letter-box shape, the contact of the lips forming a nearly horizontal line," chestnut-brown hair and beard, and a small wart on his right cheek "just above the line of the beard." His left eye was slightly lower than his right eye, and "his gait in walking might have been called decidedly unmilitary; he never carried his body erect."[16]

17. He was born in Kentucky but lived most of his life in Mississippi. While a cadet at West Point, he was not a distinguished scholar and almost killed himself stumbling back drunk to the barracks one night after visiting the local tavern. He married the daughter of a future president, but she died of malaria three months later and he blamed himself, becoming a recluse. Ten years later he began a political career that lasted the rest of his life. He served in the Mexican War under his former father-in-law and later as an adviser when the general occupied the White House. Some historians call him the best secretary of war this country has ever had. When war came he was a senator, and before resigning from

"Uncle John" was from Connecticut. He was a professional soldier who in 1861 had twenty-four years of experience.

LIBRARY OF CONGRESS

the Senate, he made an impassioned speech for which "he struck the accustomed preliminary stance of the orators of his day: high-stomached, almost sway-backed, the knuckles of one hand braced against the desk top." He was "close-shaven except for the tuft of beard at the jut of the chin." His forehead was high and square, "etched with the fine crisscross lines of pain and overwork." His deep-set gray eyes were "large and lustrous, though one was partly covered by a film." He had high cheekbones, a wide jaw, and the nostrils of his aquiline nose were "broad and delicately chiseled."[17]

18. When he was struck by a bullet at Spotsylvania, he was the third corps commander of the Army of the Potomac to be killed in action. Because this bachelor seemed to be kind and gentle, many of his men referred to him as "Uncle John." He was described as being "a stocky, solid man of medium height with thick black hair and bushy beard tinged with gray. His mustache, also dark, had a hint of a twist at the ends, and probably was waxed. His bright and sparkling eyes reflected his kindly nature. His dress was a bit unorthodox—he often wore a pork pie hat, civilian pants, and a

long uniform coat with a velvet collar. On special occasions he donned a formal full uniform, which gave him a very soldierly appearance." The highlight of his career was at Gettysburg, and many speculated that he might be given command of the Army of the Potomac.[18]

19. This Union rear admiral entered the navy in 1815 and in 1861 was considered by some to be too old to fight. He was, however, described as "a hale, well-set-up aristocrat with a dignified but genial manner and a growth of luxuriant whiskers describing a bushy U about his chops and under his clean-shaven mouth and chin." In command of the South Atlantic Blockading Squadron, he directed the victory at Port Royal. In the bid to take Charleston, he led a fleet of monitors into Charleston Harbor in April 1863. After a two-hour battle, he withdrew and was removed from command.[19]

20. This Confederate general inadvertently started the battle of Gettysburg when his troops made contact with the enemy while looking for shoes. He graduated at the bottom of his West Point class of 1847, and during fourteen years of frontier duty rose to the rank of captain before switching uniforms in April 1861. He is described as "of medium height" but trim in figure, wearing a "dark, brushy mustache, which soon turned gray." His "receding hairline, and deep-set, contemplative eyes made him appear considerably older than his 35 years."[20]

21. He was born in Kentucky but grew up in Indiana. The only military service he ever knew was as a captain of militia during the Black Hawk War. He had a checkered poltical career, losing more elections than he won. When not in public office, he practiced law. Gov. Oliver P. Morton of Indiana described this man, whose height forced most folk to look up to him, saying, "He's a queer-looking figure. His trouser legs are several inches too short; the sleeves of the gray check coat are only halfway down to his wrists and the swallow-tails are too short. His roughly chiseled features, befitting a man much older than he, made him look as if carved out of wood." Only a few of his contemporaries took note of the fact that when this man was excited his left eye was likely to jerk upward. When he sat for an 1864 portrait, he parted his hair on the right rather than the customary left side.[21]

Answers to questions in Chapter 11

1. Charles S. Winder
2. William Anderson
3. P. G. T. Beauregard
4. Henry W. Halleck
5. Benjamin F. Butler
6. Benjamin Grierson
7. Nathan Evans
8. Charles H. Davis
9. David G. Farragut
10. Richard Ewell
11. Nathan Bedford Forrest
12. Richard Taylor
13. George E. Pickett
14. Robert E. Rodes
15. Andrew Hull Foote
16. Ulysses S. Grant
17. Jefferson Davis
18. John Sedgwick
19. Samuel F. Du Pont
20. Henry Heth
21. Abraham Lincoln

12

UNSOLVED MYSTERIES

AND ENDURING MYTHS

Names and Papers

THE STORY of how the quiet former professor at Virginia Military Institute, Thomas Jonathan Jackson, was turned into the mythic figure of Stonewall Jackson is the stuff of legend. At the first major battle of the war, First Manassas, Gen. Barnard Bee's Alabama regiments were taking heavy losses near Henry House Hill. Bee reportedly rallied his men by saying something like, "Look! There stands Jackson like a stone wall. Let us resolve to die here, and we shall conquer."

Shortly after that, Bee was mortally wounded, but the Mighty Stonewall lived on as a truly legendary figure. Not quite two years later Jackson himself was mortally wounded on the Chancellorsville battlefield, losing first his left arm to amputation and then his life after pneumonia set in. When news of Jackson's wounding and surgery reached Robert E. Lee, the Confederate commander said, "He has lost his left arm; I have lost my right."

For decades it was assumed that Bee's exclamation was a compliment for the way Jackson was standing strong; however, Col. J. C. Haskell, who was at Manassas, published his opinion that Bee spoke in anger, that he meant that Jackson was "standing like a stone wall" when he should have been coming to Bee's assistance.

Because Bee died the day after the battle, no one knows unequivocally whether he was praising or condemning his comrade in arms. Scholars continue to debate and discuss Bee's intent; however, Jackson's subsequent actions are a strong testimony regarding his abilities on the battlefield regardless of whether Bee was admonishing him or commending him. The discussion of Bee's intent adds little more than a minor footnote to the legacy of a true military genius.[1]

Drewry's Bluff on the James River was sketched by an artist on the day the five Confederates guns were pitted against two mighty Federal ironclads.

Drewry's Bluff on the James River should not be omitted from any tour of Virginia's Civil War sites. A Confederate battery was positioned there to close the river to Federal navigation. Perched two hundred feet above the river, these guns could be trained upon any vessel that trespassed, but Federal gunners could not elevate their weapons sufficiently to seriously trouble the gray-clad gunners above. With only five pieces in place on May 15, 1862, the Southerners halted two ironclads, the USS *Galena* and the well-known *Monitor*. Most of the Rebels' eight-inch round shot was directed toward the *Galena,* which was hit forty-three times. After both vessels withdrew, Lt. William N. Jeffers of the *Monitor* reported, "It was impossible to reduce such works except by the aid of a land force."

A few months later when the position the Rebels called "the battery at Drewry's" fell into Union hands, the name was changed to Fort Darling. Yet no one knows why the position took so distinctive a name after changing hands. No solid evidence supports the speculation that Gen. George B. McClellan may have used the name as some kind of code to keep the Southerners from knowing when he might refer to Drewry's Bluff. More than a score of men

LIBRARY OF CONGRESS

When the citizens of Frederick, Maryland, welcomed George B. McClellan's troops, few if any of them realized that Lee's lost order had just been delivered to the Federal commander.

named Darling were involved in the conflict, but none is known to have had any link with the spot on the James River.

Some have suggested the name was an expression of Yankee relief that the guns in place there no longer presented a menace to them. Whatever the reason, once the position was dubbed Fort Darling, the unusual name stuck and entered the *OR*.[2]

Robert E. Lee's Special Order No. 191 of September 9, 1862, ranks among the best-known documents of the war. It was found near Frederick, Maryland, wrapped around three cigars. Pvt. Barton W. Mitchell of the Twenty-seventh Indiana discovered it when his regiment halted briefly on ground occupied earlier by Confederate Gen. Daniel H. Hill's troops.

Mitchell had never before seen a special order, but he realized that the paper signed by Col. Robert H. Chilton, Lee's adjutant general, might be important. He took it to his sergeant, who took it to Col. Silas Colgrove, who transmitted it to George B.

McClellan's headquarters. The lost order detailed the movements of the various elements of the Army of Northern Virginia, thus the Federal commander revised his plans to thwart Lee. Meanwhile, a Southern sympathizer was among a group with McClellan when he received the order. This person allegedly rode to Lee's headquarters, and Lee revised his strategy.

There's no mystery about the discovery of the lost order and the events that followed, but to this day no one has found out what careless Rebel officer wrapped one of only seven copies in precious tobacco and then lost it.[3]

Had it not been for papers found on his body after he was ambushed and killed, Col. Ulric Dahlgren would rate little space in Civil War literature despite the fact that his father devised the famous Dahlgren gun. Fighting in blue, Dahlgren received a serious wound while trying to block Lee's retreat from Gettysburg. A few months later, equipped with a wooden leg, he was back in action. During the spring of 1864 he joined with Judson Kilpatrick in a raid on Richmond.

Kilpatrick's thirty-five hundred men formed one wing of the operation, and a special five-hundred-man unit headed by Dahlgren formed a second. All went well until the raiders closed on Richmond. At that point, nearly everything that could go wrong went wrong. On the night of March 1, 1864, the two units separated and then became lost. Disoriented and frustrated by swollen streams, snow, and sleet, Dahlgren's group retreated from the Richmond area. Late the next day his unit rode headlong into elements of the Virginia militia, and the young colonel died almost instantly from a hail of bullets.

A small boy searched Dahlgren's body and found a set of papers detailing a plan to murder Jefferson Davis and his cabinet. Immediately published in Richmond newspapers, the so-called Dahlgren Papers were promptly denounced in Washington as forgeries. Decades later a questionable signature used to prompt the forgery claim was said to have resulted from the ink on one side of the thin paper "bleeding" through to the other side. Later tests by the National Archives established that Dahlgren's signature was authentic, which implies that Kilpatrick's Richmond raid must have been approved at the very highest level in Washington—perhaps by the president himself.

Lincoln's surviving works, however, give no hint that he had any role in a plot to assassinate the top Confederate leaders or that he even knew of it. Yet the Kilpatrick raid may have had subsequent ramifications upon his own life. John Wilkes Booth had many opportunities to scan portions of the Dahlgren Papers as they were printed by newspapers; the plot to kill Jefferson Davis could have influenced him to assassinate Lincoln.[4]

Twenty-one-year-old Sam Davis could have saved his life by revealing where he got papers he was carrying when captured by the Federals late in 1863. Once a private in the First Tennessee, Davis had left the Confederate army after being wounded at Shiloh. When his wound healed, he became a member of an irregular unit known as Coleman's Scouts. Operating in his native state, Davis served as a courier. He was carrying information concerning Union troop movements when he was captured by men of the Seventh Kansas Cavalry.

Jailed at Pulaski, Tennessee, the youthful courier withstood many hours of interrogation. At one point he was visited by Gen. Grenville M. Dodge, who underscored warnings that Davis would be hanged as a spy if he refused to talk. His last words on November 27, 1863, were, "I would rather die a thousand deaths than betray a friend or be false to duty." Lauded as "too brave to die," he was revered as a martyred Southern hero, and his family home in Smyrna, Tennessee, was later converted into a museum.[5]

Death Stalked His Prey

Gen. Earl Van Dorn, a West Pointer from Mississippi, was given command of the Army of Tennessee's cavalry division on February 25, 1863. Ten weeks later he was shot at his Spring Hill, Tennessee, headquarters by Dr. George B. Peters when he returned home on April 12 from Memphis. The "aggrieved" husband claimed that Van Dorn had dallied with his wife, Jessie. If official documents are accurate, Van Dorn's romance could have lasted only about three weeks.

Briefly a fugitive, Peters soon convinced authorities that he shot the general to defend the sanctity of his marriage. Relatives of the dead man, however, protested that the notion of an affair was nonsense. Peters, they insisted, shot the Rebel commander to curry

After delivering a single shot to Lincoln's head, John Wilkes Booth made a successful escape from the Federal capital. He was shot and killed on April 25, 1865.

favor with Union authorities and thereby prevent his property from being confiscated. Since the Peterses later reconciled, the motive for Van Dorn's murder remains controversial.[6]

Like the death of John F. Kennedy, the assassination of Abraham Lincoln is surrounded by rumors and unanswered questions. In April 1865 detectives Luther B. Baker and Everton J. Conger were sure that they had guided the Federals to John Wilkes Booth's hiding place in a tobacco shed near Port Royal, Virginia. After the death of the fugitive, authorities paid substantial rewards to those who participated in the apprehension. Within a few months, however, tales that Booth escaped and some other man had been shot were widely circulated. Over a century later, the debate still rages. Some historians contend that the man who was central to the first assassination of a president died of old age in a foreign haven.

This is not the only mystery linked with Lincoln's death. Before the so-called Lincoln conspirators went on trial, stories surfaced that the membership of the loosely organized gang included a person or persons "high in the Lincoln administration."

Louis H. Powell had been a Confederate guerrilla who forced his way into Secretary of State William H. Seward's home and tried to kill the secretary. He fled into the night but was quickly captured.

HARPER'S HISTORY

The night Lincoln was killed, Louis H. Powell attempted to murder bedridden Secretary of State William H. Seward, but his effort was pitifully feeble. Some of Seward's enemies charged that Seward had helped to eliminate his long-time political rival and then covered his tracks by arranging the Powell incident. Secretary of War Edwin M. Stanton was also accused of being the mastermind of the plot or an ally of Booth. Like the Kennedy assassination, allegations and innuendoes refuse to die. Some Americans still regard the death of Lincoln to be surrounded by questions that they hope some day may be answered.[7]

Federal forces conducted two strikes against the enemy on May 24, 1861. While numerous regiments were moving upon Alexandria, Virginia, other units headed for a site nearer Washington. The Arlington estate—owned by Mrs. Robert E. Lee, a great-granddaughter of Martha Washington—was barely three miles from the U.S. Capitol. Built on a high bluff overlooking the Potomac, the grounds could have been used by Confederate artillery to shell the Executive Mansion and other government buildings. Although there was no immediate threat to the capital,

Mrs. Robert E. Lee inherited the Arlington estate, whose massive Doric pillars dwarfed Federal soldiers who occupied the house in April 1861.

the president and his advisers agreed that the potential for danger should be removed.

On taking command of Virginia's troops, Lee had urged his wife to leave the estate; she would be safer in their home at White House hamlet on the Pamunkey River. Mary Lee resisted at first, but just before Virginia seceded she decided to take her husband's advice. Almost an invalid, Mrs. Lee found travel taxing under any circumstances. With talk of war growing louder every day, it took great fortitude to leave the home she loved. Still she packed what she could, leaving behind numerous relics associated with George and Martha Washington, and vacated Arlington.

Almost as soon as she left, Federal troops moved in. On May 26 engineers cut a new road through the woods from outposts near the rear of the mansion to a position on the Leesburg road. In some parts of Washington there was joy over the news that the Lees' home was the first property to be occupied by the military. Hence on May 31 a picnic of sorts was held on the grounds. Having been given special passes for their expedition, three residents of the Executive Mansion visited the estate to see the Custis mansion, long occupied by George Washington's adopted son, George Washington Parke Custis—Mrs. Lee's father. Robert Todd Lincoln, along with presidential secretaries John Hay and John G. Nicolay, found the mansion "of surpassing dignity and beauty." It

Long after his visit to Arlington, Robert Todd Lincoln was a corporate lawyer and president of the Pullman Company.

was fitting, they agreed, that it should have been a special target of the earliest officially authorized thrust into Virginia.

Immediately after he was named to head the Union army, Gen. Irvin McDowell took up residence in the Arlington mansion and pledged to protect the property belonging to the Lee family. It wasn't long before the Federal commander noticed that several Washington family artifacts were disappearing. Expressing concern over what seemed to be the theft of priceless national relics, he packed a few items—china and crystal, a washstand, and a pair of breeches worn by the first president—and sent them to the capital for safekeeping. They were displayed in the Patent Building under the label, "Captured at Arlington."

During the many chaotic months in which Lincoln reassigned one commander after another, Arlington was occupied by some of McDowell's successors. George B. McClellan, however, refused to establish his headquarters there. He had too much respect for Lee to sully his old residence, he said.

On January 6, 1864, tax commissioners were ordered "to Bid in the Arlington Estate of Robert E. Lee." The title to eleven hundred acres and the stately mansion was acquired by the U.S. government when $26,800 was transferred from one account to another. Crushing as that blow was, it did not prepare Lee and his family for what soon took place. Arlington was placed on a special list and henceforth could be used only "for war, military, charitable and educational purposes."

Brig. Gen. Montgomery C. Meigs, quartermaster general of the U.S. Army, presided over a scandal-ridden procurement and transportation system. Under his direction, subordinates dispensed the then astronomical amount of more than $1.5 billion. Yet their chief had time to pay special attention to the property seized from the commander of the Army of Northern Virginia.

On May 13, 1864, the body of Pvt. William Christman of the Sixty-seventh Pennsylvania was interred at Arlington. One month later Secretary of War Stanton signed an order setting aside two hundred acres around the main house for use as a cemetery for Federals killed in action. Somehow, Meigs managed to bypass regulations and select for himself and his immediate family two choice sites almost in the shadow of the mansion.

In August he rode across the river to take a look at the plots in which he and his family members were to be buried. To his consternation, he discovered that numerous small headstones had been set, not close to the mansion as he wished, but adjoining the old orchard and slave quarters. Furious, the quartermaster general sent to the capital for more bodies. When they arrived, he personally supervised their burial in the rose garden immediately adjoining the mansion.

It seems to have been no accident that one of the first pieces of property seized by Federal authorities for nonpayment of a special tax was the estate of Robert E. Lee and his wife. Strenuous efforts to learn who was ultimately responsible for turning it into a splendid graveyard have turned up little concrete evidence, but the chain of command that endorsed the burial of Christman clearly started at a very high level. Hence an unsolved riddle confronts present-day visitors to Arlington National Cemetery: Did Abraham Lincoln or Edwin M. Stanton or William H. Seward initiate actions by which a once-splendid plantation became the nation's most noted repository for military dead?

Part 4

Blood Was Cheaper Than Water

Rebels under Sterling Price fought continuously for fifty-nine hours before they succeeded in crossing the Federal breastworks.

13
WATERWORKS
STRONG MEN WEPT

ON MAY 22, 1865, a prisoner of war who had been held temporarily on the steamer *Clyde* was moved to a casemate of Fort Monroe. The improvised cell's windows and doors were heavily barred, and the first shift of around-the-clock sentries was on duty. Standing orders were that an officer was required to check on the prisoner at fifteen-minute intervals. Furniture in the improvised prison cell was limited to an iron bedstead, a chair, a table, a Bible, and "a movable stool closet."

Having been transported from Georgia in irons after his capture there, former Confederate president Jefferson Davis was under no illusions about the conditions under which he would live for the immediate future. He showed little emotion, but according to war correspondent Charles A. Dana, he shed tears when forced to leave the staff officers who had remained with him.[1]

Countless thousands of men wept when they left their homes and loved ones to go to war. Many of those men shed tears of joy when they returned. The idealized image of Civil War soldiers and civilians has no place for such emotions but emphasizes courage and eagerness to fight to the death. Many a man as strong, if not as stern, as Jefferson Davis was described as shedding tears in public, however.

A major factor leading to tears was defeat of one kind or another. At Antietam, stationed not far from the Dunker Church, Stephen D. Lee's battalion became the target of merciless Federal fire early in the action. He watched as officers and men fell like stalks of corn before a scythe, then he received word that they were nearly out of ammunition. Having no other choice, Lee ordered his men to retire. As they obeyed, "Stephen D. Lee wept openly."[2]

At Lexington, Missouri, Col. James B. Mulligan and his men fought against Southerners under Gen. Sterling Price for fifty-nine hours without any water except what they carried into the fray. When Mulligan's foes crossed his breastworks, they shouted with joy as they seized the U.S. flag and trailed it in the dust. Although he had suffered no bodily injuries, "The brave colonel wept like a child when he found himself compelled to surrender." Lt. Thomas D. McClure of the Twenty-third Illinois recorded a slightly different description of the same incident: "I went round the corner; there stood Colonel Mulligan, that brave, true-hearted man. There he stood, tears washing the dust and gunpowder smoke off his manly cheeks."[3]

At Fredericksburg, stubborn Ambrose E. Burnside continued to launch futile assaults upon Marye's Heights after the first two suicidal waves crumbled. Everything else having failed, the general proposed another charge that he would personally lead. When his aides vehemently objected to this plan, "he gave it up, and with tears running down his cheeks ordered the evacuation of Fredericksburg."[4]

Much earlier, Col. Rodney Mason of the Seventy-first Ohio saw his men scatter and run for safety under the riverbank when Southerners hit the regiment. Humiliated and angry, the officer who had spent five terms in the legislature of the Buckeye State requested a personal interview with Ulysses S. Grant. "Begging to be given another chance," Grant wrote, "Mason came to me with tears in his eyes."[5]

At Fort Wagner, South Carolina, Federals and Confederates stood within fifty yards of one another as they fired. During one such murderous exchange, 191 officers and men of the Seventh Connecticut "marched out to attack the foe"; only 88 returned to camp. According to Capt. Sylvester H. Gray, Gen. George C. Strong learned of the debacle and "with tears in his eyes he said we had done our whole duty and covered ourselves all over with glory."[6]

Stephen Lee was not the only officer who left Antietam with tear-stained cheeks. Maj. Thomas Hyde led the Seventh Maine in a doomed effort to move into Piper's Swale. After he managed to lead remnants of his regiment out of the blistering Confederate fire, Hyde "cried himself to sleep."[7]

On the outskirts of Atlanta, officers and men of the Fifty-seventh Ohio and the Fifty-fifth Illinois seized and for a time held a position in a cut of the Georgia Railroad. A sudden shift by a column of advancing Confederates meant that any Federal along the railroad line would be lucky to get out alive. A hasty retreat followed, leaving only three defenders standing. One of them saw their desperate plight and "roared like a wild man." Hastily withdrawing against his will, he "broke into tears and wept like a child."[8]

In the struggle for Atlanta, one of Gen. W. B. Hazen's artillery batteries, commanded by Capt. F. De Grasse, was a prize for which the Confederates struggled manfully and successfully. Battery H, made up of twenty-pound Parrott guns, was taken and retaken during hours of hand-to-hand struggle. Described as "a mere beardless boy," De Grasse spiked his guns when he realized they could not be saved, as all of his horses had been killed by enemy bullets. As the Federal officer "looked upon the wreck and slaughter of his battery, he wept like a child."[9]

At Enterprise, Mississippi, shortly after the fall of Atlanta, Nathan Bedford Forrest led his cavalry in an attack upon a fort manned by 469 men from three regiments of the U.S. Colored Infantry. Forrest's strength was augmented by 150 members of the Third Tennessee Cavalry and two twelve-pound howitzers. Union Col. Wallace Campbell, who was in command of the strongest installation in the region, took a look at the attacking forces and told some of his officers, "The jig is up; pull down the flag." Enlisted men, who had expressed eagerness "to try conclusions with General Forrest," could hardly believe their eyes when they saw the flag lowered. Knowing that this meant they would become prisoners, "with tears [they] demanded that the fight should go on."[10]

Trying to move upon Vicksburg two years earlier, Federal gunboats faced potential destruction by a huge ironclad, the CSS *Arkansas*. Built at Memphis, the 165-foot ram had successfully fought three Union warships on July 15, 1862. She then made her way through Rear Adm. David G. Farragut's main force, a flotilla of thirty

THE SOLDIER

An iron-plated ram, the CSS *Arkansas* (right) fought the USS *Carondelet* on July 15, 1862, as the Confederate vessel made its way to Vicksburg.

vessels, and pulled into Vicksburg for repairs. Shortly afterward, the *Arkansas* was dispatched to take part in a combined land-sea attack upon Baton Rouge. Within sight of her destination, her engines failed completely, and Lt. Henry K. Stevens decided to set fire to her rather than permit her to be captured. Once flames began to roar through the vessel, the *Arkansas* was cut adrift with the hope that it would take down one or more enemy craft. According to Confederate Gen. Earl Van Dorn, Stevens could not restrain his tears when he gave an account of the death of his ship.[11]

The loss of another Confederate warship, the *Nashville,* came about under different circumstances. When she was captured after a stiff fight, arrangements were made for a formal surrender ceremony. Among those present that day was George S. Waterman, who later wrote: "Past Midshipman George A. Joiner, being officer of the deck of the Nashville at the hour of surrender, received at the gangway Lieut. Hamilton, U.S.N. The officers and crew assem-

The CSS *Nashville* was forced to surrender after having captured the merchantman *Harvey Birch* in the British Channel.

bled on deck, and our colors came down and were saluted with raised caps, while tears flowed freely."[12]

With the war over, Confederate Maj. Pollock B. Lee was assigned a special task by Gen. Braxton Bragg. A native of Charlotte, North Carolina, Lee was ordered to surrender his city to Federal forces. A comrade in arms described the ceremony as the last official act of the Army of Tennessee in North Carolina and said of its principal figure, "It was the only time I ever saw him let fall a tear."[13]

In Baltimore early in the war, Union. Brig. Gen. James Cooper, who was in command of Maryland volunteers, received a stream of orders that kept his men busy within the state. Taunted by secessionists as disloyal, many of them pled with Cooper to do whatever it might take to let them enter active service under the Federal government. "Both officers and men have besought me, and on more than one occasion with tears," Cooper reported in a dispatch that was forwarded to the secretary of war.[14]

Robert E. Lee, described as seeming to be "a man of steel," said to aides after the death of Jeb Stuart, "I can scarcely think about him without weeping."[15]

William Tecumseh Sherman could face failure with composure, but the death of handsome young Maj. Gen. James B. McPherson was too much for him. On July 22, 1864, Confederate forces launched a counterattack against Union forces closing upon the railroad center of Atlanta. Riding forward to investigate, McPherson blundered into the Southern line and was killed trying to escape. Several officers at Federal headquarters reported the reaction of their commander. One wrote that as Sherman wept unashamedly, he managed to say to his aides, "I had expected him to finish the war." Another remembered that Sherman angrily blurted, "The whole of the Confederacy could not atone for the sacrifice of one such life."[16]

After being wounded in the thigh, Confederate Gen. T. R. R. Cobb died at the infamous stone wall at Fredericksburg. R. K. Porter, chaplain of Cobb's brigade, escorted the body to their camp and had it dressed for burial. A "coarse box was made, some ladies brought a linen shirt, and we took the body to Richmond," he later wrote. "At the undertaker's shop we were putting him in the case when Mr. [Christopher] Memminger [the secretary of the treasury] came in and wept over him as a brother."[17]

In May 1863, Union Gen. Lloyd Tilghman was standing near the rear of one of his batteries, directing gunners in the elevation of one of their pieces, when he was killed by an enemy shell. Command devolved upon A. E. Reynolds, the senior colonel present. Reporting about the clash, Reynolds wrote, "The tears shed by his men on the occasion are the proudest tribute that can be given the gallant dead."[18]

Col. Elmer Ellsworth of the New York Fire Zouaves, a close friend and protégé of Abraham Lincoln, was the first Federal casualty in the taking of Alexandria, Virginia. When handed a War Department telegram telling him of the incident, the president wept openly. He drove to the Navy Yard to view the body, then made arrangements for it to be taken to the Executive Mansion for the funeral. Numerous observers reported that the president wept repeatedly while mourners filed by the open casket. Retreating to his office, he personally penned a May 25, 1861, letter to Ellsworth's parents in which he said: "In the untimely loss of your noble son, our afflic-

Christopher Memminger, Confederate secretary of the treasury, wept without restraint when he was led to the rough box in which the body of Gen. T. R. R. Cobb lay.

tion here, is scarcely less than your own. . . . My acquaintance with him began less than two years ago; yet through the latter half of the intervening period, it was as intimate as the disparity of our ages, and my engrossing pursuits, would permit. May God give you that consolation which is beyond all earthly power. Sincerely your friend in a common affliction—A. Lincoln."[19]

When Col. J. L. Kirby Smith fell during a Federal assault on July 4, 1862, Brig. Gen. D. S. Stanley reported that "in the very moment of battle," he saw "stern, brave men weeping as children as the word passed, 'Kirby Smith is dead.' "[20]

At Gaines's Mill, John Bell Hood obeyed Lee's request that he should try to break the enemy's line. Personally leading a charge, the youthful general took the Federal position, but the price of victory was high. So many of his brigade were killed or wounded that one of his officers said, "A railroad accident is slight," compared to such a Pyrrhic victory. Five houses on the contested field were quickly filled as field hospitals. Hood wandered about the ground won at so great a cost, found a box, and sat down on it. One of his

Youthful Elmer Ellsworth's death triggered what one observer called "a spasm of uncontrollable tears" from his close friend, Abraham Lincoln.

LESLIE'S ILLUSTRATED

staff officers, James W. Ratchford, searched for his missing commander and soon found him weeping over the casualties inflicted upon his brigade.[21]

A Northern brigade, smashed in a futile assault upon a ridge at Utoy Creek, fell back after having pushed to within one hundred feet of its objective. James Reilley, commander of the unit, soon learned that the thrust had led to more than three hundred casualties. When the tally was announced to him, he burst into tears. At Antietam, Confederate Col. Alfred H. Colquitt reacted in the same way when more than half of the men in the brigade that included his regiment fell on the field. Later in the same battle, two of his comrades—William H. French and Edwin V. Sumner—shed copious tears when a brigade led by Nathan Kimball suffered so many casualties that it became useless. Men of that brigade who were able to walk from the field described "Bull" Sumner as weeping so hard that he could not speak.[22]

Under the right circumstances, a dramatic loss of any kind was enough to reduce a strong man to tears. At Antietam, thirteen Confederates died trying to defend the flag of the First Texas regiment. Union soldiers had to roll a dead officer off the flag so they could seize it as a prized trophy. When the triumphant Yankees carried the banner past captured Lt. William E. Garry of the Fourth Texas, Garry asked for permission to reach out and touch it. As he did so, his eyes welled with tears.[23]

Lt. Thomas B. McClure's diary of the 1861 siege of Lexington, Missouri, includes a highly personal passage: "At three o'clock our noble flag was taken down and handed to General [Sterling] Price, and as the deafening cheer of the rebels went up, again my eyes filled with tears [as they had when surrender was seen to be inevitable]."[24]

14

FACTOIDS

THE NUMBERS GAME

NO ONE knows how many men in blue and in gray served as file closers during 1861–65. With the conflict nearly over, Robert E. Lee directed that the Army of Northern Virginia should use one file-closer for every ten men in the ranks, but that ratio probably was not standard. These functionaries were essential to the operations of both Federal and Union forces, yet they are mentioned only seventeen times in the *Official Records.*

A conspiracy of silence may stem from the duties that were assigned to file-closers. Often keeping "two paces behind the rear rank of their squads with loaded guns and fixed bayonets," they were under orders to shoot to kill if any soldier straggled or tried to run to safety. Lee told his subordinates, "It will be enjoined upon file-closers that they shall make the evasion of duty more dangerous than its performance."

Much earlier, at Prairie Grove, Arkansas, in December 1862, Union Gen. James G. Blunt noted that a file-closer selected for this special duty should put plunderers and stragglers to death "upon the spot." Long after the shooting stopped, former Confederate D. B. Easley ventured to guess that around six hundred men who took part in Pickett's Charge at Gettysburg did so only because file-closers ran alongside them with drawn pistols.[1]

A typical regiment of Federal volunteer infantrymen numbered around 1,000 men when it left the state in which it was raised. Of this number about 96 percent were enlisted men and the remainder were officers of all grades. Despite the fact that an average regiment received about 300 replacements during its term of service, by 1864 its strength had dropped to 872, of whom only 781 were present and fit for duty. For reasons that made sense only to those who drew up the regulations, an infantry regiment of the U.S. Army included about twice as many men (2,020 to 2,452) as did a regiment of volunteers.[2]

Even the most adept players of the numbers game do not know precisely how many men were killed in battle, received mortal wounds, or succumbed to disease. Although Federal records are more accurate and more nearly complete than those of the Confederacy, Washington never received a full accounting from every unit. It's generally acknowledged that the Civil War saw more fatalities than all other U.S. wars combined, but estimates of the total vary from a low of 560,000 to a high of more than 625,000.

When the long-dominant Democratic Party split three ways in 1860, the election of the Republican presidential nominee—whoever that might be—was virtually guaranteed. Thus, a one-term congressman who had held no elective office for more than ten years and whose views on major issues were not widely known was swept into office in November. When one out of every sixteen Americans voted for him, Abraham Lincoln became the sixteenth president—receiving just over 39 percent of all ballots cast. In the Electoral College he received 180 votes against 123 for all three of his Democratic opponents combined.[3]

How many times did the two sides clash in battle? The answer depends upon who provides it. Frederick Phisterer tabulated only 2,261 "Battles, etc." Frederick Dyer concluded that there were 10,455 "campaigns, battles, engagements, combats, actions, assaults, skirmishes, operations, sieges, raids, expeditions, reconnaissances, scouts, affairs, occupations, and captures."[4]

Confederate cavalry wizard Gen. Nathan Bedford Forrest, who had no military training or experience before joining the Southern army as a private, fought throughout the entire war and compiled a numerical record that has no counterpart. He is credited with having killed thirty men in personal combat and having twenty-nine horses shot from under him.[5]

George D. Ramsay, who became the Union's chief of ordnance in September 1863, was contemptuous of the man he succeeded—

J. W. Ripley. Ramsay said more than once, Ripley was too cheap to buy decent weapons for Federal fighting forces. Harsh as it sounds, that verdict was actually mild. During his first fourteen months in office, Ripley issued purchase orders for more than 700,000 rifles—of which 8,271 were breech-loaders.

Rushing pell-mell into the munitions market, Ramsay is credited with having almost instantly doubled the number of breech-loading rifles and carbines issued to soldiers in blue. In the single year during which he made purchasing decisions, the number of breech-loaders available to Yankee troops jumped to the colossal total of about 65,000, or one for every ten to fifteen men then dodging Rebel bullets.[6]

Federal regulations required fighting men to be at least eighteen years old but no more than forty-five years old. Although this age range was well known, findings of the U.S. Sanitary Commission indicate that 2,366 fighting men were fifty or more years old. At the bottom end of the age range, 6,425 soldiers were listed as being seventeen years old. The names of 2,758 sixteen-year-olds were recorded, and 2,758 adolescents went into the ranks at age fifteen. From that point, numbers drop sharply. Only 773 fourteen-year-old soldiers in blue were tabulated, thirteen-year-olds numbered only 330, and a mere 127 boys were toting muskets by the time they were twelve.[7]

How many general officers fought in blue and in gray? More than one expert has played the numbers game here and has found more than one way to enumerate general officers. If every man from the rank of lieutenant colonel to full general falls in this category, about 2,549 officers wore blue, while Virginia alone produced more than 100 generals who fought in gray. If brevet generals are counted, as some authorities insist they must be, the total number of men who wore shoulder straps during 1861–65 was in the range of 3,700 Yankees and 450 Rebels.[8]

According to the 1860 census, there were 2,216,744 African-American males in the thirty-four states then constituting the Union. Black females were only slightly more numerous, at 2,225,086. Free blacks who lived in states and territories where slavery was banned numbered 225,973. Another 129,243 reportedly resided in Border States that permitted slavery but did not secede. In the eleven states that formally seceded, there were 132,760 free blacks just before the outbreak of hostilities.

States that seceded from the Union held 3,521,110 slaves. The Border States had only 432,586, with a grand total of 64 found in seventeen free states and eight free territories. These data strongly suggested to Lincoln and his generals that the Union armies stood to gain a substantial number of more or less eager recruits once men of color were permitted to don uniforms of blue.[9]

Some officers probably fudged a little when they compiled casualty counts after a battle. Others seem to have tried various stratagems to keep their tallies low. Typical reports treated the dead, the wounded, and the missing as casualties; in a few instances, missing men were divided between stragglers likely to return to the ranks and soldiers of whom no trace could be found. Since many stragglers stayed away from their units only a day or so and large numbers of deserters were captured, all estimates are suspect. One of the most reliable suggests that 432,000 Federals were battle casualties compared to 288,000 Confederates killed or wounded. These totals do not include miscellaneous deaths.[10]

One of the favorite weapons of Union officers, the Parrott gun, was widely used on both land and sea. At least 1,553 of them were purchased by military officers during the war with muzzle sizes ranging from 2.9 inches to 10 inches. In proportion to the strength of the fighting force that used them, naval officers bought many more—a total of 790, of which the smallest was the 3.67-inch and the largest were mammoth 8-inch guns.[11]

A single ambulance train belonging to the Union's Fifth Corps reportedly hauled 7,985 wounded men from battlefields. Of this number, 1,500 were picked up in front of Petersburg, but only 300 were rescued at Spotsylvania. Surprisingly, the 1,800 men transported from the Wilderness comprised barely more than half the 3,000 they took to field hospitals from comparatively obscure Laurel Hill, all in Virginia.[12]

No two sets of data concerning prisoners are identical. James I. Robertson Jr. came to the conclusion that 408,000 men were short- or long-term captives. He is the authority for the fact that about 14 percent of these men—56,000, to be exact—"died

LIBRARY OF CONGRESS

Members of a Federal ambulance corps demonstrate that one vehicle could transport two or more wounded men easily.

painfully and neglected while locked in the remote and makeshift compounds of North and South."[13]

Market Heights at Petersburg was so minor in scope that it seldom appears in lists of battles. Yet of the sixteen Medals of Honor bestowed upon African Americans, thirteen stemmed from gallantry at Market Heights.[14]

The second major clash in the region of Manassas, Virginia, lasted for two full days of about fourteen hours each. Such was the fury of Second Bull Run that every minute of the conflict saw an average of fourteen men killed or wounded.[15]

During about fourteen hundred days of conflict, the U.S. Army is believed to have lost less than 6,000 men in battle. This means that in the four years following April 1861, sixty times as many volunteers as regulars fell—354,000.[16]

Southerners who deserted are believed to have numbered slightly more than half the total of men who fought in blue. So many Northerners took to the woods or fields and then went home that Washington established a special deserters' branch of the provost marshal general's office. Data compiled by this office suggest that 89 Union soldiers deserted each week in 1863, while the figure jumped to 141 per week the next year.[17]

During the long siege of Charleston, South Carolina, heavily armed Union warships took Fort Sumter as their primary target. The first of several great bombardments, spread over a period of only sixteen days, saw nearly seven thousand projectiles thrown at the fortress. Since most of them were one-hundred- and two-hundred-pounders, the total iron fired from warships during this period amounted to about 1 million pounds. Inside the Confederate bastion, this rain of iron wounded fifty men but killed only two. Calculations indicate that it took just over ten tons of Federal iron to inflict one casualty among men in gray during this drawn-out cannonade.[18]

Top officials of the Confederacy were determined to have a fully rounded military force, so they organized a marine corps. Its entire personnel, officers and enlisted men, numbered just 539.[19]

Gettysburg is rightly remembered as the bloodiest battle of the entire conflict, yet fatalities during the three-day struggle came to less than 10 percent of the number of men who were captured during 1861–65 and who died in prisons and stockades.[20]

Stonewall Jackson and his men were responsible for the largest capitulation of U.S. troops before World War II. When he led his men into Harpers Ferry on Monday, September 15, 1862, he accepted the surrender of about 12,000 men in blue.[21]

Compared with the Rebel loss of Vicksburg to U. S. Grant and his troops, the fall of Harpers Ferry was minor in scope. At the Mississippi River port, so many men in gray were forced to surrender that Grant had no way to transport them to Federal prisons. In this dilemma, he approved the largest parole of the war. As a result, approximately 29,000 men in gray solemnly swore that they would not fight again unless and until they were formally exchanged.[22]

HARPER'S WEEKLY

Wounded at Murfreesboro, Chickamauga, and Jonesboro, Joseph B. "Hard Luck Joe" Palmer was given command of a hastily formed brigade to fight in the Carolinas against Sherman.

At the outbreak of hostilities, the Medical Bureau of the U.S. War Department was made up of 114 officers and one hospital with forty beds.[23]

Joseph B. Palmer, one of many Confederates who surrendered at Fort Donelson, was shipped as a prisoner to Boston's Fort Warren, where he stayed until September 1862. Back in uniform, he took three wounds at Murfreesboro and one each at Chickamauga and Jonesboro. By this time called "Hard Luck Joe," the brigadier general fought against Sherman in the Carolinas. In a desperate reorganization of shattered Southern forces, Hard Luck Joe was given command of a new brigade formed from what was left of two battalions and thirty-eight regiments.[24]

No one knows how many wet-plate glass negatives were personally exposed by famed photographer Mathew B. Brady. The truth is that his visual problems may have prevented him from taking part in this process, so the number may be zero. Nevertheless, hundreds of images taken by members of his organization are credited to him rather than to the Mathew Brady Studio.[25]

A. McDowell McCook was one of
seventeen members of a closely knit
family from the Buckeye State.

PICTORIAL FIELD BOOK

The McCooks of Ohio may have topped all other family groups in
the number of close relatives who fought in blue. Seventeen of
them ranged in rank from private to brigadier general. Ten of these
men were sons of Daniel McCook, who was killed when he took
part in a futile attempt to capture John Hunt Morgan during his
famous 1863 raid into Ohio. One of Daniel's brothers and five of
his nephews also served in Federal forces that fought on land and
on the sea.[26]

Probably the best known of many units of partisan rangers was the
Rebel outfit organized by John S. Mosby in January 1863. When
this force went into action, it consisted of its commander and nine
men who had been detached from Jeb Stuart's cavalry.[27]

According to one count, eight states in 1860 in which slavery was
permitted but secession was not then envisioned included more
than twice as many white males of military age as did the seven
states that initially formed the Confederacy. According to the
census count, the former group had potential capacity to field 1
million soldiers, while the states that seceded immediately after
Fort Sumter included only 531,000 potential fighting men.[28]

On the fringes of the action at Fair Oaks, a captain of the 102d Pennsylvania accidentally encountered a party of six Confederates who were headed toward the rear with a wounded officer. According to the *Springfield Republican,* the officer from the Keystone State politely offered to guard his captors through the battle lines. Soon he was challenged by Union pickets who called out, "Who goes there?" The captain replied in just five words: "A friend, with seven prisoners."[29]

What was the total of Union losses during the climatic last months of the war? No reliable numbers are available for this period. Brig. Gen. Joshua L. Chamberlain of Little Round Top fame is the authority for the fact that officers in blue "were not called upon or permitted to report casualties during that whole campaign from the Rapidan and Rappahannock to the James and Appomattox, for fear the country could not stand the disclosure."[30]

While records of Union activities are comparatively complete, those of the Confederacy are not. Hence it is anyone's guess as to how many volunteers and conscripts from the South died of disease during the war years.

It's well established that members of the regular U.S. Army fared remarkably well in this respect, with 3,000 of them succumbing to tuberculosis, yellow fever, malaria, camp fever, dysentery, and other common maladies. Among the volunteers, however, the death toll from disease was nearly one hundred times as great with the final count being around 221,000.[31]

During 1860 U.S. cotton exports ran to 1 billion pounds valued at $192 million. During 1865 exports from northern ports had dropped to 9 million pounds whose worth was $7 million. There are no trustworthy records concerning exports from Southern ports during 1862–65, since the only way to get the fibers from Charleston or New Orleans to England or France was by means of blockade-runners.[32]

The Confederate States of America confidently expected to build its new nation upon cotton and slavery, which had become inextricably intertwined when northerner Eli Whitney invented the "engine" that came to be known as the cotton gin. The world monopoly of the South ended when India and Egypt began to produce cotton in large quantities, but prior to that cotton enabled the Confederate government to receive the largest of its remittances from abroad.

Late in 1861 Emile Erlanger and Company, a financial house based in Paris, contracted to market a Confederate bond issue worth $14 million, backed only by cotton. French officials shrewdly demanded a 5 percent commission on sales and the right to purchase one-hundred-dollar bonds for only seventy-seven dollars.

The largest of all Confederate loans was floated simultaneously on January 29, 1863, in Paris, London, Amsterdam, and Frankfurt. Within sixty days, the value of cotton-backed bonds began a dramatic fall. When news of Federal victories at Vicksburg and Gettysburg reached Europe, bonds with a face value of one hundred dollars became readily available at sixty dollars.

Precisely how much money poured into Richmond's coffers as a result of the Erlanger loan is a matter of debate, but the total is widely believed to have exceeded $6 million. Some analysts say that this figure is too high, that the bonds yielded $4 million at most.[33]

Maine sent fewer soldiers than the larger New England states, only 70,107 compared to 146,730 men from Massachusetts. These data ignore the fact that Maine's fifty-three military units represented 11 percent of her population. Mortality among fighting men from Maine became legendary. Total losses, along with those of Massachusetts, Vermont, New Hampshire, Connecticut, and Rhode Island, reached 40,121—of which Maine lost 9,398 during the years in which Massachusetts families received only 13,942 death notices.[34]

According to the U.S. Pension Record Office, 462,634 Southerners were taken prisoner during the war years, some of them being counted separately for each of the three or more times they were captured. Nearly half of all Confederates who surrendered—a total of 247,769—were paroled on the field. The remainder were sent to prisons and stockades, where Federal authorities admitted that 25,976 of them died.[35]

Authorized by Congress in 1907 as an adjunct to the coveted Medal of Honor, the Civil War Campaign Medal was claimed by only 554 veterans.[36]

Having repeatedly warned leaders of state militia units not to purchase inferior weapons abroad, late in 1863 Washington spent four dollars each on 18,000 Prussian-made muskets. None of them were supposed to go into battle; they were designed to be used instead of sticks and wooden guns by members of militia who were learning to drill.[37]

Although exact figures were not preserved, Confederate reports indicate that nearly nine thousand men died during the Vicksburg campaign. Federal losses were slightly higher. Since all who surrendered when the siege of Vicksburg ended became prisoners and were counted as casualties, the river city was the focal point of action during which about fifty thousand men lost their lives or their freedom on or before July 4, 1863. Three days of furious fighting at Gettysburg, ending on July 3, led to an estimated fifty-one thousand casualties. Combined, the battle in the East and the siege in what was then known as the West produced the most deadly four-day period in the annals of the nation—casualties at the rate of 833 per hour around the clock during July 1–4.[38]

During the war Connecticut native Samuel Colt found a massive market for his .36-caliber Navy and .44-caliber Army revolver. Colt's six-shooters, already nearing obsolescence in many respects, used loose powder and balls or cartridges made of paper or linen. Regardless of the merits and demerits of the Colts, the Ordnance Bureau of the U.S. War Department purchased 146,000 of them at an average rate of about 3,173 per month from start to finish of the conflict.[39]

All Civil War buffs know that only one man—Lt. Gen. U. S. Grant—held the highest rank in Union forces. Only nine of his subordinates achieved the rank of major general in the U.S. Army. Among Confederates, fourteen were of the same rank as Grant, while half a dozen topped him by one grade. Full generals in gray were greatly outnumbered by major generals, however, with at least sixty-three gaining permanent rank and ten others holding it temporarily.[40]

At least 9,000 men tried to become commissioned officers in the Federal forces. The majority of these applicants sought commissions

Samuel Colt had struggled to keep his factory from bankruptcy, but the war made him wealthy.

UNIVERSITY OF OKLAHOMA LIBRARY

through the states in which they lived. Nearly two-thirds of them never received a hearing, and of the 3,790 who were examined only 2,318 won appointments.[41]

Commander in chief Abraham Lincoln towered several inches above most of the men who made up the Union armies. The average soldier who wore blue stood just over five feet eight inches tall. Had the president ever encountered Capt. Van Buskirk, even he would have had to look up to the officer of the Twenty-seventh Indiana who was the only soldier who stood six feet ten and one-half inches tall. The shortest soldier was an unidentified twenty-four-year-old member of the 192d Ohio, who was only three feet four inches tall.[42]

Tests revealed that the maximum weight that could be borne by a properly built Federal pontoon bridge—regardless of its length—was 7,865 pounds.[43]

Perhaps the most unusual Civil War monument was conceived by war correspondent George Townsend, who sent battlefield dispatches to the *Philadelphia Inquirer,* the *Philadelphia Press,* and the *New York Herald.* After the war, as a syndicated columnist and freelance writer, Townsend raised five thousand dollars to erect a memorial arch to journalists on his South Mountain estate. A remote prototype of the Vietnam Wall in Washington, the Townsend monument was found to be covered with names. Since he decided to include artists as well as correspondents, he personally selected and then memorialized the names of 9 Confederate and 142 Unionist civilians who "took the war to the people by means of newspapers."[44]

Regulations on both sides stipulated that the penalty for desertion was death. Incomplete Confederate records suggest that slightly more than 100,000 desertions took place, compared to approximately 268,000 desertions in the Union forces. A total of only 267 Federal enlisted men are reported to have paid with their lives for desertion, murder, and other capital offenses. Most who lit out for home or the far West or some obscure point in between correctly judged that they would never dangle from a rope or face a firing squad.[45]

An unidentified officer counted the Union dead after the Wilderness and reached a total of 5,597, a number that exceeded U.S. battle deaths during the five years across which the War of 1812 and the Mexican War stretched.[46]

The final tabulation of the U.S. Commissary of Prisoners was not made public until April 1869. It revealed that during four years of almost daily fighting, Federal troops captured 1 lieutenant general in gray, 5 major generals, 25 brigadier generals, 168 colonels, 146 lieutenant colonels, 244 majors, 2,496 captains, 5,811 lieutenants, 63,563 noncommissioned officers, 121,056 privates, and 5,800 civilians.[47]

A mass promotion of U.S. military officers in the Civil War has no close competitor in other wars. On March 3, 1863, Congress authorized the brevet (honorary) boost in rank to seventeen hundred men.[48]

An official report stated that 3,559 units took part in land-based Federal military action during the war. Of these, all but 86 were state groups whose officers were chosen by elections held in the ranks or were appointed by governors.[49]

As U.S. secretary of war from 1853 to 1857, Jefferson Davis increased the number of fighting men by nearly 50 percent—from 10,745 when he took office to 15,752 when he left.[50]

15

LEE TO THE REAR!

DEATH AND ITS VICTIMS, FACE TO FACE

Around 3:30 a.m. on May 6, 1864, Confederate Gen. Cadmus M. Wilcox was alarmed that reinforcements being led by Gen. James Longstreet had not yet reached the Wilderness. Knowing himself to be hopelessly outnumbered, Wilcox put his pioneers to work digging trenches, but that action came too late. At first light Federal forces opened blistering musket and rifle fire at close range. Panic-stricken Southerners ran from the lines, singly at first and then in clusters of eight to a dozen.

Wilcox sent repeated urgent messages to Gen. Robert E. Lee, beseeching help that his commander did not have to send. Lee saw that the day could be lost before it was started, so he rode among the stragglers and rallied them as best he could.

"Longstreet must be here," Lee assured Gen. Samuel McGowan after chastising the South Carolinian for having permitted his men to run "like a flock of geese."

Dispatching Wilcox to find Longstreet, the commander of the Army of Northern Virginia turned into a field adjoining a lone house belonging to a Mrs. Tapp. Soon Lee was surrounded by swirling smoke from artillery, officers waving their swords, and stragglers trying to get away. Suddenly a score of men wearing ragged uniforms came into sight. Asking their identity, Lee was told that they were "Texas boys" under Gen. John Gregg, who had succeeded to the command of Hood's Texas Division of Longstreet's corps.

With reinforcements at hand, Lee took off his hat, waved it, and shouted, "Hurrah for Texas!"

The new arrivals formed a line of battle close to their gun pits and prepared for a countercharge. As the infantry started forward,

HARPER'S WEEKLY

Astride Traveller, Robert E. Lee had to be restrained from riding into enemy fire during the battle of the Wilderness.

Lee guided his horse Traveller into the line and spurred the animal forward.

When the Texans realized what was happening, spontaneous shouts went up. Ignoring frantic warnings to go back, Lee acted as though he had heard nothing. Some said, "His face was aflame and his eyes were on the enemy in the front."

Gregg failed to turn Traveller's head, but at a signal from him, a sergeant seized the bridle rein of Lee's horse. This action slowed Traveller, but Lee continued to move toward the head of the line until Col. Charles S. Venable rode to his side and shouted, "Longstreet has arrived!"

Described as looking "like a man coming out of a trance," Lee reined his animal back as Longstreet's men raced forward and appeared to return to his normal countenance. Turning in the direction of artillery, he paid only perfunctory attention to Longstreet's signals to his officers as they advanced.

Four days later, near Battery 45, Lee exposed himself to a hail of Yankee bullets while standing near the Whitworth House on Town Creek. That day no high-ranking subordinate was at hand to ask and then to force him to get out of the line of fire.

Gregg, widely credited with having saved the life of his commander, led a counterattack near Petersburg five months later and was killed in the saddle.[1]

Lee's potentially fatal actions soon gave rise to a host of oral accounts and a poem entitled "Lee to the Rear!" John R. Thompson, author of the stirring lines, described the central figure as "a gray-bearded man, with a black slouch hat." Oblivious to danger, said Thompson, Lee "rode to the space where Death and his victims stand face to face."[2]

Had the poet been more familiar with battlefields, he would have known that in the Wilderness Lee violated not only common sense but standard military procedures. It was axiomatic in European and British military schools, as well as at West Point, that a commander should not expose himself to enemy fire except in an extreme emergency.

Pickett's Charge at Gettysburg is by far the most familiar action of its sort. Although some critics contend that George E. Pickett did not lead the spectacular but futile attempt to break through the Federal lines on July 3, 1864, historian Glenn Tucker claimed that the Confederate leader moved forward with his doomed men and did not turn aside until within about a hundred yards of the enemy.[3]

Lt. Col. William H. Stewart, who participated in the Confederate charge at the Crater in Petersburg, described that action in vivid detail. In doing so, he made it clear that Gen. William Mahone did not come near the action but remained at a command post well to the rear. In doing so, the Rebel leader was obedient to guidelines with which every general officer was or should have been familiar.

Brave or foolhardy general officers frequently seemed to be guided by the principle, Let the enemy's bullets be damned! Hence documented instances in which both blue and gray commanders accidentally or deliberately exposed themselves to enemy fire are numerous.

Action at Petersburg's Crater was watched from a distance by William Mahone and other general officers.

Many of these rash leaders lived to tell of their exploits, but most accounts of such incidents come from junior officers who were present when their conduct took an unconventional turn. Early in the war, however, some rash or boastful generals wrote about their foolhardy actions or those of others.

At the battle of First Manassas (Bull Run) an unidentified correspondent for the *Richmond Dispatch* described P. G. T. Beauregard as "the fearless general whose reputation as a commander was staked on this battle." As the newspaperman watched, the Creole general "rode up and down our lines, between the enemy and his own men, regardless of the heavy fire."

In his own summary of the battle, Beauregard wrote: "Between half past two and 3 o'clock p.m, our re-enforcements pushed forward, and, directed by General Johnston to the required quarter, were at hand just as I had ordered forward to a second effort for the recovery of the disputed plateau the whole line, including my reserve, *which at this crisis of the battle I felt called upon to lead in person.*"[4] Beauregard's dash brought him what he wanted. On August 31 he became a full general, ranking from the date of the battle.[5]

Gen. Joseph E. Johnston, whose Confederate commission was dated ten weeks after Beauregard's, did not reach Manassas until the battle was well under way. Deferring to the younger man, Johnston rode with him to the rear of the Robinson and Henry houses about noon. There they found the commands of Barnard Bee, Francis S. Bartow, and Nathan G. Evans to consist only of "mingled remnants." In this crisis, wrote Beauregard, "General Johnston impressively and gallantly charged to the front, with the colors of the Fourth Alabama Regiment by his side, all the field officers of the regiment having been previously disabled."[6]

Less than four months later, at Belmont, Missouri, three Federal officers threw away their copies of Hardee's *Tactics* and followed the example of Beauregard and Johnston. John A. Logan of Illinois was awed by the courage of a man from his own state. Like Logan, Gen. John A. McClernand had no military training but owed his commission to friendship with the president. After a lengthy struggle that Logan called "really terrific," his green troops charged an enemy position "with a will and a yell." They then formed a line of battle "on a high piece of ground overlooking the [Confederate] camp." After a hurried council of war, the Federal leaders decided to charge the camp.

Some of their men reached the encampment, but Capt. Alexander Bielaski was killed "while planting the flag of our Union." Two regiments of men in blue rushed forward at this juncture, and Logan said that he saw "General McClernand, with hat in hand, leading as gallant a charge as ever was made by any troops unskilled in the arts of war."[7]

Although the Federals subsequently claimed victory, late in the afternoon of November 7, 1861, it was obvious to them that they had to abandon their position or be overrun by a counterattack. As a result, they decided to drive through the enemy ranks and take refuge on the gunboats *Tyler* and *Lexington* and the transports that they guarded. This daring breakthrough was accomplished under the leadership of Logan, McClernand, and U. S. Grant. According to one account, "Grant acted as his own rear-guard, was the last man on the shore, and at one time found himself not more than one hundred and fifty feet from a line of the enemy."[8]

In reporting the engagement to Washington, Grant rather casually noted that his horse was shot under him but said nothing about his exposure to Confederate fire. Of McClernand, the future commander in chief wrote, "[He] was in the midst of danger throughout the engagement . . . his horse was three times shot under him."[9]

Stonewall Jackson, whom Lee called his right hand, was at least as daring as his commander. On May 25, 1862, he headed troops engaged in a furious fight near Winchester, Virginia. After ordering three regiments to take a hill, he accompanied Col. John A. Campbell and men of the Second Brigade who obediently moved up from Abraham's Creek.

A moment of sublime courage or irresponsible leadership followed: "Up the hill went the two officers. By the time the Federal skirmishers had withdrawn in the face of the advancing line, Jackson was on the crest. Bullets screamed past him from a Union line 400 yards in front, on the ridge near the town. Federal artillery was plastering the position." Campbell "received an ugly wound" but "the General seemed to wear magic armor. Not a bullet touched him or his garments."[10]

Two weeks later, at Cross Keys, Gen. Richard Taylor found Jackson riding at his side between a Confederate column and the Federal line. Ignoring his own disregard for safety, Taylor tried to tell Jackson that "this was not the place for the commander of the army." If Jackson heard, he did not heed. According to Col. Evander M. Law, the Mighty Stonewall soon "was on the road, a little in advance of his line, where the fire was hottest, with reins on his horse's neck, seemingly in prayer." Although Jackson was often seen motionless with his head bowed, Law said that when the general led a charge "he became the very incarnation of battle."[11]

Two weeks after Jackson's daring exposures at Cross Keys, Union Gen. George B. McClellan—normally cautious—threw discretion to the wind at Oak Grove. For several hours on the afternoon of June 25, he watched the action from a parapet of Redoubt No. 3. A newspaper reporter observed that "bullets whistled rather dangerously" at this vantage point.[12]

By August 1862 many commanders had a year of Civil War battlefield experience behind them. Yet Confederate Gen. John C.

Breckinridge acted as though he did not know his life was considered to be worth that of scores of infantry privates.

According to the account in the *Grenada (Miss.) Appeal,* at a Confederate base "in the pine woods of St. Helena, Louisiana, parish," plans were made for an attack upon Baton Rouge. By the night of August 4, wrote a Southern correspondent, "the boys were following the retreating Yankees with fixed bayonets." Charles Clarke, who reportedly commanded the right wing, was accompanied by Breckinridge himself. The presence of the former vice president of the United States, wrote a correspondent who signed his dispatches as Se De Kay, "had a magical effect upon the men." Having watched Breckinridge in action, he rejoiced: "There was no danger he did not share with fighting men. His tall form seemed ubiquitous—here, there, and every where in peril, where there was an enemy to drive or a position to gain."[13]

In late August 1862 two more general officers risked their lives. At Second Bull Run, Brig. Gen. Maxcy Gregg's brigade fought hand-to-hand in a desperate attempt to hold off a Federal force under Maj. Gen. Philip Kearney. According to Lt. Col. Edward McCrady of the First South Carolina, Gen. Lawrence O. Branch saw the critical situation and "came to our assistance with one of his regiments, and, literally, with coat off, personally took part in the affray."[14]

In a different segment of the same swirling conflict, a brigade commander rode at the head of his men in a spectacular charge. Like generals on both sides, Confederate Lt. Col. Thomas T. Munford of the Second Virginia Cavalry seemed almost to be miraculously shielded from enemy bullets.[15]

At least four daredevils, two in gray and two in blue, were exceptionally lucky at Antietam. About 9 A.M., Confederate Gen. Daniel H. Hill rode toward the crest of a hill east of Sharpsburg, Maryland. Federal batteries were throwing shells rapidly from a thicket across a creek, creating a situation in which a horseman made a conspicuous target. Some of Hill's officers dismounted, but "with typical bravado" Hill remained in the saddle until he reached the top.

Later on the same eventful day, another Southern general, James Longstreet, spied a battery whose gunners were so exhausted that they moved very slowly. On the spur of the moment,

Gen. Winfield Scott Hancock was enraged when he learned that one of his officers, Capt. Thomas Huling, was hiding behind an oak during the battle of Antietam.

NATIONAL ARCHIVES

Longstreet galloped to them and for a time "sighted and primed the pieces himself."[16]

On the same battlefield, Union Gen. Winfield Scott Hancock's brigade was for a time the target of Confederate gunners. Described as "quivering with anger," Hancock castigated Capt. Thomas Huling, who had stayed behind an oak tree while sending his men forward. Defying protocol, Pvt. Benjamin Clarkson stepped to Hancock's side. "Come away, general," urged the member of Company C. "You really ought not to be here!"

On the same day Maj. Gen. Joseph Hooker guided his horse to the side of Col. Jacob Higgins of the 125th Pennsylvania. Facing the Dunker Church with his men, Higgins was given a peremptory order to advance toward a nearby clump of trees and hold the site.

Hooker had barely finished barking his orders when Confederate snipers opened fire. Some of them who took his highly visible white horse as a target hit their mark with nearly spent balls. As the animal jerked with pain, Higgins urged his commander to seek safety. As Hooker pulled on the bridle to ride away, a Confederate ball clipped the lower left leg of "Fighting Joe."[17]

In October 1862 at Perryville, Georgia, Confederate Gen. Leonidas Polk mistook Federal troops for Rebels firing upon their own comrades. Riding to them, the bishop-general demanded to know the identity of the unit. According to Col. Phil B. Spence, Polk recognized his blunder when an officer responded, but he bluffed his way out.

Shouting a forceful order to "Cease fire!" he turned his horse back toward the Confederate lines—expecting every instant to be hit by a minié ball. When he reached a colonel in gray, the general reported, "I have reconnoitered those fellows pretty closely, and there is no mistake as to who they are; you may get up and go for them."[18]

At Stones River on the last day of 1862, Union Gen. William S. Rosecrans rode across an open field in clear view of the Confederates. He then led his men in a complete change of front, an action described by a correspondent for the *Cincinnati Commercial* as "executed at awful personal hazard."[19]

In February 1863 Gen. William T. Sherman tried to dispel his wife's fears: "As to my exposing myself unnecessarily, you need not be concerned," he wrote. "I know where danger lies and where I should be." Then he added, "Soldiers have a right to see and know that the man who guides them is near enough to see with his own eyes, and that he cannot see without being seen."[20]

Despite his assurances to his wife, Sherman clearly felt that under some circumstances a general officer should risk his life—hoping not to fall. According to Confederate cavalry Maj. Heros Von Borcke, two of Sherman's enemies did just that at Chancellorsville in May 1863.

During the fighting on the right side of the Federal line, Jeb Stuart saw a color-bearer falter, so he raced to the spot and snatched the battle flag from his hands. Waving the emblem over his head, he gestured for his men to follow him.

When Gen. Robert E. Rodes saw the men behind Stuart falter, he led his own troops in a race to the front, an action that gave the Confederates a temporary respite from fierce fighting. Instead of receiving a reprimand for having put his life at risk, Rodes was promoted.[21]

At Gettysburg Confederate Gen. James H. Lane "fought like a demon." On the second day he succeeded to divisional command,

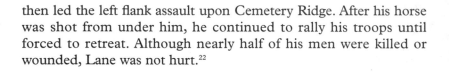

Confederate Gen. James H. Lane of Kansas fought valiantly at Gettysburg. His horse was shot out from under him and he lost nearly half his men, but Lane escaped without a scratch.

NICOLAY & HAY, LINCOLN

then led the left flank assault upon Cemetery Ridge. After his horse was shot from under him, he continued to rally his troops until forced to retreat. Although nearly half of his men were killed or wounded, Lane was not hurt.[22]

Far to the south in May 1863, at Tunnel Hill, Georgia, Union Gen. George H. Thomas was equally fortunate. Directing movements of Battery C, First Ohio Artillery, Thomas "personally went out under a brisk sharpshooters' fire, and pointed out the position to be taken." Thomas said nothing about his near miraculous escape, but it was described by newspaper correspondent A. J. Daugherty.[23]

Near Resaca, Georgia, three days later, Thomas and a party of fellow officers became the target of a Rebel gunner. Along with Gens. John Schofield, John Palmer, Washington Elliott, and William Whipple, he was standing in an open field when "a round shot was sent whizzing within a few feet of the gnarled and knotty old war horse." Daughtery, the sole source of this account, dryly noted that the missile caused the five general officers to engage in what he called "a scatterment."[24]

Near Resaca, Georgia, a single Rebel shell caused five Federal generals to run for their lives.

At a different moment of the same engagement, Hooker and Gen. Mahlon Manson ventured too close to a Confederate battery. According to Maj. Clem Landgraeber, fragments of a shell hit both of them but neither was seriously wounded.[25]

Following the retreating Army of Tennessee, Sherman and his commanders again saw spirited action at Dallas, Georgia, late in May 1864. There, according to an account by a Northern correspondent, the Fourth Corps commander, Gen. Oliver O. Howard of Maine, "exposed his person recklessly, and came sufficiently near being a one-legged, as he is already a one-armed veteran. A ragged piece of shell contused his foot severely while he was riding coolly outside the skirmish line, and another piece slightly bruised his forehead."[26]

In July 1864 Gen. Mortimer Leggett of New York led an assault upon Bald Hall, close to Atlanta. Although he was not injured, the man who could have been killed in the charge was rewarded by having his fellow soldiers rename the eminence Leggett's Hill.[27]

At Jonesboro, Georgia, on September 1, 1864, Gen. Absalom Baird led the men of Este's Brigade directly toward heavy defensive works made of logs and earth. His objective, screened by a heavy growth of underbrush, could not be seen when Baird snapped his order, "Boys, pile your knapsacks, fix bayonets, and charge those works!"

Characteristically, Sherman did not rebuke his subordinate for having displayed daring disregard for his life. Instead he recommended him for the Medal of Honor.[28]

A veteran of wars in Latin America and Italy, Confederate Maj. Chatham R. "Rob" Wheat led his Tiger Rifles at Bull Run. Spurring his horse to a gallop while leading his battalion in a charge, he was shot down and was soon told that his wound was mortal. This time the surgeon was wrong. Wheat recovered and fought until June 1862, when he was fatally wounded at Gaines's Mill.[29]

During the same battle, Southern Gen. Arnold Elzey personally directed the fire of one of his batteries for a time. He relinquished control of these guns only after he was seriously wounded after having his horse killed by a single ball.[30]

At Port Hudson in May 1863, Union Gen. Thomas W. Sherman (no relation to William Tecumseh Sherman) had a furious argument with his commander, Nathaniel P. Banks. "With steam coming out of both ears," Sherman mounted up and signaled for the Zouaves of his division to follow him. They did so at a terrible price. Soon Slaughter's Field was littered with the dead and wounded. Sherman lost a leg as a result of his foolhardiness, a punishment that some officers said "was too good for him, since he was dead drunk that day."[31]

Although George E. Pickett did not get a scratch during Pickett's Charge at Gettysburg, the leader of Gen. William Pender's Division was seriously wounded. Gen. Isaac R. Trimble earlier took a ball at Second Bull Run and was laid up for many months. Soon after Trimble returned to duty, Pender foolishly conducted a reconnoiter; hit by a shell fragment, the twenty-nine-year-old lost a leg and did not survive the amputation. At the head of Pender's men as they moved toward Cemetery Hill, Trimble received a wound that cost him a leg. In a Federal hospital he recuperated and waited many months to be exchanged.[32]

Death was the price paid by several general officers who willingly—even eagerly—disregarded the principles about a leader's caution in battle. Confederate Gen. Barnard Bee, who commanded a brigade under Joseph E. Johnston at First Bull Run, "led each regiment and seven companies of his command into the hottest fire" before receiving a mortal wound. At Wilson's Creek, Union Gen. Nathaniel Lyon swung his hat in the air, rallied his troops, and led them toward a Rebel position. Seconds after the movement got under way, a ball tore through his chest and killed him.[33]

Edward D. Baker, a close friend of Abraham Lincoln, turned down a commission as major general to retain his seat in the U.S. Senate. Fighting at Ball's Bluff at the head of his men, he rode directly into Rebel fire and death.

At Pea Ridge, Confederates James M. McIntosh and Ben McCulloch died while heading columns. Albert Sidney Johnston, often called the ablest of all Confederate commanders, led an attack near the Peach Orchard at Shiloh and bled to death as a result of his impulsive decision to leave a sheltered position.

Isaac I. Stevens, first in the class of 1839 at West Point, knew how a general should conduct himself. Yet in the last exchange of fire at Second Bull Run he seized the flag of the Seventy-ninth New York, dashed in front of a column, and signaled for his Highlanders to follow him. He took only a few steps before meeting instant death from a single ball.

Gen. Lawrence O. Branch helped to restore the Confederate right at Antietam, then remained so close to the skirmish line that a Federal sharpshooter dropped him with one shot.[34]

Another general who died at Antietam was fifty-eight-year-old Gen. Joseph F. K. Mansfield, commanding the Twelfth Corps, Army of the Potomac, as he prodded his men forward to help stop Lee's invasion of Maryland. Two hours after the Cornfield became strewn with dead, the white-haired Mansfield led his command through the East Woods. Thomas L. Livermore described the veteran soldier as "a gallant old fellow" and was astonished when he saw him advancing on foot and almost alone. "With his bare sword in his hand, and his face as black as a thunder cloud," Livermore reported, he ignored men who shouted a warning, "Behind the haystack!" Soon dead on the field from enemy fire, Mansfield was posthumously promoted to the rank of major general.[35]

While some generals died as a result of careless or deliberate exposure to enemy fire, others were killed in highly dramatic ways. During the siege of Vicksburg, Isham W. Garrott reputedly became so bored that he borrowed a rifle from a picket. Taking a place in a skirmish line, he was killed a few days before his commission as brigadier general reached the Confederate bastion.

One of his Vicksburg colleagues who had already received his commission, Martin E. Green, never described himself as bored. Still, on June 25, 1863, he sauntered within rifle range of the enemy to take a look and was also dropped by a sharpshooter.[36]

At Gettysburg, Confederate Gen. Lewis A. Armistead helped to lead Pickett's Charge. As the men in gray moved forward, the general "threw away his cravat, and placed his old black hat upon the point of his sword and held it high in the air, and walked with measured step toward the enemy." Armistead soon fell, mortally wounded, and the Federals nursed him for two days before he died.[37]

During eight weeks that began in early May 1864, five Confederates demonstrated that veteran commanders were not bulletproof. At Mansfield, Louisiana, Gen. Jean Jacques Mouton led a successful charge that cost seven hundred casualties—himself included.

Thomas Green took Federal gunboats as his targets and was at the head of a cavalry column that made an attack at Blair's Landing four days after Mouton died. Hit while charging at top speed, Green was later described as having been "well fortified with rum" before he rode to his death.

If Jeb Stuart was drunk at Yellow Tavern, it was with the excitement of battle rather than alcohol. After watching the Federals capture a battery, the famous cavalryman went to a spot on the Telegraph Road held by fewer than one hundred Confederates. They "held steady during a Federal charge," and the men in blue soon retreated. According to Henry B. McClellan, a fleeing and dismounted cavalryman "turned as he passed the general, and discharging his pistol inflicted a fatal wound."[38]

During the Atlanta campaign, indiscretion cost Gen. Charles G. Harker his life. Harker was leading his men against Joseph E. Johnston's entrenchments on a steep tree-covered slope. No one in blue saw the spot from which a concealed Confederate marksman dropped their commander from the saddle.

Near Atlanta on July 22, 1864, Confederate Gen. William H. T. Walker led a division against Sherman's left. Drifting too close to pickets of the Federal Sixteenth Corps, while "swinging his hat and cheering his men forward," he was hit several times and died instantly.[39]

At Franklin, Tennessee, more generals died than during any other battle. Six of them were Confederates who knew better than to take chances that might make their brigades leaderless. Yet both Irish-born Patrick Cleburne and States Rights Gist of South Carolina led charges on foot. Hiram Granbury died at the head of a column whose assault on a Federal position was doomed before it was launched.[40]

Near West Point, Georgia, one of Sherman's foes may have been the last general officer deliberately to expose himself to enemy fire. After Robert C. Tyler supervised the construction of earthworks, it was named Fort Tyler in his honor.

Unable to walk without the aid of crutches, due to a wound suffered earlier, Tyler had a motley band of 120 ragged convalescents and civilians under his command. About 10 A.M. on April 16, 1865, cavalry under Union Col. Oscar H. LaGrange moved within rifle range of the installation.

Pulling out his field glasses, Tyler hobbled toward a portcullis "in order to view the enemy." Standing there immobile, in plain sight, he took a fatal shot from a Federal sharpshooter. Before his body reached the ground, a second ball cut one of his crutches in two.[41]

Numerous naval officers also took great risks that they considered to be necessary. One of them used the life-threatening situation to issue an unforgettable command.

At Mobile Bay on August 5, 1864, Rear Adm. David G. Farragut had ample firepower—guns on four monitors and fourteen wooden warships. Yet he was confronted by the ironclad CSS

Tennessee, three gunboats, and artillery at Fort Morgan. Nevertheless, the most formidable threats that the Federal commander faced were the scores of floating mines that dotted the waters of the bay.

Soon after the battle began, Farragut saw that smoke from his own guns prevented him from getting a clear view of the bay. Rapidly climbing rigging, the admiral went "as far as the furrock-shrouds, immediately below the maintop." Pilot Martin Freeman of the USS *Hartford* ordered a quartermaster aloft to fasten a rope around Farragut so he would not topple to the deck.

When the crippled USS *Brooklyn* was unable to obey his orders, the admiral decided to take the lead and ordered his flagship to move ahead at full speed. As he passed the *Brooklyn,* a warning was shouted concerning Confederate torpedoes.

Back on deck, Farragut reputedly responded, "Damn the torpedoes! Full speed ahead!" Then he submitted to Flag Lieutenant Watson, who "slipped a rope around him and secured it to the rigging, so that during the fight the admiral was twice 'lashed to the rigging.' "[42]

The Federal guns were soon victorious, and Farragut's contemptuous dismissal of danger—often not fully understood in an age when torpedoes move rapidly instead of floating in position—is still quoted throughout the Western world.

An unscientific survey of some of the literature suggests that among those who died as a result of exposure to enemy fire, Confederate general officers outnumbered Federals by a ratio of more than two to one. That could mean that men from the South were braver than men from the North. Then it might signify that marksmen from the North were better shots than those from the South or had superior weapons and ammunition. Whatever the reason, the Civil War exceeds other modern conflicts in the proportion of commanders who risked all by refusing to remain in safe positions.

Part 5

Battles with Fate Are Never Won

During the administration of Thomas Jefferson, the size of the U.S. Army was enlarged, but it remained pitifully small.

16

DESTINY OR PROVIDENCE

OR CHANCE?

DURING 1808–9 Thomas Jefferson, our nation's third president, occupied the Executive Mansion, and his vice president was George Clinton of New York. As tension between Great Britain and the fledgling nation formed of her former American colonies was rising steadily, one of the most important steps taken then by the federal government was to increase the size of the U.S. Army. As enlarged, it consisted of five regiments of infantry, one of riflemen, one of light artillery, and one of light dragoons. In this period of growing uncertainty—a prelude to the War of 1812—both Jefferson Davis and Abraham Lincoln were born.[1]

Once the thirteen colonies had "formed a more perfect union," the stage was set for growth. Vermont was admitted to the United States in 1791 as the fourteenth state. Kentucky followed in 1792, Tennessee four years later, and in 1802 the nation pushed westward by admitting Ohio as the seventeenth state.[2]

Sprawling over 1 million square miles—more or less—the nation was three times as large as England, Germany, and France combined. Census takers estimated that in 1810 the population would come very close to 7 million persons and might even exceed that number. Immense numbers of them were crowded into the huge port cities of New York, Philadelphia, Baltimore, Charleston, and New Orleans. Two of these urban centers exceeded 50,000 inhabitants, two more fell between 25,000 and 49,999, and seven smaller cities exceeded 10,000 but fell short of 25,000 in size.[3]

Into this geographic entity, more than a half-million infants were born annually. One of them, a son of Samuel and Jane Davis, first saw the light of day on June 3, 1808, in rural Christian County,

New York, Philadelphia, Baltimore, Charleston, New Orleans, and other port cities held the bulk of the population of the nation.

Kentucky. Just eighteen months later a son of Tom and Nancy Lincoln was born in Hardin County, Kentucky, on February 12, 1809. In the nation that stretched from Canada to the Gulf of Mexico and from the Atlantic Ocean to unexplored regions west of the Mississippi River, these two boys were born about 125 miles apart.

This coincidence of place and time that bound Davis and Lincoln together has been noted many times. There are other similar early experiences of the two. When the Davis boy named for the sitting president was about three years old, his parents took him out of Kentucky. The boy who bore the name of the Old Testament patriarch was taken out of Kentucky by his parents when he was about seven years old. Both Blue Grass State birthplaces of the future chief executives were subsequently renamed. Once in Christian County, the Davis place later became a part of Todd County—and attorney Lincoln later took Mary Todd as his

Zachary Taylor was responsible for the fact that Jefferson Davis was linked with Chief Black Hawk.

wife. His own home in infancy, Hardin County, later became Larue County.

Before the future chief executives were born, the Sauk and Fox Indians had ceded their tribal lands east of the Mississippi River to the United States. The Native Americans, however, found their new lands to be less fertile than those they had abandoned, so they sided with the British in the War of 1812. A generation later, Chief Black Hawk led remnants of his tribe to their old fertile lands in Illinois in time for the spring planting. A white settler, never identified, soon shot an Indian brave and the fracas known as the Black Hawk War ensued.

At the outbreak of trouble, a local militia unit formed in Illinois to fight the Indians and elected Abraham Lincoln as its captain. Sworn into service by Lt. Robert Anderson, he drilled, marched, and shouldered a musket for about six weeks but had no combat experience. A stunning victory by the settlers brought the struggle to an abrupt end on August 2, 1832.[4]

By now a lieutenant in the U.S. Army, Jefferson Davis was on furlough during the brief struggle and took no part in it. Yet his name is prominently linked with it because Black Hawk escaped and was soon captured by Davis, who was ordered by Zachary Taylor to become his jailer. Very early in September 1832, Davis and a small band of soldiers escorted Black Hawk to a stockade at Fort Armstrong on Rock Island.[5]

Lieutenant Anderson, a good friend of Davis, was a member of the party that guarded the Native American chief. Nearly three decades later, Anderson was placed in command of Federal installations at Charleston, South Carolina. There, his decision to move his command from Fort Moultrie to Fort Sumter without authorization led to the confrontation that led to civil war.

Strange Encounters

The intertwined lives of Davis and Lincoln were not the only Civil War examples of events that appear to have been statistically unlikely. Strange encounters occurred repeatedly.

The vital role played in the Civil War by legislation enacted to subdue Pennsylvania's Whiskey Rebellion of 1794 is generally overlooked, despite the fact that Lincoln's April 1861 call for volunteers was both based upon and limited by congressional actions designed to end the trouble in the Keystone State.

Alexander Hamilton had sponsored an excise tax upon whiskey that triggered an attack upon a federal marshal in Allegheny County and enraged a band of several hundred protesters who burned the home of Gen. John Neville. Soon an estimated fifteen thousand armed men prepared to defy the government whose capital was then in Philadelphia. Alarmed, President George Washington used the powers conferred upon him by Congress to call for the militia to quell the insurrection.[6]

Henry "Light-Horse Harry" Lee, a distinguished veteran of the American Revolution and a member of the Virginia legislature, was selected to lead the militia of his state against the insurgents in Pennsylvania. He played a leading role in quickly ending the Whiskey Rebellion, which remained nearly bloodless when its condemned leaders were pardoned. Lincoln almost certainly used his power to have field command of the U.S. Army offered to recently promoted Col. Robert E. Lee through the agency of elder statesman Francis P. Blair. It is doubtful, however, that he then knew that the soldier he wanted to lead his forces against the secessionists was the son of the man who had put down the first armed revolt against the federal government and thereby paved the way

Henry Lee of Virginia played a crucial role in putting down the nation's first revolt against federal authority.

for Lincoln's call for seventy-five thousand volunteers to end the secession movement.[7]

Since inland transportation in the mid-nineteenth century was dominated by rivers, it is logical that many river names were bestowed upon the armies. Federal authorities made their Army of the Potomac a major fighting force, while in Richmond military and political leaders chose the identical name for the Confederate force into which Virginia militia units were transferred.[8]

This confusion of nomenclature continued for at least six months. Dates of Confederate dispatches suggest that an unofficial name change took place at the end of 1861 or early in 1862. It was the son of Henry Lee who initiated the change in nomenclature without first securing official sanction to do so. Once men on both sides began to accept this change, Lincoln no longer had to wonder whether or not directives sent to the Army of the Potomac might somehow fall into Rebel hands.[9]

Two decisive Federal victories were scored within an extremely narrow time frame. In Pennsylvania, while the battle of Gettysburg was raging in its third and final day, at 3 P.M. on July 3, 1863, in faraway Mississippi, a white flag fluttering in the breeze marked a

VICKSBURG HISTORICAL SOCIETY

Pennsylvania-born
John C. Pemberton became a
Rebel and was given
command of all-important
Vicksburg, Mississippi.

period of truce. Confederate Gen. John C. Pemberton, a
Pennsylvania native, was conferring with Ulysses S. Grant under
an oak tree. Their parley led to the surrender of Vicksburg on July
4. The events at Gettysburg and Vicksburg persuaded many British
and European observers that the Confederacy was doomed.[10]

Chief Executives

No other pair of Americans became commanders in chief of armies
by sets of circumstances so strange as those that elevated two
Kentuckians to the top positions. Resting briefly at his Brierfield
plantation in Mississippi, Jefferson Davis knew that momentous
decisions were being made in Alabama. He knew that delegates
from six seceded states were scheduled to convene at Montgomery
on February 4. Like most well-informed southerners, he believed
that a sectional war was likely to be waged. That being the case,
Davis hoped and expected that the members of the Provisional
Confederate Congress would choose him for a military role.

Davis and members of his family were therefore not surprised when a messenger appeared at Brierfield with a telegram
that had been sent to Vicksburg from Montgomery. When Davis
read the message, however, his face showed such anguish that

Varina Davis knew that her husband was far from pleased at his unexpected elevation to the presidency of the Confederacy.

his wife, Varina, initially thought he might have received word of a family tragedy.

It was nothing of the sort. The delegates had voted on the morning of February 9 to make Davis the first provisional president of the new nation. Like the first six chief executives of the United States, he was swept into office without a popular election having been held.

On the following day, slaves rowed Davis downriver to a packetboat landing, where he became a passenger on the *Natchez*. The vessel reached Jackson before nightfall. Davis remained there until a telegram led him to begin his preinaugural journey immediately. He estimated that during the two days he had to travel by train to reach Montgomery, he would have to make at least a dozen speeches at junctions and railroad towns. He underestimated. On the way to his inauguration he made about twenty-five speeches.[11]

David Davis ran the campaign that sent Lincoln to the Executive Mansion, but he may have acted without the knowledge or consent of the man from Springfield.

If Lincoln had serious aspirations for the presidency, he kept such thoughts to himself. A seasoned politician, he never forgot that his previous highest office was a single term in the U.S. House of Representatives. He knew that the Republican National Committee had voted to hold the 1860 convention in Chicago only after receiving a pledge that Illinois would not field a favorite son as a candidate. It was common knowledge that William H. Seward of New York—nationally famous as "Mr. Republican"—was likely to receive the nomination on the first ballot. Nomination was considered tantamount to election, for the Democrats were divided into three warring factions.

Many citizens of Illinois were surprised when their own state Republican convention ignored earlier promises and made Lincoln a candidate as a result of support that surged to him when he began to be called "the Rail Splitter." Still, there was no reason to believe he had a national following. A vote cast for him was likely to be a token vote.

David Davis, who had assumed the role of campaign manager for Lincoln, was scheduled to preside over the early sessions of the national Republican convention. He managed to delay the printing presses so that it was impossible to take a ballot on the first evening, May 16, 1860. On the following morning, jubilant adher-

Chicago's Wigwam was the first building erected for the purpose of housing a national political convention.

ents of Seward took to the streets and marched behind brass bands. Bogus admission tickets to the meeting place of the convention had been hastily printed and distributed in order to pack it. When Seward's followers made their belated appearance on May 17, only a few of them were able to find seats. While these shenanigans were taking place, Davis and his aides were busy promising contenders for the nomination that their support of Lincoln would bring them cabinet posts.

No evidence indicates that Lincoln, who remained in Springfield, knew what was taking place in Chicago. He seems to have been greatly surprised to receive a telegram informing him that on the third ballot he had become the Republican nominee for the nation's highest office. It is uncertain whether or not he was ever fully informed about the chain of events that virtually guaranteed him four years in the Executive Mansion in Washington.

Clearly, however, he knew at least the broad outline of events that took place on November 6. A total of 1,375,157 Northern Democrats put their influence and their votes behind Stephen A.

Douglas. Southern Democrats and Independent Democrats cast 847,953 ballots for John C. Breckinridge. Supporters of the Constitutional Union Party gave 590,631 votes to John Bell of Tennessee.

Lincoln of Illinois did not have a single recorded supporter in the states of the Cotton Belt. Although the national population was 31 million in 1860, the electorate was tiny. Voting was confined to white males, twenty-one years of age or over who had served in the military or who owned property. Lincoln's total of 1 million votes constituted a little over 39 percent of all that were cast, but he became president of the United States as a result of being supported at the polls by only one American in sixteen.[12]

Spending many a nearly sleepless night in his Springfield home, making no speeches concerning his positions on crucial national issues and giving no interviews to reporters, candidate Lincoln was keenly aware that his nomination resulted from unprecedented events. Despite his poor showing in the general election, he received almost 60 percent of votes cast by members of the Electoral College. Although he seems never to have used the modern term, he had received a clear mandate to lead the nation in a time of grave crisis.

Lincoln started for Washington and his inauguration on February 11, 1861, about one day before Davis started for Montgomery and his inauguration. As he rode, he meditated on the highly improbable series of events in which he played a passive role. Small wonder, therefore, that Lincoln later said over and over that he was an instrument of forces that guided his path in life. If he pondered the ways in which his path in life had paralleled that of Jefferson Davis, he said nothing about it. Although Lincoln was not a churchman in a conventional sense, his conviction that he was an instrument of God (or fate) echoes over and over in his speeches and letters.[13]

17

ANONYMOUS AID

NAMELESS AFRICAN AMERICANS

Capt. THEODORE F. ALLEN of the Seventh Ohio Cavalry followed Ambrose E. Burnside into Tennessee in 1863 and at Rogersville was seriously wounded during an engagement that ended in a Federal rout. How long he lay unconscious on the ground Allen never knew. His first postbattle recollection was the realization that a Rebel soldier was trying to pull off his prized boots. For fifty dollars in Union greenbacks, worth an estimated three thousand dollars in Confederate currency, his captor permitted him to keep his boots.

Aware that Ulysses S. Grant had suspended the exchange of prisoners, Allen was resigned to a lengthy imprisonment. He was not, however, prepared for the news that he and other men of his unit would have to march all the way to the Belle Isle compound in Richmond. On an evening when their captors relaxed their vigilance, Allen and Lt. A. A. Carr managed to join a column of Rebel cavalry, having no idea where their attempted escape would take them. Days later they entered familiar territory in the valley of the Holston River, so they turned their horses toward the heavily forested foothills of the Smoky Mountains and set out for freedom without food, weapons, or anything except the clothing on their backs. After more than two days, they were famished, having eaten nothing except an apple that they had shared. If they could make it to Rogersville, county seat of Hawkins County, Tennessee, they were sure that Unionist John R. Netherland would help them reach a place of safety.

At the Netherland home, the lady of the house introduced herself as a native of Vermont and warned them that her home was searched at regular intervals. On one occasion a fugitive, pursued by Confederates was seen to enter the house—where he literally disappeared. Mrs. Netherland, Allen later wrote, had guided the hunted man into a cabin occupied by a slave.

From "a colored woman who was rocking her baby to sleep in the cradle," Allen learned how the hunted man escaped capture:

> Grasping the situation, this colored woman moved the cradle aside, lifted a board in the floor and put the soldier in this opening in the floor. She replaced the board, put the cradle in place over it, and resumed her lullaby.
>
> Confederate soldiers entered this little one-room cabin and asked the colored mother if she had seen the Union soldier. She replied, "Yes," that he had come to this cabin and had gone right on through, whereupon the Confederate soldiers continued the search elsewhere. In relating her experience, the young colored mother stated that she was afraid that the loud beating of her heart would betray the presence of the man under the floor.

Leaving the Netherlands, Allen and Carr proceeded to the home of Unionist John Blevins—"a handsome mansion in the Tennessee River Valley." From there the fugitives followed what Union soldiers knew as "the underground railroad for escaped prisoners," and after four days of constant danger reached the Federal lines about two miles from a ford of the Holston River.

Allen's narrative, filled with vivid details and including a tribute to "a young colored woman" is like many other wartime accounts, but he did not record the name of the woman who risked her life and that of her child to help two Union soldiers evade capture.[1] Such omissions are not that unusual in the official accounts, which include scores of incidents in which slaves, former slaves, or escaped slaves supplied information to Federal soldiers and sailors. In only a minority of these personal accounts are the informants named.

Stationed on Louisiana's Plaquemines Brule Bayou, Lt. Col. S. A. Bean of the Fourth Wisconsin Regiment was warned by "negroes" in April 1863 that fifteen hundred to two thousand enemy troops were nearby.[2]

During the Federal siege of Wilmington, North Carolina, two blockade-runners managed to come close to the port under cover of darkness, announcing their arrival to Confederates on shore through signals. "A captured contraband understood the signals" and told Gen. Alfred H. Terry what reply "would bring them in." When that reply was flashed, the commanders of the blockade-runners "came in, entirely unconscious they were falling among Federal forces" and unaware that a black resident of the coastal region was responsible for their capture.[3]

From Martinsburg, Virginia, in 1864 Union Col. George D. Wells sent information to Harpers Ferry that "three negroes in from Strasburg report that [Confederate Maj. Harry W.] Gilmor is wounded, that [Gen. John D.] Imboden and [Gen. Thomas L.] Rosser have received orders to join [Gen. James] Longstreet, and it is believed that they have gone."[4]

Almost simultaneously, Capt. Lemuel Norton, stationed in the same region, learned from other contrabands that cavalrymen in gray were "collecting for a raid on our right."[5]

Comdr. William Budd, charged with helping to clear the Potomac River of Rebel gun batteries, "learned from the negroes" where three hundred Southerners were concentrated. This information led him to take the gunboat *Resolute* up a creek, where he captured twenty-five or thirty men.[6]

Gen. George B. McClellan was given "information from contra-bands" that included details as to the whereabouts of forces commanded by Stonewall Jackson, D. H. Hill, and some of their subordinates.[7]

Fighting on the west bank of the Mississippi River, Col. T. W. Parmele of the 174th New York learned from contrabands that all-important help was close at hand. Adm. David D. Porter, with the warships *Hartford* and *Albatross,* was only a few miles away. He took "one of them to Captain Alden, of the *Richmond,* who dispatched him with some communications" to Porter.[8]

During the 1862 blockade of Charleston, South Carolina, Comdr. Percival Drayton sent news to Comdr. Samuel F. Du Pont: "Two contrabands came in to-day from Charleston. Like the rest I have seen, they represent the harbor as completely blocked up, the ordinary channel stopped, and vessels obliged to come over the middle ground (probably at high tide only) and close to a palmetto fort erected there recently. They say that in front of the piles are iron-pointed snags at an angle of 45 degrees, and that off [Fort] Moultrie they saw some torpedoes placed as large as the gunboat's cabin. Charleston is evidently not to be given up without a struggle."[9]

Far to the west in Louisiana, Col. Stephen Thomas of the Eighth Vermont learned at his Algiers headquarters that men at Bayou Des Allemands were confronted by an "immensely superior force." In this situation, fearing that "his first fire might prove fatal to his own men," the commander of the post surrendered. "This I learned by an intelligent contraband that escaped," Thomas said.[10]

Aboard the USS *Potomska*, in Saint Catherine's Sound, Georgia, the commanding officer may have owed the safety of his ship to an unidentified informant. Searching for a Confederate vessel thought to be at anchor seven miles up the Ogeechee River, the *Potomska* managed to avoid an ambush by "keeping a lookout for a battery and row of piles reported by a contraband."[11]

In April 1862 the *New York Tribune* reported that men from the First New Jersey Cavalry had captured ten prisoners at a courier station not far from the Rappahannock River. "They were surprised in their beds," reported the newspaper. "The information which led to their capture was volunteered by a loyal black, who guided the Jersey men through the rebel picket line."

In May 1862, Gen. Thomas Williams, whose expeditionary corps was in action near Vicksburg, "learned from negro runaways that the rebels had a battery of four guns" at a railroad bridge that otherwise might have been approached without caution.[12]

Not far from Charleston the ship *Dale* managed to escape damage from "a barricade of piles driven across the river" by Southerners. Again, this maneuver was performed as a result of information given to a member of the crew "by the negroes."[13]

In June 1862, men aboard the USS *James Adger* received word from contrabands that "a floating battery was seen over Morris Island [in Charleston Harbor] having a couple of guns mounted."[14]

From Dividing Creek, Virginia, during the first month of 1863, Comdr. T. J. Linnekin of the USS *Currituck* reported his seizure of "a large manufactory for salt in a steam sawmill, owned by a man named Oscar Yerby" based on "information obtained from a negro."[15]

Near Culpeper, Virginia, late in the winter of 1863, Gen. Wesley Merrit warned nearby officers that contrabands "coming into infantry lines" had given sure word that "the rebels are preparing for a raid with the intent to demonstrate on our right flank, while [Jeb] Stuart crosses the river below on the left flank of the army."[16]

About the same time a paymaster aboard the USS *Currituck* received vital information concerning illicit trade between Virginia and Maryland. When a party of sailors were dispatched to find a canoe used in that trade, they triumphantly returned with two canoes and three civilian prisoners. This blow against forbidden exchanges of merchandise was struck as a result of what the naval officer "learned from a negro."[17]

Early in February 1863 the Union warship *Diana* managed to capture "one of Fuller's negroes, who says there are three guns in Butte-a-la-Rose, commanded by Burbank and manned by the crew of the steamer *Cotton*." Lt. A. P. Cooke, who transmitted this information to Gen. Godfrey Weitzel, noted that it came "from contrabands near Indian Bend, who left there yesterday."[18]

An August 23, 1863, entry in the abstract log of the USS *Jacob Bell* states, "At 9:25 PM. a colored man came on board with the information that a schooner had run into Rosier's Creek."[19]

With New Berne, North Carolina, as an important 1864 target, Gen. John J. Peck sent a dispatch to Gen. Benjamin F. Butler: "Nine contrabands have just come from Kenansville and Warsaw, where they were raised," he wrote. "They report troops passing to Wilmington from Virginia on three days in large numbers. The soldiers said they were going to advance from Wilmington on New Berne. [My informants are] well posted and intelligent and honest."[20]

Near Sayler's Creek, Virginia, on April 5, 1865, a Federal body was forced to retire when attacked by Confederates. This temporary

At Cairo, Illinois, unidentified blacks provided vital military intelligence to Ulysses S. Grant.

setback was more than offset, in the opinion of Gen. Wesley Merritt, by receipt of a letter written by a Confederate colonel at Amelia Court House. "Brought into the lines by a negro," it conveyed the welcome news that "our Army [of Northern Virginia] is ruined, I fear."[21]

Even Ulysses S. Grant owed at least a trifle of his fame to information given him by persons whose names he did not preserve. Near Cairo, Illinois, he reported to superiors: "The rebels left Secession last Monday; had there four regiments of Tennessee and Mississippi troops, ten or twelve pieces of artillery drawn by horse, one large piece drawn by five yoke of oxen, and one mortar drawn by three yoke. In addition to this Jeff Thompson had 1,500 men [who were headed toward] New Madrid and then to Memphis."[22] That evening, the future commander of Union armies telegraphed that troops could be spared from Cairo.

The collective impact of these and hundreds of other informants much like them made a significant contribution to Federal movements of troops and warships. In most instances geographical names are carefully listed, but the names of the informants who put their lives on the line are rarely noted. In addition to providing information that was often eagerly volunteered, blacks who remained anonymous frequently served as guides on land and as pilots on water.

In January 1863 Acting Master T. J. Linnekin was almost totally dependent upon locally reared pilots who knew the Potomac and Rappahannock Rivers well. When he learned from two contrabands that a sloop and two canoes—almost certainly being used in forbidden trade—were "lying in Tabb's Creek," he said that he acted promptly. "I at once sent a party in search of them, the negroes acting as pilots. They succeeded in capturing them, and all the crew, with one exception. The canoes were full of freight, and I found on the person of the captain $1,314."[23]

Four months later men of the Fourth Wisconsin, moving out from Washington, Louisiana, were led by their chief of cavalry who "was furnished with a negro guide, who was acquainted with the woods and paths."[24]

During the siege of Petersburg the Ninetieth Ohio was sent on a flanking mission that took them to abandoned trenches. "An old Negro ran up to them" and hurriedly babbled that the Rebels were gone. "The Negro offered to guide them and the men agreed to follow. Sure enough, he led them right into the unsupported and unguarded rear of Southern artillerymen."[25]

Headed directly toward a beleaguered Confederate city, Gen. David Birney found his map to be worthless, making it difficult or impossible to cross Harrison's Creek. In this dilemma, he found that "none of the white natives would or could give him any information." Finally, however, "he obtained some Negro guides and the column started toward Petersburg."[26]

One of the reports about an 1864 foray by Gen. Judson Kilpatrick's cavalry was filed by Capt. Joseph Gloskoski of the Twenty-ninth New York. Advancing toward the South Anna River from Beaver Dam Station, the cavalrymen moved forward in pitch darkness with wind and sleet so fierce that they tried to close their eyes. "So complete darkness I never saw," Gloskoski wrote. "Men depended entirely on the instinct of their horses, and the whole command on a negro to guide them."[27]

Acting Master William T. Street of the USS *Primrose*, searching the Rappahannock River for Southern "blockade boats and goods" in May 1863 got word of a heavy trade that was being conducted from Dividing and Indian Creeks. Since he had no pilot who knew that channel, he "took on board a colored man who was oystering near the mouth" and used him as a pilot in his successful hunt for the ship *Sarah Lavinia*. Although the vessel was abandoned and nearly empty, seven packages of gold lace were found in the cabin. Seized as a prize of war, the *Lavinia* was sent to Washington, where it was sold and the proceeds were divided among the officers and men of the *Primrose*.[28]

Acting Rear Adm. Theodorus Bailey, stationed at Key West, Florida, sent the bark *Restless* on a mission early in 1864. Members of the crew led by Ens. James J. Russell blundered upon a schooner stationed where the Confederates could watch the movements of the Federal ship. The capture of the schooner and seven of its men proved easy, but the task of getting the vessel out of the creek was seen to be difficult. In this dilemma Bailey reported: "Not venturing to trust to the pilotage of any of the captured party, Mr. Russell sent two negro boys, who were oystering near by, for their father, who, it appeared, knew the channel well. [He] got the schooner—a valuable prize—underway and out into the bay."[29]

In perhaps one out of every twenty instances in which blacks spontaneously aided Federal forces, one or more names of these civilian volunteers went into the record. Strangely, this occurred far more frequently in naval incidents than in land actions. Occasionally, but not regularly, the name of a black who aided a Federal operation appears in an official cumulative index to events of 1861–65.

Off Charleston in early June 1862 Comdr. J. B. Marchand of the USS *James Adger* saw a rickety canoe approaching. It proved to hold six men, all of whom were slaves belonging to Charleston owners. They were field hands who had been hiding in the woods for months, so they could provide no helpful information. Hence Marchand decided that if they seemed useful, he would enlist them as members of his crew; if not, he would send them to Port

Royal as laborers. This naval officer carefully noted that the "six contrabands" who escaped to a Federal ship were named Alexander, Robert, Samuel Quamer, Tony Duhar, Monday, and Thomas Hamilton.[30]

Less than a month later, Comdr. George A. Prentiss of the USS *Albatross* found that members of his crew knew nothing of the waters they were ordered to patrol. Fortunately, reported Prentiss, "My pilot, Prince, upon whom I shall have mainly to depend," was intimately familiar with the waters near Waccamaw, South Carolina.[31]

Capt. R. S. Davis, a member of the staff of Benjamin F. Butler, departed from custom and recorded both the name and the reward of a black who provided valuable news about a cache of concealed arms. "The negro boy who gave the information—George Washington Walker—will be emancipated," he wrote.[32]

Rear Adm. Samuel F. Du Pont gave no hint of emancipation or any other reward, but he did record the name—Nelson Anderson—of "a contraband pilot" who aided one of his warships.[33]

Compensation of any kind was rare, even after a black volunteer provided important service or gave significant information. An exception to this pattern took place after the shooting stopped. Comdr. Foxhall A. Parker of the Potomac River Flotilla, aboard the USS *Don,* seized an unspecified number of small boats. When no valid claims of ownership were presented, he "directed that the boats should be distributed among officers, seamen, and pilots who had served faithfully during the rebellion, and to some contrabands who had acted as guides. These were of course given, not sold."[34]

Although it probably was not unique, Col. Ulric Dahlgren's "reward" to a black guide was both dramatic and violent. As he led a picked force of five hundred men to Richmond (see chapter 12), Dahlgren realized that the James River was his most formidable barrier. Uncertain about where he might ford the river, he accepted an offer of guidance from an adolescent black. When led to a place of crossing, the Federal officer eyed the swollen river doubtfully for a long moment before deciding to remain on the

Former slaves, widely known as contrabands during the war years, fared little but not much better during Reconstruction years.

north bank to try to join forces commanded by Gen. Judson Kilpatrick.

Angry at his failure to effect the planned southern approach to his target, Dahlgren concluded that his black volunteer had betrayed him. As a result, he had the boy—later identified as Martin Robinson—shot on the spot.[35]

18
NUMERO UNO
FIRST EVENTS AND ACHIEVEMENTS

THE LITERATURE of the Civil War is so vast, so colorful, and so varied that any reader can expect to encounter accounts of first events and achievements in everything from colossal engagements to trivial actions.

Fateful Encounters

The first general officer to receive a mortal wound while retreating after having led an immortal charge was James J. Pettigrew. During Pickett's Charge at Gettysburg, Pettigrew took over the leadership of a division when Henry Heth was shot from the saddle. Somehow surviving that murderous charge, during the retreat of the Army of Northern Virginia, Pettigrew was hit at Falling Waters, Maryland, and clung to life for three days.[1]

Capt. William Latane was the only Confederate to be killed during Jeb Stuart's famous June 1862 ride around McClellan's army.[2]

Lt. Albert B. Rowland of the Sixth Massachusetts was the first soldier in blue to die from a bullet. He took a direct hit from a civilian on the streets of Baltimore on April 19, 1861.[3]

Col. Nathan Bedford Forrest planned and led the first major raid of the war. On November 14, 1861, he brought his men into Kentucky—officially neutral but actually tilting toward the Union. Whooping Confederates hit Caseyville, Eddyville, and numerous smaller settlements before leaving the state on December 5.[4]

Lt. Col. John Q. Marr, who fell at Fairfax Court House on June 1, 1861, was the first Southern officer to die. Not yet a Confederate, Marr held a commission in the Virginia Volunteers, a militia force not under the control of the government headed by Jefferson Davis.[5]

Mrs. Judith C. Henry was the first woman to die in battle. Living on Spring Hill Farm near Manassas, Virginia, she was the widow of a physician who once served as a surgeon's mate on the famous frigate *Constitution*.

When the Union and Confederate armies converged on July 21, 1861, Mrs. Henry, her son, her daughter, and a servant were the only occupants of the farmhouse. They hastily moved out when the shooting started, but it was impossible to pass through the military lines. They had to return to the Henry house and soon a ball believed to have come from one of the guns of U.S. Capt. J. B. Rickett's battery took off one of Mrs. Henry's legs. She clung to life until late afternoon. When she had breathed her last, her son John reputedly moaned over and over, "They've killed my mother!"[6]

Debate over who pulled the lanyard to fire the first shot at Fort Sumter early on the morning of April 12, 1861, began immediately after the Confederate victory and is still going on. Little more is positively known about the first artillery shot at First Bull Run.

About 5 A.M. on the day of the first major battle of the war, Capt. J. Howard Carlisle's Company E of the Second Artillery, U.S. Army, opened the action with a mighty blast from a 30-pounder Parrott gun. Some authorities credit Lt. Peter C. Hains with having directed the shot, but claims have been advanced for other members of the battery.[7]

According to Judson Kilpatrick, then a captain in the Fifth New York, the first Federal officer to die in a pitched battle was Lt. John T. Greble. A member of the Second Artillery, U.S. Army, Greble took a direct hit at Big Bethel, Virginia, on June 10, 1861.[8]

During the engagement that claimed the life of Greble, Pvt. John Baines of the Wythe Rifles (Virginia state troops) is believed to have been the first Rebel soldier to kill a Yankee officer. Shortly

Fierce but chaotic fighting at Big Bethel, Virginia, produced a number of firsts.

after Greble was mortally wounded, reported Gen. Ebenezer W. Pierce, a shot from Baines's musket felled Maj. Theodore Winthrop, a member of Maj. Gen. Benjamin Butler's staff.[9]

A Tar Heel is believed to have been the first Confederate soldier to die in battle. Henry L. Wyatt of the First North Carolina, called "a brave soldier and devoted patriot" by Col. John B. Magruder, lost his life at Big Bethel on June 10, 1861.[10]

Students at the Virginia Military Institute won a special kind of immortality by their gallantry during the May 15, 1864, battle of New Market. They were not the first of their kind to go into combat, however. That distinction was earned by a group of fifteen cadets from the North Carolina Military Institute. Like Greble, Baines, and Watt, they took part in the battle of Big Bethel, Virginia, that ended in a decisive Confederate victory.[11]

At Iuka, Mississippi, men in blue under E. O. G. Ord encountered an estimated twenty thousand Rebels led by Sterling Price. On the afternoon of September 19, 1862, the Eleventh Ohio Battery went into battle with ninety-seven enlisted men and five officers. Before night brought a close to its duel with Confederate gunners, only eight men of this unit were still in action.

Capt. Henry M. Neil, who was there, said that eighteen men died; thirty-nine more were wounded—many mortally. Among cannoneers, forty-six out of fifty-four were listed as casualties; many were bayoneted at their guns.

Their dead and wounded made the Ohio unit first among all light batteries in one-day losses. According to Fox's *Regimental Losses,* Buckeye casualties at Iuka exceeded the closest competitor for an unwanted "first" by 22 percent.[12]

At Stones River, near Murfreesboro, Tennessee, Confederates led by Braxton Bragg clashed head-on with Federal troops under William S. Rosecrans. Fighting began on the last day of 1862 and continued for seventy-two hours. When the carnage stopped, the opposing forces counted their losses. The Confederates suffered more than 10,000 casualties among just under 38,000 men engaged; of the 43,400 Union men who entered the conflict, 13,249 were dead, wounded, captured, or missing. Horrendous losses at Antietam and Gettysburg are far more widely known than those in Tennessee. Yet Stones River saw the highest percentage of casualties relative to numbers engaged of any Civil War battle.[13]

Most reports by officers, Union and Confederate, are relatively cold and dispassionate in tone. An exception is Col. N. B. Buford's account of the Twenty-first Illinois at Belmont, Missouri, submitted to Gen. John A. McClernand. Compared to later clashes between entire armies, Belmont was minor in scope, but it seemed colossal to the men fighting here for the first time. Early in November 1861, wrote Buford, his green troops had an awesome experience: "It was our first action. We encountered great odds; the enemy in his fortified position, the thunder of the heavy artillery from Columbus, the whizzing of rifled cannon; we had no guides. How could soldiers who had volunteered only a few days ago be expected to brave such odds?" *But they did brave them.*[14] In their first battle, these Illinois volunteers lost ninety-five men. Buford registered his profound gratitude that "Chaplain Rev. Dr.

S. Y. McMasters accompanied the expedition, and was unwearied in consoling and dressing the wounded."

Numerous commentators count Mill Springs, Kentucky, as the first Union victory of the war. Fought in January 1862, the win came after a brief but bloody clash with Confederates under Felix Zollicoffer.

Ephraim A. Otis, who was present as an officer under George H. Thomas, later wrote, "The contest was short, sharp, and decisive, and was ended by a bayonet charge from the Ninth Ohio and Second Minnesota; and the Rebel Army was routed, their leader killed, and their camp, artillery, and supplies captured."[15]

On May 6, 1862, one of many ship-to-shore encounters involved a Confederate battery and the USS *Mound City* on the White River. On both sides, gunners initially missed their targets. Then an accurate or a chance shot from a Rebel gun made a direct hit on the Federal vessel. Often described as "first among the most deadly shots of 1861–65," a thirty-two-pound shell hit the casemate of the warship close to a forward gun port. Three gunners died upon impact, but the shell went on to blow a hole in the boiler, causing 82 men to die from scalding steam.

That should have ended the slaughter, but it did not. While the vessel drifted helplessly down the river, frightened survivors abandoned ship. As soon as a few of them hit the water, Confederate sharpshooters put their rifles to work. In a matter of minutes, 43 men in blue drowned or were killed by rifle fire, while 25 more were severely wounded. A total of 150 casualties resulted from a single shot that may have found its mark by chance.[16]

Durance Vile

Lt. John L. Worden of the U.S. Navy was the first sailor to become a prisoner of war. Maj. Robert Anderson surrendered Fort Sumter on April 14, 1861, but members of the garrison were not treated as prisoners. Instead, they were allowed to board waiting ships and return to the North.

Worden took an urgent message to Fort Pickens during the artillery duel at Charleston. He then managed to board a train and pass through Confederate lines to Montgomery, Alabama. Seized at the provisional Confederate capital on the day after Confederates occupied Fort Sumter, he addressed a plaintive plea to the

Inventor John Ericcson built the ironclad commanded by former prisoner of war John L. Worden.

Confederate secretary of war, L. P. Walker: "Very unexpectedly I find myself a prisoner of war at this place. May I be permitted to request that you will do me the kindness to inform me of the grounds upon which I am so detained?"[17]

If Walker responded to this memorandum, his reply was not preserved. After seven months Worden was exchanged and soon took command of John Ericcson's experimental ironclad, the USS *Monitor*.[18]

The first soldiers to become prisoners of war were members of Capt. A. T. Lee's company of the Eighth U.S. Infantry. Under the command of Lt. E. W. H. Read, these members of the U.S. Army surrendered to Capt. James Duff and a company of citizen volunteers. Read protested that their arrest would constitute a violation of an agreement between the state of Texas and brevet Gen. David E. Twiggs. Duff waved objections aside and on April 23, 1861, sent the entire company to a Confederate stockade near San Antonio.[19]

Numerous other persons mistakenly believed that they had a role in taking the first soldier to become a prisoner of war. One of them was Col. Alfred H. Baird of the First North Carolina. He died thinking that a Federal picket captured near Fort Monroe on

Gen. John A. Dix signed for the Union when the first cartel for the exchange of prisoners was approved.

A. H. RITHIE ENGRAVING

June 9 by one of his details was the first Yankee soldier to throw up his hands in surrender.[20]

The first cartel for formal exchanges of prisoners was not perfected until July 22, 1862. Part of the delay stemmed from President Lincoln's fear that adoption of such a process would constitute tacit recognition of the Confederate States of America as an independent nation. Gens. John A. Dix and Daniel H. Hill signed for the Union and Confederacy, respectively.

The agreement, which lasted only briefly without modification, required that all prisoners were to be exchanged within ten days of their capture. Johnny Rebs were swapped for Billy Yanks on a one-for-one basis, but officers were valued according to rank. Six captured privates or two lieutenants were considered equal to one captain, and the release of a single major general meant freedom for thirty of the enemy's enlisted men.[21]

Clement L. Vallandigham of Ohio was the first former member of the U.S. Congress to be ordered into close confinement for the duration of the struggle. His sentence stemmed from findings of a commission of officers who concluded that he had publicly declared "disloyal sentiments." Lincoln did not like the uproar that resulted, so he agreed to have him set free on condition that he leave the Union. Vallandigham accepted the offer and went into a

Former Congressman Clement L. Vallandigham was asleep when soldiers broke down the door of his home in Dayton, Ohio, to arrest him.

Rebel-held section of Tennessee. The authorities in Richmond, doubting Vallandigham's sympathies, sent him to Wilmington, North Carolina, for deportation. That made the former law-maker—briefly an exile in Canada—the first and only person to be banished from both Union and Confederate soil.[22]

Camp Douglas in Chicago had the dubious distinction of being first in the monthly mortality records of all large Federal prisons. During just twenty-eight days in February 1862, 387 of its 3,884 inmates died.[23]

According to the Washington Navy Yard commandant, John A. Dahlgren, on May 24, 1861, the *Baltimore* returned from Alexandria, Virginia, with a very special cargo. She transported to the Federal capital thirty-six prisoners of war, the first large group of captives taken after the war began.[24]

Henry Wirz, a native of Zurich, Switzerland, entered Confederate service on June 16, 1861, as a private in Company D of the Fourth Louisiana Battalion. A series of promotions took him to Seven Pines (or Fair Oaks), Virginia, as a captain. A direct hit nearly took off his right arm, which never recovered from the wound. Handicapped as a fighting man, the physician who had been educated in Zurich, Paris, and Berlin was made a major and assigned to duty as a staff officer at a military prison in Tuscaloosa, Alabama. Although he did not want the post, Wirz became commandant of Andersonville prison in March 1864.

After he surrendered at the prison whose name has become synonymous with starvation and brutality, his role was reversed and Wirz became a prisoner. During eight months of captivity, the former prison commandant was tried by a military tribunal and given a death sentence. Much evidence suggests that he could have saved his life by testifying that Jefferson Davis was a conspirator in a plot to murder prisoners, but he refused to perjure himself.

On November 10, 1865, Wirz was taken to the Old Capitol Prison under heavy guard and led to the scaffold. He was the only Civil War soldier to be executed as a war criminal.[25]

Col. William S. H. Baylor, commanding the Fifth Virginia —a militia unit—stopped a train near Harpers Ferry, Virginia (now West Virginia), and demanded that the conductor lead him to Federal soldiers on the train. Soon he was surprised to find himself facing "one old fellow in uniform asleep on the mail-bags in the first car." This passenger, now listed as the third prisoner of war taken in Virginia, admitted his identity. To Baylor's surprise, he learned that he had in his hands the first Federal general to be captured. At that time Tennessee native William S. Harney was one of only four general officers of the line of the U.S. Army. Headed toward Washington from his former post as commander of the Department of the West, the sixty-one-year-old officer informed his captor that he had decided to resign his commission.

John B. Imboden, himself later a general, reported that the prisoner told his captors that no troops were en route from the West. That assurance was received with delight, for Thomas J. Jackson and his men feared that large numbers of men in blue might have been dispatched to their state.

After a single night as a prisoner in comfortable quarters, Harney promised to report to authorities in Richmond and was

"Professor" Thaddeus S. C. Lowe, age twenty-seven, became a pioneer military "aeronaut" after his release from a South Carolina jail.

HARPER'S WEEKLY

paroled. According to Imboden, "He was a fine-looking old soldier . . . [who] was accompanied socially by two or three of our generals and a swarm of staff-officers" as he walked to a train about to leave for Winchester. No other captured general and few officers on either side spent so brief a period as a captive or were treated more like a guest of honor than a prisoner of war.[26]

At least one account of imprisonment turned out to be bogus. It was made by "aeronaut" Thaddeus S. C. Lowe, who bestowed upon himself the title of "Professor." Just eight days after the first shot of the war was fired in Charleston, Lowe guided one of his big gas-filled balloons into the air at Cincinnati. Not a military mission, his voyage was undertaken to test his theory that currents in the upper air (now known as the jet stream) consistently move from west to east.

After having traveled nine hundred miles and finding support for his theory, Lowe came down, to his surprise, on secessionist soil. South Carolinians arrested him as a spy.

When his papers proved his identity as a scientist, he was put on the first train headed north. His brief detention was spent in a public house whose windows were not barred, and he suffered no inconvenience except a short delay. Yet Lowe boastfully insisted upon being recognized as "the first prisoner of the Civil War."[27]

Big gas-filled balloons were used by Lowe in the world's first aerial reconnaissance missions.

HARPER'S HISTORY

Sails and Steam

The first nineteenth-century Americans to face possible death sentences on the charge of piracy were Thomas H. Baker and twelve members of the crew of the Southern privateer *Savannah*. Captured near Charleston by the USS *Perry* on June 3, 1861, they were taken in irons to "the Tombs" prison in New York.

Their trial started on October 23, 1851, in the Federal Circuit Court of the Southern District of New York. The jurors were not wholly convinced by the prosecution; some of them wondered why soldiers should become prisoners of war, while sailors should be charged with piracy.

Given a reprieve by a hung jury, the Charlestonians remained in their cells until a lengthy confrontation between Federal and Confederate officials led to their exchange for captured Union officers being held as hostages.[28]

Long before the fierce conflict drew to a close, the USS *Monitor* was famous throughout the Western world. Because of its duel with the CSS *Virginia* (aka *Merrimac*), it is often called the first iron warship.

Those who adhere to this belief overlook a sister ship that was completed a few days before the *Monitor*. Built at Mound City,

Illinois, by James B. Eads, the 512-ton USS *Cairo* was commissioned as a part of the army's Western Gunboat Fleet. Its original battery consisted of three 8-inch guns, six 32-pounders, four 42-pounders, and one 12-pounder howitzer, but its big guns failed to protect it from an encounter with two Confederate explosives. After a brief but notable operation on the Mississippi River, one of the first Federal ironclads struck two Southern mines on the Yazoo River and went to the bottom in December 1862.[29]

The first capture of a U.S. steamer took place near Indianola, Texas, on April 17, 1861. Troops led by Col. Earl Van Dorn, who soon transferred his allegiance from the Lone Star State to the Confederacy, mastered their opponents and took possession of the *Star of the West*. Rear Adm. David D. Porter considered the captured steamer to be among the best of the Rebel-operated ships and rejoiced when it was sunk in March 1863 in an effort to block the Tallahatchie River.

Although never classified as a warship, the symbolic importance of the little vessel was enormous. It was this ship that President James Buchanan dispatched to Charleston in January 1861 in the first futile attempt to resupply the Fort Sumter garrison. In its prewar encounter with hostile gunfire, the *Star* was the target of a battery manned by cadets from Charleston's military school, the Citadel.[30]

19

ARMED PROTECTORS

ESCORTS AND BODYGUARDS

DURING THE July 20, 1864, battle of Atlanta, much of the afternoon fighting took place close to Peachtree Creek. Although it was comparatively small, the stream had high banks that dropped sharply, and seasonal rains had made it exceptionally deep. Terrain leading to both sides of the creek was described by William T. Sherman as being "very hilly and stony," and severely limited the use of horses.

At his Howard House headquarters, Sherman was the center of constant going and coming of messengers and subordinates. Among the latter was Gen. James B. McPherson, the handsome and brilliant young commander of the Army of the Tennessee. When an unusually loud burst of gunfire punctuated a conference between the two men, McPherson abruptly broke away to try to find out what was happening.

Although he could have had an escort made up of an entire regiment with weapons at the ready, the thirty five-year-old West Pointer dashed off in such haste that only two or three aides accompanied him. Some accounts state that he was headed not toward the source of the gunfire but toward his own command with a single orderly.

Although aware that dense thickets were likely to be giving shelter to Confederate sharpshooters, McPherson acted as though he had no sense of danger. When a cry of "Halt!" came from the nearby underbrush, he wheeled his horse and dug his spurs into the animal's side. As he raced toward the safety of Federal lines, a volley dropped him from the saddle. Pvt. George J. Reynolds of the Fifteenth Iowa later received the Medal of Honor for his heroism in recovering McPherson's body.[1]

The use of armed guards whose sole mission was protection of the man they surrounded was standard practice among soldiers in both blue and gray. Although the terms *escort* and *bodyguard* were used interchangeably, the former was much more commonly employed in military dispatches. The *OR* refers to escorts more than two thousand times, but bodyguards rarely appear in these pages.

Armed escorts also frequently guarded mail, gold, caissons, ammunition, civilians of importance, women, and cattle. A supply train of any size was likely to have an escort of fifty or more men headed by a captain. When off the battlefield, the movement of a flag might involve an escort. Troops proceeding along the bank of a river were likely to be escorted by a gunboat. When militant Unionist "Parson" Brownlow of East Tennessee was expelled from Confederate territory, high-ranking officers in gray disagreed over whether or not to provide the lone traveler with an escort on his enforced journey to Kentucky.[2]

Few Guards . . . or None

Every general officer could use an escort if he wished to do so, and some line officers and an occasional field officer also resorted to them for protection. The number of men who surrounded an officer was not specified.

Stonewall Jackson had an official bodyguard, but on the morning of his death at Chancellorsville, Jackson sent Capt. William F. Randolph with members of his bodyguard to deliver a dispatch to Lee. When Randolph and his men returned after an absence of several hours, Jackson ordered them to scout Federal pickets. As a result, Lee's "right arm" was unguarded when he rode into a line of fire from North Carolina troops. Had he been accompanied by his full escort, Jackson might not have been fatally wounded during a burst of "friendly fire."[3]

When James Longstreet left his New Mexico post to take part in the first major battle of the war, he rode off with a few other officers. After they pitched camp on the Rio Grande near Fort Craig, a sergeant from Virginia came to see the travelers. Since several other men from the South wanted to return to their respective states, the sergeant suggested that they be formed into an escort. Officers, Longstreet explained to his new friend, were free to resign their commissions at any time. Privates had less freedom; they could not leave their posts without permission from the War Department. Hence Longstreet regretfully declined the offer and went on his way, unguarded.[4]

Confederate Gen. Jeb Stuart had an officially designated escort, although he may have followed Jackson's example and used the men for other purposes at times. After the December 1861 engagement at Dranesville, Virginia, Stuart reported, "Redmond Burke, Chief Bugler Steele, Privates Lewis, Barnes, Harris, Barton, Landstreet, Routh, Brigman, Thompson, and Carrol, of my escort, deserve my thanks for their promptness and accuracy in conveying orders and instructions."[5]

When Confederate congressman-elect Thomas A. R. Nelson left East Tennessee late in July 1861 for Richmond, he was captured in Lee County, Virginia, by a Unionist company of home guards. The secretary of war, L. P. Walker, reported to Gen. Leonidas Polk about this incident, implying that Nelson might have reached his destination had he not traveled with an escort of only three men.[6]

Headed toward the western mountains of the Old Dominion in September 1861, Robert E. Lee rode through the town of Louisbourg and received the plaudits of civilians living there. Reporting this to Jefferson Davis, W. H. Same noted that the general, who was still in Virginia's service, "had with him only an escort of cavalry."[7]

After the debacle at Ball's Bluff, Virginia, Federal officials sought someone other than Col. Edward D. Baker—who held a commission as major general that he neither accepted nor declined—on whom to place the blame. They chose Brig. Gen. Charles P. Stone, so he was placed under arrest and sent by Gen. George B. McClellan to Fort Lafayette guarded by an escort whose size was not reported but which was considered to be suitable for the mission.[8]

A very cautious Lt. James Curtis was charged with making an inventory of the "subsistence stores" of Gen. Irvin McDowell as his fellow men in blue moved toward Bull Run. Accordingly, Curtis acquired an escort of "twenty men from the New Jersey regiment stationed there."[9]

Charles P. Stone and two other officers were blamed for the Ball's Bluff disaster and escorted to Fort Lafayette under guard.

NICOLAY & HAY, LINCOLN

Serving as a bearer of dispatches to Irvin McDowell from P. G. T. Beauregard, Confederate Col. Thomas H. Taylor rode under a flag of truce—surrounded by "an escort of twelve men and an officer."[10]

Gen. Philip Kearney, operating in Virginia early in 1862, seems to have believed that he was safely in Union territory. When a band of about 150 Rebels suddenly swooped upon him, Kearney's escort made a swift countercharge. Although they were only "a small detachment of Lincoln Cavalry," these men in blue whose official duty was to protect their commander routed the attackers and took fourteen prisoners.[11]

Gen. Samuel R. Curtis and his Army of the Southwest clashed violently with a Confederate force at Pea Ridge, Arkansas, on March 7–8, 1862. Reporting about events that took place when heavy fire erupted near nightfall on the second day of the battle, Curtis noted, "One of my bodyguards fell dead, my orderly received a shot, and General [Alexander S.] Asboth was severely wounded in the arm."[12]

Large Escorts

Joseph Conrad, captain of a rifle company in the Third Missouri, surrendered himself and his men at Neosho on July 5, 1861. After

J. C. BUTTRE ENGRAVING

Gen. Philip Kearney's bodyguard defeated a Rebel body and took fourteen prisoners.

their arms had been stacked in the county courthouse, the prisoners were told they would be freed if they would swear "not to serve any more against the Confederate States of America during the war." Following the example of their leader, every man in the company gave the required parole, although they realized that many civilians of the region would shoot them if they had a chance to do so.

Col. T. J. Churchill of the Arkansas Rangers was aware of the difficulty facing his former foes, so he took decisive action. On the evening of July 8, the paroled but unarmed former soldiers were given an escort of thirty men. After having covered about four miles, the escort turned back to Neosho. Thus Conrad and his men were abandoned to their fate in a countryside filled with farmers and hunters who despised all Unionists.[13]

While commanding troops in Kentucky, Confederate Gen. Felix K. Zollicoffer prepared a roster of thirty-three recently captured prisoners that he wished to send to headquarters in Bowling Green. As the dispatch was considered to be of considerable importance, he protected the messenger with an escort of sixty cavalrymen.[14]

At Pea Ridge, Arkansas, Union Gen. Samuel R. Curtis must have been in grave danger, for one of his bodyguards was killed and a staff member and an orderly were wounded.

J. C. BUTTRE ENGRAVING

Gen. Albert Pike went to the Indian Territory in 1861 to recruit Native Americans to fight for the Confederacy. Creek, Choctaw, and Cherokee regiments were soon raised. These recruits were without arms, however, and there was no other Rebel force in the region. Therefore Pike decided that his personal safety warranted precautions on a significant scale. Although he could give them nothing but promises as pay, he formed a personal escort consisting of sixty-four warriors.[15]

On July 4, 1861, a division led by Gen. Monroe M. Parsons of the Missouri State Guard made camp on Cowskin Prairie. Then Parsons directed an officer to go into Carthage and "take possession of the mills" in the town. Although he did not expect serious trouble from civilians, Parsons provided the man with an escort of ninety-five men when he started on his mission.[16]

Capt. John F. Lay eagerly led a squadron of secessionist cavalry toward Manassas Gap, Virginia, in July 1861. Many units were not yet formally organized, so his men were known only as the Powhatan Troops. Accompanied by Capt. K. E. Utterback and his Little Fork Rangers, Lay and his comrades had the brief but significant honor of acting as escort to P. G. T. Beauregard when the

Confederate Gen. Albert Pike had a sixty-four-man bodyguard made up entirely of Native Americans.

Confederate commander moved toward a new command post near Mitchell's Ford.[17]

Two months later, Confederate Gen. Simon Buckner instructed Gen. J. L. Alcorn to form another large but short-lived escort. This time, the body of one hundred men who marched with their weapons at the ready were assigned to guard, not an officer wearing shoulder straps, but an unspecified number of pieces of field artillery.[18]

Sent by Union Gen. Thomas W. Sherman to inspect Savannah, Georgia, and its vicinity, Capt. Quincy A. Gillmore of the engineers took the steamer *Ben DeFord* down the Savannah River. His short voyage was scheduled to end at Tybee Island, where an important lighthouse stood. Since he could not arrive before early evening at a spot where Rebels might still be lurking, Gillmore wanted and got protection. His escort for this noncombat mission consisted of three companies of the Fourth New Hampshire.[19]

The exact size of an escort is seldom specified, but most involved only a few men. Records of Gen. Nathaniel P. Banks and the Department of the Gulf mention one such body. In June 1864 units "not brigaded" because of special assignments included "[Charles] Hamilton's Body Guard, Lieut. Alexander Roberts." Presumably this special body consisted of one hundred or more men, but accounts concerning their activities are not included in reports.[20]

Lt. Orlando M. Poe of the topographical engineers of the U.S. Army headed an escort of undesignated size whose special job was protection of Gen. William F. Smith. At least once Poe and his men abandoned Smith in mid-September 1861. Responding to a sudden attack by the enemy, Poe took command of the Federal rear guard. In that role, he moved swiftly to place 12-pounder guns at a point where they could be used against the Confederate cavalry in case of a charge. Once Smith arrived at the scene of conflict, he detached the leader of his escort "for duty under his immediate direction."[21]

In at least one instance, the driver of an ambulance was given an escort as large or larger than those of many generals. Col. Timothy Sullivan of the Twenty-fourth New York reported directly to Irvin McDowell about action around Upton's Hill, Virginia. About 7 A.M., a train of six wagons proceeded toward the front under the protection of a 50-man escort. As was usual for bodies of that size, the enlisted men were led by a captain and a lieutenant. Twenty hours later, a much larger escort was formed and put into action. This time, five companies of the regiment—250 to 400 men—formed a protective cordon around a single four-horse ambulance that was sent to the battlefield "to bring in the dead and wounded."[22]

Records concerning escorts to protect Yankee officers are much more numerous than those about their Rebel counterparts. Federal records were more carefully preserved, and many a gallant Confederate general disdained mentioning his bodyguards, while others refused to have their movements encumbered by such a unit.

During the early fighting in western Virginia, Maj. Gen. George B. McClellan was protected by a bodyguard made up of the Western Virginia Sourness Rifles under Lt. N. E. Sheldon. After being elevated to general in chief, McClellan for a time used Major Barker's Dragoons for protective purposes. At Antietam men from the

J. C. BUTTRE ENGRAVING

At Antietam, Union Gen. William B. Franklin was surrounded by riders of the Sixth Pennsylvania Cavalry.

Fourth U.S. Cavalry, led by Capt. Daniel P. Mann, comprised his escort. These and other men under his command later reported that although their commander was fearless, he seldom rode close to a line of fire.[23]

Late in 1862, Union Gen. C. C. Washburn filed a report about some of his activities in Mississippi. He noted that his bodyguard "had six horses killed" but did not indicate the size of the unit.[24]

At Antietam, at least five Federal major generals were protected by escorts. Edwin V. Sumner was shielded by two companies of the Sixth New York Cavalry. Fitz John Porter's escort was a detachment of the First Maine Cavalry. William B. Franklin was protected partly by Companies B and G of the Sixth Pennsylvania Cavalry. Ambrose E. Burnside rode in the center of Company G, First Maine Cavalry. Joseph E. Hooker was escorted by four companies of the Second New York Cavalry. Records fail to report that any Confederate general who fought at Antietam had a bodyguard on hand for the action.[25]

Civilian Joshua Green was astonished to find that Major Gen. William T. Sherman seemed to have no bodyguard at Jackson,

Mississippi. This observation may have been erroneous, as Sherman was protected by twenty-five or thirty cavalrymen at Shiloh and by the Seventh Ohio Sharpshooters at Atlanta.[26]

Numerous other Federal officers used bodyguards all or part of the time. Gen. Samuel R. Curtis was shielded by his bodyguard at Pea Ridge, but at Batesville, Arkansas, he sent the unit into combat. Members of the Benton Hussars protected Gen. Charles Hamilton at Iuka, Mississippi. Gen. John M. Pope used members of the First Ohio Cavalry as living shields, while Gen. Franz Sigel relied upon infantrymen of the First Indiana.

Six horses were killed under members of the First Texas Legion, Gen. C. C. Washburn's bodyguard, at Coldwater River, Mississippi. At Chickamauga, Gen. George B. Crook relied upon a cavalry division. Near Smithfield, Virginia, a lowly captain— Drake DeKay—took his bodyguard along when he entered a hostile area.[27]

At Appomattox Lee's escort was large: thirty-three men of the Thirty-ninth Battalion of Virginia Cavalry plus Capt. S. B. Brown and bugler Joseph Michen. In this instance, the body functioned primarily as its title implies rather than as a bodyguard.[28]

Although the term *escort* was frequently applied to it, the special unit formed by Confederate Gen. Nathan Bedford Forrest was actually "a fighting bodyguard." Led by Maj. William D. Bowen and sometimes accompanied by four mountain howitzers, this escort played an important role in engagements near Rome, Georgia.[29]

Its size does not appear in the record, but "a suitable escort" formed late in July 1861 by order of Irvin McDowell must have been very large. The short-term function of this special detail was to be at "the Georgetown Ferry at one o'clock to-day to meet the President of the United States, and accompany him throughout lines to visit the troops."[30]

When Gen. Horatio G. Wright left Hilton Head, South Carolina, on a night expedition to Braddock's Point, he was "escorted by five companies of the Seventh Connecticut" with Col. Alfred H. Terry at their head. The Federal leader who dared to move through

Rebel country at night reached Lawton's Plantation about midnight, and there halted for a four-hour rest.[31]

When Maj. Gen. John Charles Frémont commanded in Missouri early in the war, his bodyguard, apparently handpicked, was commanded by Maj. Charles Zagoni, a native of Hungary. This elite unit included at least 150 men and at times may have numbered twice that many.

Following Frémont's orders, Zagoni once led the bodyguards against Confederates whose number was ten times their own. A report that this tiny band of Federals "routed and fearfully slaughtered" their enemies was vouched for by Frémont but was scornfully challenged by Southerners.[32]

Called by whatever name, men whose short- or long-term duties were designed to be protective played a major but widely overlooked role during 1861–65. The life of many a general officer was extended because he was surrounded by a cordon of bodyguards; many such units are listed in Dyer's *Compendium*. Although they are notably conspicuous, the deaths of unguarded Stonewall Jackson and James B. McPherson came as a result of only a fraction of the instances in which generals did not use escorts who were readily available to them.

20
FAMILY TIES
BLOOD LINES

THE FORMER Martha Ellen Young exclaimed with wonder when she wandered through some of the ornate rooms of a Washington, D.C., mansion. On her first visit there, she was guided to a bedroom and told that she would have the honor of sleeping in the bed Abraham Lincoln had slept in.

"No, sir! Not on your life! I wouldn't be caught dead in that thing!" she exploded. Responding to her obviously unbending decision, President Harry S. Truman led his mother to another bedroom.

Mrs. John A. Truman was born on a farm that now lies within the city limits of Kansas City, Missouri. It was there that she had felt the full wrath of Yankee invaders led by Gen. Thomas Ewing Jr. A native of Ohio, Ewing was both a foster brother and a brother-in-law of William Tecumseh Sherman. An attorney who had moved his practice to Kansas in 1856, Ewing recruited the Eleventh Kansas Cavalry and became colonel of the unit. His leadership at Prairie Grove brought him a star and command of the Union-held region called the District of the Border.

Many residents of this region along the Missouri-Kansas border were known to be Confederate sympathizers. Some of them were believed to be harboring guerrillas commanded by the notorious William Quantrill. This situation was considered to be so serious that it was called to the attention of the president. Lincoln referred the matter to Gen. John M. Schofield, urging him to take "appropriate action," and Schofield delegated the action to Ewing.[1]

Thus Martha Young, age twelve, had been forced to leave her home. She mistakenly believed that Lincoln had personally approved of Ewing's action but was correct in thinking that the

231

Gen. Thomas Ewing forced many families to leave their homes in Missouri and Kansas because the area was rife with guerrilla activity.

president was aware of the tumult in the region where she lived. At the time the Missouri girl could not foresee that she would live to age ninety-four and see her son become the thirty-third president.[2]

In addition to Truman's mother, a surprisingly large number of those caught up in the chaos of 1861–65 were related to U.S. presidents. Of men who fought in the Civil War, Confederate descendants of presidents outnumbered Union descendants by a ratio of about five to three.

John A. Washington, whose plantation lay near Mount Vernon, usually kept at least eight thousand pounds of bacon and seventy-five barrels of fish in his storehouses. When Virginia seceded, he left his life of ease and as a volunteer was made a lieutenant. Washington helped to work Virginia's guns at Carrick's (or Corrick's) Ford, now in West Virginia, on July 13, 1861. For this and other actions he was assigned to the staff of Robert E. Lee and soon became a colonel.

In September near Cheat Mountain, Virginia (now West Virginia), Washington led a patrol in a probe of the Federal lines. Union pickets ended the military career of George Washington's

Mount Vernon is still close to
some of Virginia's finest plantations
and farms.

closest living relative; he was also the first member of Lee's staff to
die. His body was left on the field when the Virginians retreated.

George Washington had no children, so his relatives descended
through his brother John Augustine Washington. It was John's
great-grandson bearing the same name who shouldered a musket
to fight for secession. On his mother's side, Colonel Washington
was a great-grandson of Richard Henry Lee, a Revolutionary War
hero and relative of Robert E. Lee.[3]

George Wythe Randolph, also of Virginia, began his military service by founding the Richmond Howitzers. He fought at Big
Bethel, one of the earliest engagements of the war. In 1862 he
became a Confederate brigadier general but was then called to a
civilian post. Chosen as secretary of war, his tenure was brief. After
just eight months he sailed for France in a futile attempt to recover
from tuberculosis. Born at Thomas Jefferson's home, Monticello,
the Confederate general was a grandson of the third president and
is buried at Monticello.[4]

Attorney Samuel Garland Jr. of Lynchburg organized a unit of the
Home Guard before Virginia seceded. His company was later

Big Bethel, Virginia, was the first significant military clash of the war. There blue-blooded George Wythe Randolph directed a Rebel battery.

mustered into the Eleventh Virginia, and Garland became its colonel. After fighting at Bull Run, Dranesville, and Williamsburg, he was assigned to command a brigade in Daniel H. Hill's division. Garland is described as having "fought with distinction" at Seven Pines during the Seven Days' battles and at Second Bull Run.

At Fox's Gap in September 1862, in an action designed to halt the advance of McClellan's forces toward Sharpsburg, Maryland, this collateral descendant of James Madison became the second Confederate descendant of a president to be killed in action.[5]

Attorney Charles Francis Adams Sr. played a relatively quiet but extremely important role in the war. Sent to England in 1861 as U.S. minister, he remained in the island kingdom for seven years. When he reached London, he found that many political leaders leaned toward the Confederacy, some of them favoring diplomatic recognition. He had been at his post only a short time before he became involved in the *Trent* Affair. Some historians credit him with having resolved the international crisis over the seizure of Confederate commissioners James M. Mason and John Slidell from the British mail steamer.

Monticello, where George Wythe Randolph was born, suffered little damage during four years of bitter fighting.

Having won the support of Prince Albert, Adams eventually succeeded in stopping Britain from building ships for the Confederacy. This action did not come until after the ship that became the CSS *Alabama* was launched, however. In the lengthy legal contest now known as the *Alabama* Claims, Adams was one of the arbitrators who awarded the United States $15.5 million in gold.

Grandson of John Adams, the second president, and son of John Quincy Adams, the sixth president, Charles Francis had a son and namesake in the Union army. Early in 1865 Lieutenant Adams became colonel of the Fifth Massachusetts Cavalry (Colored), and his leadership at Secessionville, South Carolina, South Mountain, and Antietam brought him a brevet promotion at war's end.[6]

Col. Benjamin Harrison of Ohio, a grandson of President William Henry Harrison, was named for his great-grandfather who signed the Declaration of Independence. Like his grandfather, he occupied the Executive Mansion when he became the nation's twenty-third chief executive. Harrison launched his military

Benjamin Harrison entered the fray as a second lieutenant. After rising to the rank of colonel, he became noted for strick discipline.

BRADY STUDIO

career as a second lieutenant of the Seventieth Indiana and later served as a brigade commander without having been given the appropriate rank. Partly because his men resented his strict discipline, his promotion to the rank of brigadier was by brevet only. After fighting at Atlanta he led a brigade to Nashville, then rejoined Sherman in the Carolinas. More skillful as a politician than as a leader in combat, the Civil War veteran won the presidency in 1888.[7]

Richard "Dick" Taylor is sometimes identified as the only son of a president who fought for the Confederacy. A native of Kentucky, he entered the ranks of fighting men in gray from his Louisiana plantation. One of Colonel Taylor's lasting regrets grew out of his arrival at First Bull Run "too late to help send the Yankees packing." By October 1861 the son of Gen. Zachary Taylor (known as "Old Rough and Ready") and the brother of Jefferson Davis's first wife was a general. He received another promotion just eight months later and became a lieutenant general in May 1864. His subordinates claimed that his May 1865 surrender was the last one east of the Mississippi River.[8]

Robert Tyler Jones, a nephew of President John Tyler, enlisted in the Fifty-third Virginia as a private. Since he did not rise above the

William Henry Harrison fought Indians; his grandson fought Rebels.

rank of captain, little is known about his military career. At Gettysburg, however, Jones served as officer of a color guard. According to a postwar account, he and his men lay on their faces "in a broiling July sun for several hours, with the artillery playing over them." Gen. Lewis A. Armistead then shouted to his men that they were fighting for their homes, firesides, and sweethearts. According to Jones, when the day was over, "Out of the sixty-five men in the Charles City company, to which I belonged, but five escaped death or capture."[9]

Capt. John Taylor Wood of the Confederate navy never achieved the prominence of his uncles, Dick Taylor and Jefferson Davis. Wood was a gunnery instructor at the U.S. Naval Academy in 1861. As a lieutenant during the battle between the USS *Monitor* and the CSS *Virginia* he commanded the aft gun of the Confederate ironclad. He was a commander by August 1864 when his ship, the CSS *Tallahassee,* was credited with having captured at least thirty-one prizes. Upon the fall of Richmond, he joined the party of the fleeing Confederate president and was captured with him in Georgia.

Among relatives of presidents, Wood stands alone in two respects. He is the only one of them who escaped while a prisoner of war, and he fought on both water and land. His brief experience as a soldier came after the scuttling of the *Virginia*. Unwilling to be idle while waiting for another berth, Wood commanded sharp-shooters at Drewry's Bluff while still wearing a naval uniform. Soon afterward he was made a colonel of cavalry but relinquished that commission when he returned to the sea to launch small-boat attacks against Union warships.[10]

Famous Ancestors

Fighting men on both sides had distinguished ancestors. Lt. Col. Charles A. Hamilton of the Seventh Wisconsin was a grandson of Alexander Hamilton. Because he stopped a Confederate bullet, he was mentioned in a lengthy report by Gen. Irvin McDowell. Gen. John Gibbon's much shorter summary of Second Bull Run commended him for remaining on the field after being wounded. Hamilton, he said, "brought off his [shattered] regiment in the best possible manner."[11]

Fletcher Webster, surveyor of the port of Boston and son of Daniel Webster, raised the Twelfth Massachusetts in June 1861 and was elected colonel of the unit. He immediately found himself in a dilemma: His state had met its quota in the call for seventy-five thousand volunteers and it looked as though his men would remain at home.

Sen. Henry Wilson, however, appealed directly to the president, saying, "Fletcher Webster has raised a capital regiment." He urged Lincoln to accept it and requested, "Telegraph me at once." Thus Colonel Webster and his men left for Washington. He fought with distinction at Cedar Mountain but was killed at Second Bull Run.[12]

Confederate Col. Henry Ervin of the Sixth Missouri does not appear on most lists of prominent military leaders, although he fought in several major battles. A lieutenant at Pea Ridge, he discovered a Federal gun, which led to its capture. After having been seriously wounded at Corinth, he had a single brief moment of glory during the siege of Vicksburg. When a Federal mine was triggered underground to breach the Confederate line, "overwhelming numbers of infantry" stormed the Southerners. Some of the attackers succeeded in getting inside the fortifications, but Ervin led a charge regaining the position for the Southerners. In furious hand-to-hand fighting, the military career of a grandson of statesman Henry Clay ended when his body "was lacerated with bullets."[13]

One member of the staff of Confederate Gen. John H. Morgan was described by acquaintances as "a rather dudish grandson of Henry Clay." Although named for his grandfather, little is known about the Rebel soldier.[14]

John Cook was mayor of Springfield, Illinois, when he offered his services to the Union. As a general he commanded a brigade at Fort Donelson, but his four years in uniform brought him little recognition despite his good connections. His grandfather, a governor of Illinois, was President Lincoln's brother-in-law, Ninian Edwards.[15]

Born in Alabama, David B. Birney grew up in Cincinnati and when war came was elected colonel of the Twenty-third Pennsylvania. He won a star early in 1862 and was promoted to major general in May 1863. Birney's military career, however, was stormy. He quarreled with Samuel Heintzelman at Fair Oaks and was charged with dereliction of duty at Fredericksburg. At the peak of his career he was as famous as his father, abolitionist James G. Birney. Long the executive secretary of the American Anti-Slavery Society, in 1840 James Birney had been the Liberty Party's candidate for the presidency but lost to John Tyler.[16]

Beginning in November 1861 John Jacob Astor Jr. served as an aide to George B. McClellan for about eighteen months. He is credited with having kept complete records of all transport vessels used by the Army of the Potomac, and he was made a brevet brigadier general in 1865.

Before becoming a soldier, Astor was head of the New York City Union Defense Committee where he offended the secretary of war, Simon Cameron, by proposing to send rifled cannon to Fort Pickens without having consulted military leaders. There's no record, however, that Washington was offended by his offer of money—said by Confederate sources to be $10 million.

Grandson of the fur trader and financier, Astor managed the family fortune for fifteen years, beginning in 1875. His son and namesake fought in the Spanish-American War and went down on the *Titanic* in 1912.[17]

Confederate Col. Churchill Clark, a grandson of William Clark of Lewis and Clark, commanded artillery for both Sterling Price and Braxton Bragg. An account of the battle of Sayler's Creek says that on April 6, 1865, "Union troops captured the aged Clark [age 56] and most of the Richmond garrison."[18]

Oliver Wendell Holmes Jr. was the son of the poet-essayist who wrote *The Autocrat of the Breakfast Table* and dozens of other works. After graduating from Harvard, the younger Holmes became a second lieutenant of the Second Massachusetts. He fought at Ball's Bluff, Antietam, and Fredericksburg before being sent to Washington with the Twentieth Massachusetts to help defend the capital. When Confederates under Jubal Early seemed to threaten the city, Lincoln went to Fort Stevens to watch the fray. As the president stepped into the line of fire, Holmes, then a captain, is reputed to have shouted, "Get down, you fool!" In later life Oliver Wendell Holmes Jr. served thirty years as an associate justice of the U.S. Supreme Court.[19]

Robert E. Lee was the son of Henry "Light Horse Harry" Lee. Harry Lee's famous legion, made up of three troops of cavalry and three companies of infantry, won one of the most thrilling victories of the American Revolution. On August 19, 1779, they stormed and captured a British fort at Paulus Hook (now Jersey City), New Jersey.

Light Horse Harry commanded part of the Army of the Constitution that was mobilized to quell the Whiskey Rebellion of 1794. No one who was engaged in that bloodless but vital struggle knew that it would have far-reaching consequences. Legislation enacted to deal with the rebellious farmers of Pennsylvania was used by Lincoln as the legal basis for his first call for volunteers. It was this action that precipitated Virginia's secession and Lee's subsequent resignation from the U.S. Army.[20]

Theodore Lincoln was among the ranks of the Sixth Maine at the siege of Yorktown in 1862. Coincidentally he was the great-grandson of Benjamin Lincoln, who received the sword of Lord Cornwallis when the British surrendered at Yorktown in 1781.[21]

Hugh W. Mercer, cashier of the Planters' Bank in Savannah, resigned in order to become colonel of the First Georgia. Most of his career as a Confederate officer was spent as commander of districts and departments; however, he raised a regiment for the Army of Tennessee when Sherman's invasion of Georgia was launched. After William H. Walker was killed at Atlanta, Mercer took over the division. Mercer was a grandson of Gen. Hugh Mercer, credited with having suggested Washington's surprise attack upon Trenton, New Jersey, in 1776.[22]

Gen. Joseph Warren Revere's grandfather was Paul Revere of the famous midnight ride of 1775 fame. The Massachusetts native became colonel of the Seventh New York on September 19, 1861, and was promoted to general after a year of service, then ran into trouble at Chancellorsville. There his men exhausted their ammunition, and he moved them to the rear without orders. Censured and relieved, he was court-martialed and dismissed, but his case then went to the president, who revoked the sentence and accepted Revere's resignation.

Col. Paul Joseph Revere of the Twentieth Massachusetts, another grandson of the silversmith-patriot, took a Confederate bullet on the second day at Gettysburg and survived only two days. He received a brevet promotion after his death.[23]

It took John Henry Winder of Maryland forty years after his graduation from West Point to become a U.S. Army major. Soon after resigning to fight in gray, he was given the rank of brigadier. As provost marshal and commander of Richmond's military prisons, he was hated throughout the North. He was the son of Gen. William Henry Winder, who failed to turn back an attack at Bladensburg, Maryland, in the War of 1812, which enabled the British to seize Washington and burn many of its buildings. The cartel written by the elder Winder became the basis of early exchanges of Federal prisoners held in the custody of his son and other Confederates.[24]

Commo. William D. ("Dirty Bill") Porter made news by divorcing his southern-born wife to prove his fidelity to the Union in 1861. His brother David had no problem of this sort since he had been in the U.S. Navy since age eleven. William's health deteriorated as the war went on, and in May 1864 he died of heart disease.

Comdr. David Porter, father of the Civil War naval officers, had been captured by the British during the War of 1812. After peace was restored, he fought pirates in the West Indies, initiated a proposal to send naval missions to Japan, and for three years was commander in chief of the Mexican Navy.[25]

Noted Descendants

Simon Baruch immigrated to South Carolina from Schwersenz, Germany, at the age of fifteen. Upon graduation from medical school, he enlisted in the Confederate army and at age twenty-one was appointed an assistant surgeon "before ever treating a sick person or even having lanced a boil." Baruch first experienced combat at Second Bull Run, where he helped to select the site for a field hospital.

The Confederate veteran practiced medicine in Camden, South Carolina, for fifteen years, then moved north, where in 1888 he performed the first American appendectomy. His son, Bernard, a financier and statesman, served as an unpaid adviser to every president from Woodrow Wilson to Dwight David Eisenhower.[26]

In 1861 West Point graduate Josiah Gorgas left the U.S. Army as a captain, came south, and offered his services to the Confederacy. He was made chief of the Ordnance Bureau. In this role he had the enormous task of arming the Confederate armies. He bought guns in England and Europe, repaired captured Federal weapons, and boosted the capacity of Southern industrial plants. Some say that the war would have been over in 1863 had it not been for the organizational genius of the Pennsylvania native who married an Alabama woman.

Significant as was Gorgas's role in the Civil War, his accomplishments were eclipsed by those of his son, William C. Gorgas. A physician and the world's leading sanitation expert, the younger Gorgas made possible the construction of the Panama Canal by eradicating the mosquitoes that carried malaria.[27]

Born in Tennessee and reared in Missouri, Col. William C. Falkner moved to Mississippi at the age of fifteen. He led the Second Mississippi at Bull Run but was subsequently voted out of command. He returned home and raised two or more bands of partisan rangers. Falkner was in command of an estimated seven hundred men who were defeated at Coldwater River, Mississippi, early in 1863. After the war, besides building a railroad, he wrote popular romantic novels, including *The White Rose of Memphis,* which was reprinted thirty-six times. His great-grandson William inserted a *u* in the family surname before winning the Nobel Prize for literature and two Pulitzer Prizes.[28]

Russell C. Mitchell did not aspire to high rank. He knew he was not qualified to command, so he was satisfied to serve as a first sergeant. Little is known about his military career, but through his bloodline the Civil War took on new dimensions two generations later. The Pulitzer Prize–winning novel *Gone with the Wind* brought great renown to Margaret Mitchell, the granddaughter of the obscure sergeant in Hood's Texas Brigade, Army of Northern Virginia.[29]

John Rodgers Meigs, oldest son of the U.S. Army's quartermaster general, took a leave of absence from West Point to serve as an aide at Bull Run. Returning to his studies, he graduated first in the class of 1863. The next year Gen. Philip Sheridan made the young officer his chief engineer. Late in 1864, while returning from a surveying expedition, he was shot and killed by Confederate cavalrymen. His grandfather for whom he was named had been a naval officer during the American Revolution. Later made a commodore, Rodgers was the ranking active officer of the U.S. Navy during the War of 1812.[30]

A Confederate army captain's son, Richmond P. Hobson achieved fame during the Spanish-American War. On June 3, 1898, he tried to bottle up Santiago Harbor. Although his exploit was a failure and he was held prisoner in Morro Castle for three days, he became one of the most celebrated heroes of the short war.[31]

Confederate Col. George S. Patton of the Twenty-second Virginia commanded a brigade under Gen. John C. Breckinridge. In May 1864 Patton's brigade reported 2,150 men fit for duty. Four months later its decimated ranks held only 275 men. He fought at Cold Harbor without being injured, but at the battle of Third Winchester in September 1864, he took a direct hit from a Federal ball. His men later reported sorrowfully that in their hasty retreat they were forced to leave him behind "in the streets, mortally wounded." His grandson and namesake was one of the most colorful American generals in World War II. Gen. George S. Patton's toughness and rough speech earned him the nickname "Old Blood and Guts." Patton led troops in the invasions of North Africa, Sicily, and France. His leadership in the Battle of the Bulge was a classic in field maneuver and brought him a promotion to full general. His Yankee-hating grandfather would have been proud of him.[32]

Lt. Manning M. Kimmel fought in blue at Manassas then resigned and entered Confederate ranks without receiving a promotion. Fighting under Gen. Earl Van Dorn, and still a lieutenant, he was cited for gallant action at Pea Ridge. Writing to Adj. Gen. Samuel Cooper, the Confederate commander said that he would have liked to substitute Kimmel and other junior officers for higher-ranking ones who "are in false positions, without a degree of rank commensurate with their value and services." Van Dorn made Kimmel an inspector general without promotion, but later Kimmel became an assistant adjutant general with the rank of major. When Gens. John G. Walker and John B. Magruder quarreled, Kimmel helped to soothe tempers but received no promotion for his efforts. Although he was often under fire, the major never experienced anything like what his son experienced. When the Japanese attacked Pearl Harbor, Adm. Husband E. Kimmel was the senior U.S. naval commander on the scene. He and U.S. Army Gen. Walter C. Scott took the heat for U.S. unpreparedness on that fateful day. A congressional investigation resulted in a reprimand for "errors of judgment."[33]

Seventeen-year-old Arthur MacArthur had tried hard to get an appointment to West Point, but he did not have the necessary political connections. As a result, he joined the Twenty-fourth Wisconsin and soon became its adjutant. He never received a spectacular promotion, but he rose steadily in rank and was a brevet colonel at war's end. McArthur was in the thick of the action at Perryville, Stones River, Chickamauga, and Chattanooga before following Sherman from Tennessee into Georgia and then back into Tennessee. After his last big battle at Franklin, Tennessee, he decided to remain in the U.S. Army. In 1890 he was awarded a belated Medal of Honor for his courage at Missionary Ridge in 1863. In 1898 he fought in both Cuba and the Philippines and became a lieutenant general in 1906. He frequently told comrades that his most notable exploit was that of fathering a son. When the boy was born on an Arkansas army post, the Civil War veteran did not dream that Douglas McArthur would eventually wear five stars as general of the army during World War II. In 1942 Douglas also received the Medal of Honor, the only time a father and a son have won the award.[34]

Conclusion

AMAZING IS not adequate as a descriptive term for the American nation's most defining historical event, the Civil War. With more than three million men in arms, a ten-thousand-mile line separating North and South, and an estimated one thousand engagements to describe and chart, the chances of interesting, unusual, and strange happenings are almost infinite. I have included only nineteen categories in this book and a few examples under each. Much more could be added and many more categories could be defined. Thus I hope to add to the information here in the future.

There is no shortage of material, given the personal memoirs, letters, and diaries generated by the soldiers and their families during and after the war. What I find constantly amazes me. I tend to classify all of it into three major categories: battles, biographies, and personal accounts.

Every major battle and most minor ones have been treated in print—often several times. As a result, thousands of books deal with military engagements; Gettysburg alone has spawned hundreds of titles. Biographies constitute the second enormous subsection. In this category, only Abraham Lincoln towers over the life stories of Robert E. Lee, Ulysses S. Grant, Thomas J. Jackson, and William T. Sherman.

First-person narratives of the conflict have recently come to the fore. They are fascinating in their literate, emotional expressions of the immediate effect cataclysmic events like battles have on individual lives. Here random incidents, such as those recounted on the preceding pages, fill in the great voids between the big battles that usually spring to mind when the Civil War is discussed.

In recounting these events, I find myself in the footsteps of such chroniclers of the war as Burke Davis, a fellow Tar Heel, who first collected short accounts that intrigued him. Only after he found an audience did his publisher add illustrations to his work. His *Our Incredible Civil War,* first offered in 1960, is still going strong and has been reissued lately as *The Civil War: Strange and Fascinating Facts.* Other titles in this genre include Albert Nofi's *A Civil War Treasury* and *A Civil War Notebook* and Rod Gragg's *Civil War Quiz and Fact Book.* It is my hope that I have added something of interest for the general audience interested in the War Between the States that will enlarge their understanding of the conflict and enhance their admiration and perceptions of the men and women who underwent and survived the vicissitudes of the war.

Notes

In citing works, short references have generally been used. Complete bibliographical data may be found in the bibliography. Works frequently cited below have been identified by the following abbreviations:

MOLLUS   Publications of the Military Order of the Loyal Legion of the United States. Various cities and dates.

NOR   U.S. Navy Department, *Official Records of the Union and Confederate Navies in the War of the Rebellion*, 31 vols.

OR   U.S. War Department, *The War of the Rebellion: A Compilation of the Official Records of the Union and Confederate Armies*, 128 vols.

1: Never Flogged, Never Taught

1. Wiley, *Common Soldier*, 51; Shane, *Atlanta Century*, April 8, 1860; Lord, *They Fought for the Union*, 113; Sifakis, *Who Was Who*, 714.
2. *Civil War Times Illustrated*, May 1988, 26.
3. Sifakis, *Who Was Who*, 49.
4. Ibid., 489.
5. *MOLLUS*, 2:356.
6. Sifakis, *Who Was Who*, 676.
7. Miller, *Photographic History*, 8:207; Wiley, *Common Soldier*, 50.
8. Wiley, *Common Soldier*, 50; Faust, *Encyclopedia*, 220; Moore, *Rebellion Record*, 7:3.
9. *MOLLUS*, 35:170–71.
10. Denney, *Prisons and Escapes*, 120; Miller, *Photographic History*, 7:191.
11. Robertson, *Blue and Gray*, 133.
12. Wiley, *Common Soldier*, 51; *MOLLUS*, 2:360; Shane, *Atlanta Century*, April 8, 1860.
13. *Confederate Veteran*, 2:235; *Civil War*, 33:20.
14. Commager, *Blue and the Gray*, 507.
15. Moore, *Rebellion Record*, 4:15; *Civil War Times Illustrated*, July 1993, 24; *Civil War*, February 1992, 20; *Blue & Gray*, April 1991, 53; Wiley, *Common Soldier*, 50.
16. *Civil War Times Illustrated*, August 1969, 37; Shane, *Atlanta Century*, April 8, 1860; Wiley, *Common Soldier*, 50; Faust, *Encyclopedia*, 220.
17. *Civil War Times Illustrated*, August 1963, 20; March 1997, 18.
18. *Civil War Times Illustrated*, July 1993, 24; Sifakis, *Who Was Who*, 723; Shane, *Atlanta Century*, April 1, 1860; Robertson, *Blue and Gray*, 133; Wiley, *Common Soldier*, 50; Faust, *Encyclopedia*, 220.

19. *Blue & Gray,* April 1991, 53; Sifakis, *Who Was Who,* 51.
20. *Confederate Veteran,* 3:110; *Civil War,* 33:10.
21. *Civil War Times Illustrated,* August 1969, 38.
22. *Georgia Historical Quarterly,* 47:240.
23. Denney, *Civil War Years,* 55; Wiley, *Common Soldier,* 51.
24. Shane, *Atlanta Century,* November 30, 1862.
25. Higginson, *Army Life* and *Letters.*

2: Cities under the Gun

1. *OR,* 73:332.
2. *Rebellion Record* (doc), 11:282.
3. *OR,* 76:794, 838; 74:993; 78:418–19, 503; 98:33.
4. Moore, *Rebellion Record,* 3:126; doc, 3:521–23; *NOR,* 17:34.
5. *OR,* 18:80; Moore, *Rebellion Record,* 4:94; *OR,* 14:458.
6. *OR,* 6:544; 116:613–14; Currant, *Encyclopedia of the Confederacy,* 4:1141; *NOR,* 18:231–25, 822–23; *Civil War Times Illustrated,* May 1960, 4–6; May 1987, 38–40.
7. *Rebellion Record* (doc), 5:42; *Civil War Times Illustrated,* February 1983, 33.
8. *OR,* 21:736–38, 744–45.
9. *OR,* 4:497–98; 10:910–11; *Rebellion Record* (doc), 5:174–77; Denney, *Civil War Years,* 180.
10. *OR,* 31:783–85.
11. *MOLLUS,* 6:262–63.
12. *OR,* 111:290–91; *NOR,* 16:250, 258–59, 264, 370; *OR,* 99:483–84, 526, 659–60.
13. *NOR,* 16:275–77; Denney, *Civil War Years,* 538.
14. *MOLLUS,* 6:55.
15. *Confederate Veteran,* 9:25; *OR,* 103:145–46.
16. *Blue & Gray,* 232.
17. Faust, *Encyclopedia,* 233–34.

3: Henry Wilson

1. *OR,* 57:96–98.
2. Mosocco, *Chronological Tracking,* 200.
3. *Civil War,* 7:138–39.

4: Southern Yankees

1. Evans, *Confederate Military History,* 5:311–12; Sifakis, *Who Was Who,* 252.

2. Allardice, *More Generals in Gray*, 17–18; *National Cyclopedia of American Biography*, 13:493; Evans, *Confederate Military History*, 9:236–38.
3. Sifakis, *Who Was Who*, 556.
4. Faust, *Encyclopedia*, 450–51; Evans, *Confederate Military History*, 2:162–63; *Civil War Times Illustrated*, March 1993, 53; Sifakis, *Who Was Who*, 396.
5. *Dictionary of American Biography;* Warner, *Generals in Gray*, 275–76; Sifakis, *Who Was Who*, 593; *America's Civil War*, September 1994, 10f; Evans, *Confederate Military History*, 16:208–9.
6. Freeman, *Lee*, 4:48; Sifakis, *Who Was Who*, 248; Freeman, *Lee's Lieutenants*, 3:80–81, 181–83, 766, 778.
7. Faust, *Encyclopedia*, 427; Boatner, *Dictionary*, 475; Warner, *Generals in Gray*, 176; Evans, *Confederate Military History*, 8:424–26.
8. Warner, *Generals in Gray*, 347–48; Evans, *Confederate Military History*, 13:320–21; Sifakis, *Who Was Who*, 736.
9. Sifakis, *Who Was Who*, 201.
10. *National Cyclopedia of American Biography*, 6:16; Evans, *Confederate Military History*, 4:628–30; Warner, *Generals in Gray*, 190–91; Boatner, *Dictionary*, 489.
11. Sifakis, *Who Was Who*, 403; Evans, *Confederate Military History*, 4:560, 1129.
12. Sifakis, *Who Was Who*, 42, 19; Faust, *Encyclopedia*, 50; Boatner, *Dictionary*, 50.
13. Faust, *Encyclopedia*, 214; Sifakis, *Who Was Who*, 177; Warner, *Generals in Gray*, 71.
14. Faust, *Encyclopedia*, 292; Evans, *Confederate Military History*, 9:252–55; Warner, *Generals in Gray*, 93–94.
15. *Dictionary of American Biography; National Cyclopedia of American Biography*, 11:54; Warner, *Generals in Gray*, 62–63; Evans, *Confederate Military History*, 1:616–17; Faust, *Encyclopedia*, 165; Boatner, *Dictionary*, 175; Foote, *Civil War Narrative*, 1:125.
16. Faust, *Encyclopedia*, 717; Warner, *Generals in Gray*, 291–92; Evans, *Confederate Military History*, 6:419–20.
17. *Dictionary of American Biography;* Evans, *Confederate Military History*, 10:318–19; Warner, *Generals in Gray*, 157–58; Faust, *Encyclopedia*, 397; Boatner, *Dictionary*, 437; *Civil War Times Illustrated*, January 1972, 48.
18. *National Cyclopedia of American Biography*, 3:299; Evans, *Confederate Military History*, 6:418–19; Boatner, *Dictionary*, 700–701; Faust, *Encyclopedia*, 634–35.
19. Evans, *Confederate Military History*, 10:334–35; Warner, *Generals in Gray*, 295–96; Faust, *Encyclopedia*, 725; Boatner, *Dictionary*, 811; *Confederate Veteran*, 3:299f.

20. *Dictionary of American Biography; National Cyclopedia of American Biography*, 1:24; Evans, *Confederate Military History*, 12:186–88; Faust, *Encyclopedia*, 606.
21. Freeman, *Lee's Lieutenants*, 2:718; Faust, *Encyclopedia*, 647; Evans, *Confederate Military History*, 4:660–62; *Civil War Times Illustrated*, February 1981, 15.
22. *Dictionary of American Biography;* Warner, *Generals in Gray*, 235–36; *National Cyclopedia of American Biography*, 1:527; Evans, *Confederate Military History*, 16:207–8; Faust, *Encyclopedia*, 575.
23. Warner, *Generals in Gray*, 271–72; Evans, *Confederate Military History*, 9:266–67; Boatner, *Dictionary*, 729; Faust, *Encyclopedia*, 663–64.
24. Moore, *Rebellion Record* (p), 4:85; *National Cyclopedia of American Biography*, 4:178; Warner, *Generals in Gray*, 27–28; Evans, *Confederate Military History*, 13:294–95; Boatner, *Dictionary*, 68.
25. Moore, *Rebellion Record* (p), 4:100; *Dictionary of American Biography;* Evans, *Confederate Military History*, 14:408–10; *National Cyclopedia of American Biography*, 1:527; Evans, *Confederate Military History*, 14:408–10.
26. *Dictionary of American Biography;* Evans, *Confederate Military History*, 1:413; Faust, *Encyclopedia*, 377; Sifakis, *Who Was Who*, 329.
27. *National Cyclopedia of American Biography*, 19:321; Warner, *Generals in Gray*, 5; Evans, *Confederate Military History*, 8:385–86, 459–61; Sifakis, *Who Was Who*, 7–8; Faust, *Encyclopedia*, 8.
28. Sifakis, *Who Was Who*, 489; *Dictionary of American Biography;* Evans, *Confederate Military History*, 4:1094–95.
29. Sifakis, *Who Was Who*, 235; Faust, *Encyclopedia*, 298; *National Cyclopedia of American Biography*, 4:222; Warner, *Generals in Gray*, 97–98; Evans, *Confederate Military History*, 13:297–98.
30. Sifakis, *Who Was Who*, 74–75; Evans, *Confederate Military History*, 4:558.
31. *Dictionary of American Biography;* Evans, *Confederate Military History*, 8:412–15; Warner, *Generals in Gray*, 113–14; *National Cyclopedia of American Biography*, 22:277; Faust, *Encyclopedia*, 316.
32. *Dictionary of American Biography;* Evans, *Confederate Military History*, 1:424–29; *National Cyclopedia of American Biography*, 2:93, 105; Sifakis, *Who Was Who*, 598.
33. Sifakis, *Who Was Who*, 619–29; *National Cyclopedia of American Biography*, 4:207; Evans, *Confederate Military History*, 8:196–99; Warner, *Generals in Gray*, 289–90.
34. *National Cyclopedia of American Biography*, 5:96; Evans, *Confederate Military History*, 16:210; Warner, *Generals in Gray*, 282–83; Faust, *Encyclopedia*, 697; Sifakis, *Who Was Who*, 605.
35. Warner, *Generals in Gray*, 94–95; Evans, *Confederate Military History*,

12:292; *National Cyclopedia of American Biography*, 5:535; Faust, *Encyclopedia*, 293–94; Boatner, *Dictionary*, 319; *Civil War*, 19:52.

36. Evans, *Confederate Military History*, 4:210; *National Cyclopedia of American Biography*, 12:258; Warner, *Generals in Gray*, 292; Sifakis, *Who Was Who*, 623, 269; Faust, *Encyclopedia*, 718 19.

37. Faust, *Encyclopedia*, 494–95; Warner, *Generals in Gray*, 217–18; Evans, *Confederate Military History*, 16:206–7.

38. Freeman, *Lee*, 3:211–13.

39. Evans, *Confederate Military History*, 4:937–40; Sifakis, *Who Was Who*, 319; Freeman, *Lee's Lieutenants*, 1:27f; 3.29–30, 599 600, 609.

5: Hard Money

1. Moore, *Rebellion Record*, 6:49.
2. Long, *Day by Day*, 721.
3. Ibid., 725–26.
4. *OR*, 122:52; *Civil War Times Illustrated*, August 1966, 33; Catton, *Civil War*, 165ff.
5. *Statistical History*, 1104, 1118.
6. Long, *Day by Day*, 726f; *Statistical History*, 8.
7. *Civil War Times Illustrated*, May 1972, 29.
8. *Civil War*, 15:12.
9. *OR*, 4:66.
10. *Civil War Times Illustrated*, June 1981, 23.
11. Ibid., July 1992, 54.
12. Faust, *Encyclopedia*, 187, 323; Nevins, *War*, 2:371.
13. Sifakis, *Who Was Who*, 262.
14. Faust, *Encyclopedia*, 187, 197f; *Journal of the Southern Historical Society*, 55:474.
15. *Civil War*, 7:69; Faust, *Encyclopedia*, 342.
16. *MOLLUS*, 35:238f.
17. Faust, *Encyclopedia*, 163.
18. *Civil War Times Illustrated*, August 1963, 18.
19. Faust, *Encyclopedia*, 212.
20. *Civil War Times Illustrated*, February 1985, 5.
21. Ibid., October 1972, 38f.
22. Commager, *Blue and the Gray*, 2:1041.
23. *MOLLUS*, 11:228.
24. *Civil War Times Illustrated*, December 1968, 35.
25. Freeman, *Lee's Lieutenants*, 1:407.
26. *Civil War Times Illustrated*, December 1971, 23.
27. McElroy, *Jefferson Davis*.
28. *Blue & Gray*, December 1988, 48ff.
29. *Civil War Times Illustrated*, June 1971, 34.

30. *America's Civil War,* May 1995, 59f.
31. *Civil War Times Illustrated,* May 1995, 58.
32. Sifakis, *Who Was Who,* 564.
33. *Blue & Gray,* February 1995, 34f.
34. Sifakis, *Who Was Who,* 161.
35. *Civil War Times Illustrated,* December 1976, 25.
36. *MOLLUS,* 11:228.
37. *Civil War Times Illustrated,* February 1974, 75.
38. Faust, *Encyclopedia,* 373.
39. Sifakis, *Who Was Who,* 62.
40. *Civil War Times Illustrated,* December 1976, 28.
41. Lord, *They Fought for the Union,* 242.
42. *Civil War Times Illustrated,* September 1983, 6.

6: Graft and Corruption

1. *OR,* 3:409–10.
2. Ibid., 3:390, 402, 537, 540.
3. Ibid., 3:402, 444.
4. Ibid., 3:543.
5. Davis, *Great Battles,* 303; *OR,* 3:442, 502.
6. *OR,* 3:464.
7. Ibid., 3:541.
8. Ibid., 3:549.
9. Ibid., 3:550.
10. Ibid., 3:541.
11. Ibid., 3:542–43, 550–51.
12. Davis, *Great Battles,* 304.
13. Nevins, *War,* 2:313–14; Davis, *Great Battles,* 303.
14. Mathews, *Americanisms,* 2:1524.
15. Johnson, *Campfire,* 245.

7: The Overlooked Blockade

1. *NOR,* 5:152.
2. *Civil War,* 4:290, 292.
3. Ibid., 4:338–39, 346–47.
4. *Civil War Times Illustrated,* December 1960, 17.
5. *NOR,* 5:58.
6. Ibid., 5:132.
7. Ibid., 5:126, 130, 134, 136, 158, 161, 198, 208, 222, 225, 232, 232–34, 245.
8. *OR,* 37:531.

9. Ibid., 63:506.
10. *NOR*, 102:281–82.

8: Hirelings in Uniform

1. Moore, *Rebellion Record*, 5:37, 62, 7:11; Nevins, *War*, 1:237.
2. Moore, *Rebellion Record* (p), 6:32, 41; *OR*, 21:734.
3. *OR*, 22:301; *Civil War Times Illustrated*, February 1988, 34.
4. Moore, *Rebellion Record*, 6:4; Nofi, *Notebook*, 103; *OR*, 111:734–35; Nevins, *War*, 2:163; Lord, *They Fought for the Union*, 63; Faust, *Encyclopedia*, 72.
5. Lord, *They Fought for the Union*, 285.
6. *Civil War Times Illustrated*, May 1967, 32; Boatner, *Dictionary*, 74; Faust, *Encyclopedia*, 73.
7. *OR*, 125:694–95.
8. Sifakis, *Who Was Who*, 7, 612.
9. *Civil War*, September 1993, 22; *MOLLUS*, 12:126.
10. Sifakis, *Who Was Who*, 474; *OR*, 107:1278.
11. DeGregorio, *Presidents*, 323.
12. Miers, *Lincoln*, 3:286; Sifakis, *Who Was Who*, 617.
13. Nofi, *Notebook*, 93.
14. Long, *Day by Day*, 707; Boatner, *Dictionary*, 858.
15. *Civil War Times Illustrated*, May 1967, 29; Leech, *Reveille*, 230; Moore, *Rebellion Record*, 8:10.
16. Leech, *Reveille*, 230; Nevins, *War*, 2:164, 4:145; Ketchum, *History*, 485; *Civil War Times Illustrated*, May 1967, 29.
17. Moore, *Rebellion Record* (p), 4:57–58.
18. Moore, *Rebellion Record*, 6:68, 8:6, 20, 49; *Civil War Times Illustrated*, July 1991, 61; Long, *Day by Day*, 708; Nevins, *War*, 4:251.
19. Lord, *They Fought for the Union*, 6.
20. *Civil War Times Illustrated*, May 1995, 58; Nevins, *War*, 2:465.
21. *Civil War Times Illustrated*, May 1967, 35; Faust, *Encyclopedia*, 731; Nevins, *War*, 2:316; Leech, *Reveille*, 272, 349; Moore, *Rebellion Record*, 7:34; Lord, *They Fought for the Union*, 220; *MOLLUS*, 35:165; *America's Civil War*, July 1995, 8.
22. Boatner, *Dictionary*, 858; Did, 707; *Blue & Gray*, April 1991, 56; *MOLLUS*, 35:161, 169.

9: Out of Uniform

1. *OR*, 121:339f.
2. Ibid., 46:296.
3. Ibid., 117:591.
4. *Civil War Times Illustrated*, May 1993, 46; *OR*, 31:262.

5. *OR,* 87:837.

6. Ibid., 55:409.

7. Ibid., 90:547.

8. Ibid., 105:22.

9. Ibid., 84:861.

10. *Civil War Times Illustrated,* January 1994, 58.

11. *OR,* 102:837.

12. Ibid., 120:768; 121:781.

13. Ibid., 120:874.

14. Ibid., 121:167.

15. Ibid., 118:901; 121:348.

16. Fuller, *Recollections,* 61ff.

17. Miller, *Photographic History,* 8:409.

18. *OR,* 73:761.

19. Priest, *Before Antietam,* 3, 20.

20. McPherson, *Battle Cry of Freedom,* 752.

21. Gragg, *Quiz and Fact,* 178.

22. *OR,* 122:963.

23. *MOLLUS,* 5:240.

24. Faust, *Encyclopedia,* 465–66.

25. *MOLLUS,* 4:285–86.

26. Johnson, *Campfire,* 188–89.

27. Ibid., 185–86.

28. *Civil War Times Illustrated,* August 1976, 14.

29. Sifakis, *Who Was Who,* 123.

30. *Blue & Gray,* October 1988, 10.

31. Marszalek, *Sherman,* 276; *Civil War Times Illustrated,* October 1975, 36; July 1989, 24.

32. *Civil War Times Illustrated,* October 1976, 10.

10: Fear in the Field

1. *OR,* 2:311, 462.

2. *MOLLUS,* 12:156.

3. Sifakis, *Who Was Who,* 485.

4. *MOLLUS,* 4:10–11.

5. *Rebellion Record* (doc), 4:393.

6. *MOLLUS,* 10:115.

7. *Civil War Times Illustrated,* April 1989, 18.

8. *OR,* 13:563; *Confederate Veteran,* 7:224.

9. Commager, *Blue and the Gray,* 141.

10. *OR,* 13:724.

11. *Confederate Veteran,* 1:234.

12. *OR,* 27:1026.

13. Ibid., 29:54–55.
14. *MOLLUS,* 1:358–91.
15. *NOR,* 14:370.
16. *America's Civil War,* March 1992, 8.
17. *Confederate Veteran,* 2:338.
18. *OR,* 41:360; Faust, *Encyclopedia,* 49.
19. *Rebellion Record* (doc), 11:37.
20. *Civil War Times Illustrated,* March 1990, 46ff.
21. Allardice, *More Generals in Gray,* 11.
22. Moore, *Rebellion Record,* 3:46.
23. Denney, *Prisons and Escapes,* 38.
24. Sifakis, *Who Was Who,* 15.
25. Moore, *Rebellion Record,* 5:66.
26. Sifakis, *Who Was Who,* 121.
27. Robertson, *Blue and Gray,* 128.
28. *OR,* 38:762f.
29. Ibid., 26:338–40; Freeman, *Lee's Lieutenants,* 2:485–90.
30. *Civil War Times Illustrated,* January 1994, 35.
31. Boatner, *Dictionary,* 443; Faust, *Encyclopedia,* 403.
32. Sifakis, *Who Was Who,* 155; *Blue & Gray,* February 1995, 24.
33. *Civil War Times Illustrated,* July 1994, 46.
34. Boatner, *Dictionary,* 584; Sifakis, *Who Was Who,* 468.
35. Sifakis, *Who Was Who,* 691.
36. *Journal of the Southern Historical Society,* 16:144.
37. Sifakis, *Who Was Who,* 215f, 378; Boatner, *Dictionary,* 474.
38. Faust, *Encyclopedia,* 364.
39. *MOLLUS,* 14:378.
40. *OR,* 12:879.
41. Ibid., 11:326; Priest, *Antietam,* 182.
42. Faust, *Encyclopedia,* 661.
43. Long, *Day by Day,* 705.

11: Well-Known Personalities of the War

1. Freeman, *Lee's Lieutenants,* 1:326; Sifakis, *Who Was Who,* 722.
2. *Blue & Gray,* May 1988, 31.
3. Foote, *Civil War Narrative,* 1:124.
4. Nevins, *War,* 2:12; *Civil War Times Illustrated,* July 1962, 15.
5. *Civil War Times Illustrated,* December 1984, 12; May 1993, 29, 64.
6. Ibid., January 1965, 6.
7. Boatner, *Dictionary,* 268.
8. Foote, *Civil War Narrative,* 1:379.
9. Nevins, *War,* 2:95.

10. Freeman, *Lee's Lieutenants*, 1:347, quoted in Boatner, *Dictionary*, 269.
11. *MOLLUS*, 6:48
12. Freeman, *Lee's Lieutenants*, 1:366.
13. Quoted in *Civil War Times Illustrated*, July 1966, 19; Freeman, *Lee's Lieutenants*, 1:159.
14. Freeman, *Lee's Lieutenants*, 1:240; Sifakis, *Who Was Who*, 550.
15. Foote, *Civil War Narrative*, 1:184.
16. Commager, *Blue and the Gray*, 2:974.
17. Foote, *Civil War Narrative*, 1:4.
18. *Civil War Times Illustrated*, December 1966, 13.
19. Foote, *Civil War Narrative*, 2:24.
20. *Civil War Times Illustrated*, July 1966, 13.
21. Braden, *Lincoln*, 120; Randall, *Lincoln*, 1:396; Neely, *Lincoln Encyclopedia*, 237.

12: Unsolved Mysteries

1. Freeman, *Lee's Lieutenants*, 1:81–82, 733–34; *OR*, 2:408, 474, 478, 481–82, 499.
2. *NOR*, 7:358–67; *OR*, 12:36; 68:13–19, 218–27, 975–99; 108:619; Commager, *Blue and Gray*, 2:269–70; *Blue & Gray*, October 1980, 59.
3. *OR*, 28:603–4; *Journal of the Southern Historical Society*, 12:519–20, 420; Freeman, *Lee's Lieutenants*, 2:73, 201, 715–23.
4. *Richmond Dispatch*, March 1864; *OR*, 60:178; Freeman, *Lee*, 3:219, n.10, 12; Freeman, *Lee's Lieutenants*, 3:334; Priest, *Antietam*, 70.
5. *Civil War Times Illustrated*, August 1960, 15; February 1980, 44; *Blue & Gray*, March 1985, 58ff; *Civil War*, 26:50; *America's Civil War*, May 1990, 12.
6. *Blue & Gray*, October 1984, 12ff; Warner, *Generals in Gray*, 315; Sifakis, *Who Was Who*, 673.
7. *OR*, 95:1317–18; 100:287, 302, 321, 346, 403; 102:104, 136; 121:696–99, 812, 852, 855–57, 860; Gutman, *Booth*; *Blue & Gray*, March 1984, 18ff; April 1990, 8ff; June 1990, 8ff; *America's Civil War*, March 1989, 27ff; *Civil War Times Illustrated*, February 1960, 12; February 1990, 60ff; August 1990, 8ff, 26ff, 90ff.

13: Waterworks

1. *OR*, 121:595.
2. Priest, *Antietam*, 79.
3. Moore, *Rebellion Record*, 3:32; (doc) 3:83, 439–42.
4. Nevins, *War*, 2:350.

5. *Civil War Times Illustrated*, July 1992, 44.
6. *OR*, 46:361.
7. Priest, *Antietam*, 166.
8. *Civil War Times Illustrated*, September 1992, 70.
9. Moore, *Rebellion Record*, 11:258.
10. *OR*, 77:524.
11. Ibid., 21:18.
12. *Confederate Veteran*, 9:27.
13. Ibid., 7:269.
14. *OR*, 122:929–31.
15. *America's Civil War*, May 1994, 79.
16. *Civil War Times Illustrated*, September 1988, 43; July 1989, 48.
17. *Confederate Veteran*, 2:309.
18. *OR*, 37:80.
19. Miers, *Lincoln*, 3:43; *Civil War*, 4:385–86; *MOLLUS*, 11:17.
20. *OR*, 24:181.
21. *Civil War*, 51:63.
22. Ibid., 52:37; Priest, *Antietam*, 86, 209.
23. Priest, *Antietam*, 89.
24. Moore, *Rebellion Record*, 3:83.

14: Factoids

1. *OR*, 96:1249; 32:82; *Confederate Veteran*, 20:379.
2. Lord, *They Fought for the Union*, 60.
3. FAP, 92–93.
4. Phisterer, *Statistical Record*, 212; Dyer, *Compendium*, 2:582.
5. *Civil War Times Illustrated*, September 1993, 60.
6. Sifakis, *Who Was Who*, 545, 325.
7. Long, *Day by Day*, 707.
8. Phisterer, *Statistical Record*, 247, 316; *Journal of the Southern Historical Society*, 36:105–20; Boatner, *Dictionary*, 328.
9. *Statistical History*, 17; Long, *Day by Day*, 701.
10. Long, *Day by Day*, 710.
11. *Civil War Times Illustrated*, August 1966, 33.
12. *MOLLUS*, 28:84.
13. Robertson, *Blue and Gray*, 190.
14. *Civil War*, 46:31.
15. Buel and Johnson, *Battles and Leaders*, 2:497–500.
16. Lord, *They Fought for the Union*, 219.
17. Long, *Day by Day*, 714.
18. *Civil War Chronicles*, 57.
19. *Civil War Times Illustrated*, September 1985, 40.
20. *Civil War Chronicles*, February 1992, 50.

21. Long, *Day by Day*, 266; *Blue & Gray*, January 1988, 22.
22. *Civil War Chronicles*, February 1992, 48; *Civil War Times Illustrated*, July 1993, 64.
23. *Civil War Times Illustrated*, January 1978, 25.
24. Sifakis, *Who Was Who*, 486.
25. Boatner, *Dictionary*, 78.
26. Sifakis, *Who Was Who*, 409–11.
27. Boatner, *Dictionary*, 622.
28. Mearns, *Lincoln Papers*, 588.
29. Moore, *Rebellion Record*, 6:6.
30. *Civil War Times Illustrated*, June 1997, 56.
31. Lord, *They Fought for the Union*, 219.
32. *Statistical History*, 899.
33. Roller and Twyman, *Encyclopedia of Southern History*, 410; Schwab, *Confederate States*, 41.
34. Miller, *Photographic History*, 8:58.
35. *Civil War Times Illustrated*, December 1984, 36.
36. *Blue & Gray*, February 1989, 31.
37. Nevins, *War*, 2:469.
38. *Civil War Times Illustrated*, July 1993, 64.
39. Sifakis, *Who Was Who*, 135.
40. Miller, *Photographic History*, 10:302, 318.
41. Lord, *They Fought for the Union*, 220.
42. Long, *Day by Day*, 707.
43. *America's Civil War*, May 1993, 70.
44. Sifakis, *Who Was Who*, 659.
45. Long, *Day by Day*, 714; Boatner, *Dictionary*, 75; *MOLLUS* 10:523.
46. Nofi, *Notebook*, 100.
47. Moore, *Rebellion Record* (doc), 8:67.
48. Boatner, *Dictionary*, 84.
49. Miller, *Photographic History*, 8:223.
50. *Civil War Times Illustrated*, July 1991, 39.

15: Lee to the Rear!

1. Freeman, *Lee*, 3:285–88, 4:52; Faust, *Encyclopedia*, 325; Commager, *Blue and the Gray*, 984, 996–99; *Blue & Gray*, June 1995, 12; Warner, *Generals in Gray*, 118; *Journal of the Southern Historical Society*, 24:80–81.
2. *Journal of the Southern Historical Society*, 10:518–20.
3. Tucker, *High Tide*, 354–67.
4. *OR*, 2:495, italics added.
5. Sifakis, *Who Was Who*, 43f.
6. *OR*, 2:492.

7. Ibid., 3:288.
8. Commager, *Blue and the Gray*, 342.
9. *OR*, 3:267–72.
10. Freeman, *Lee's Lieutenants*, 1:396–98.
11. Commager, *Blue and the Gray*, 159, 161, 163.
12. *Civil War*, 51:56.
13. *Rebellion Record* (doc), 5:309–12.
14. Commager, *Blue and the Gray*, 181.
15. Faust, *Encyclopedia*, 517.
16. Priest, *Antietam*, 111, 217, 277; Sifakis, *Who Was Who*, 309–10, 394.
17. Faust, *Encyclopedia*, 337, 369–70; Priest, *Antietam*, 99; Sifakis, *Who Was Who*, 318.
18. *Confederate Veteran*, 9:22–23.
19. *Civil War Times Illustrated*, October 1962, 23; Faust, *Encyclopedia*, 642–43, 722–23.
20. Sherman, *Memoirs*, 239.
21. Commager, *Blue and the Gray*, 262; Sifakis, *Who Was Who*, 631–32.
22. Faust, *Encyclopedia*, 424.
23. *Rebellion Record* (doc), 11:28.
24. Ibid., 11:36.
25. Ibid., 11:49.
26. Ibid., 11:62; Faust, *Encyclopedia*, 373.
27. Faust, *Encyclopedia*, 433.
28. *Civil War Times Illustrated*, June 1976, 5f.
29. Freeman, *Lee's Lieutenants*, 1:88; Faust, *Encyclopedia*, 818.
30. Faust, *Encyclopedia*, 242; Freeman, *Lee's Lieutenants*, 1:445.
31. Faust, *Encyclopedia*, 681.
32. Ibid., 569, 763.
33. *OR Sup*, 1:193; *Civil War Times Illustrated*, April 1972, 15; Faust, *Encyclopedia*, 454.
34. Evans, *Confederate Military History*, 14:74–75; *OR*, 8:218–19; Commager, *Blue and the Gray*, 191; Faust, *Encyclopedia*, 461, 468; Sifakis, *Who Was Who*, 69, 622.
35. Commager, *Blue and the Gray*, 219; Sifakis, *Who Was Who*, 432; Faust, *Encyclopedia*, 473.
36. Faust, *Encyclopedia*, 301, 323, 338.
37. *Confederate Veteran*, 2:271; Sifakis, *Who Was Who*, 15f.
38. Faust, *Encyclopedia*, 323, 515; Commager, *Blue and the Gray*, 991.
39. Faust, *Encyclopedia*, 799; Evans, *Confederate Military History*, 4:329.
40. Sifakis, *Who Was Who*, 127, 251; Faust, *Encyclopedia*, 145, 312, 317.
41. *Civil War Times Illustrated*, January 1995, 54–59; Faust, *Encyclopedia*, 767–68.

16: Destiny or Providence

1. Lossing, *Harper's Encyclopedia*, 9:175.
2. Ibid., 9:159; *Statistical History*, 8.
3. *Statistical History*, 8, 11.
4. Sandburg, *Lincoln*, 1:203; 2:495; 3:253, 268; 4:250.
5. Davis, *Davis*, 49–51.
6. Andrews, *Concise Dictionary*, 1015.
7. Freeman, *Lee*, 1:432–38.
8. *OR*, general index, 778.
9. Ibid., 5:981, 1027.
10. Long, *Day by Day*, 377–78; *Civil War Times Illustrated*, September 1988, 16.
11. Davis, *Davis*, 301–5.
12. Kane, *Presidents*, 92–93; *Statistical History*, 8.
13. *Civil War*, 4:190, 194, 208–9, 234–35; 5:186, 332–33, 496–97; 7:431–32, 533–34; 8:55–56.

17: Anonymous Aid

1. *MOLLUS*, 6:147–67.
2. *OR*, 1:344.
3. *MOLLUS*, 1:47.
4. *OR*, 60:683.
5. Ibid., 60:689.
6. Moore, *Rebellion Record*, 2:63.
7. *OR*, 27:89; *MOLLUS*, 4:167.
8. *OR*, 21:266.
9. *NOR*, 13:116.
10. *OR*, 21:134.
11. *NOR*, 13:161.
12. *OR*, 21:22.
13. *NOR*, 13:199.
14. *OR*, 13:131.
15. *NOR*, 5:210.
16. *OR*, 60:695.
17. Ibid., 5:591.
18. Ibid., 21:245.
19. *NOR*, 5:600.
20. *OR*, 60:642.
21. *MOLLUS*, 14:120.
22. *NOR*, 22:311.
23. Ibid., 5:224.
24. *OR*, 21:375.

26. Ibid., 456.
27. *OR*, 60:189.
28. *NOR*, 5:266.
29. Ibid., 17:634.
30. Ibid., 13:77.
31. Ibid., 13:123.
32. *OR*, 21:554.
33. *NOR*, 14:152.
34. Ibid., 1:577.
35. *OR*, 129:325; Boatner, *Dictionary*, 461.

18: Numero Uno

2. *Civil War Times Illustrated*, April 1973, 9.
3. *Civil War*, 36:28.
4. Mosocco, *Chronological Tracking*, 36.
5. *Civil War Times Illustrated*, October 1981, 26.
6. Ibid., July 1980, 32f; Davis, *Bull Run*, 177, 204–5.
7. *OR*, 2:361f.
8. Ibid., 2:188–90; *Civil War Times Illustrated*, August 1980, 50.
9. *OR*, 2:81–86, 938; *Civil War Times Illustrated*, August 1980, 51.
10. *Civil War Times Illustrated*, August 1980, 50; *OR*, 2:92.
11. Ibid., August 1980, 50.
12. *MOLLUS*, 7:350.
13. *OR*, 29:201, 674; Buel and Johnson, *Battles and Leaders*, 3:611–12, 632.
14. *OR*, 3:285, emphasis added.
15. *MOLLUS*, 11:400.
16. *America's Civil War*, May 1997, 22.
17. *OR*, 1:65, 461–63.
18. Sifakis, *Who Was Who*, 731.
19. *OR*, 1:578.
20. *Confederate Veteran*, 5:406.
21. Robertson, *Blue and Gray*, 192.
22. Miller, *Photographic History*, 204.
23. Ibid., 68.
24. *NOR*, 3:483.
25. Faust, *Encyclopedia*, 837; Sifakis, *Who Was Who*, 725.
26. Buel and Johnson, *Battles and Leaders*, 1:119.
27. Wheeler, *Voices*, 51.
28. *Columbiad*, 1:128–36; *OR*, 114:387–89.
29. *NOR*, 11:1, 42, 148.

30. Mosocco, *Chronological Tracking,* 10; *NOR,* 4:220–23; 24:541; 25:755f.

19: Armed Protectors

1. Davis, *Great Battles,* 308; Sherman, *Memoirs,* 2:78; *OR,* 76:38, 232, 288, 556–57.
2. *OR,* 7:744–46.
3. *Journal of the Southern Historical Society,* 29:329–31.
4. Longstreet, *Manassas to Appomattox,* 1:29–30.
5. *OR,* 5:494.
6. Ibid., 4:383–84.
7. Ibid., 5:870.
8. Ibid., 5:541.
9. Ibid., 2:341.
10. Ibid., 2:738.
11. Ibid., 5:544.
12. Ibid., 8:201.
13. Ibid., 3:39.
14. Ibid., 7:772.
15. Ibid., 8:720.
16. Ibid., 3:35.
17. Ibid., 2:572.
18. Ibid., 4:424.
19. Ibid., 6:193.
20. Ibid., 64:615.
21. Ibid., 5:170–72.
22. Ibid., 5:438.
23. *Blue & Gray,* November 1961, 32; Buel and Johnson, *Battles and Leaders,* 2:598f.
24. *Rebellion Record* (doc), 6:230–33.
25. Buel and Johnson, *Battles and Leaders,* 2:598–600.
26. *Confederate Veteran,* 1:76; *MOLLUS,* 6:26; Buel and Johnson, *Battles and Leaders,* 4:284.
27. Denney, 63; *MOLLUS,* 15:70; Priest, *Antietam,* 23; *OR,* 8:200; *MOLLUS,* 14:234; *Civil War Times Illustrated,* July 1994, 56; Buel and Johnson, *Battles and Leaders,* 2:495, 497; *Rebellion Record* (doc), 6:230–33, Moore, *Rebellion Record* (p), 6:5.
28. Priest, *Antietam,* 23; *Journal of the Southern Historical Society,* 15:7–9.
29. *Confederate Veteran,* 9:268; 12:426; 35:278, 452–54; *OR,* 8:269f.
30. *OR,* 2:758.
31. Ibid., 6:33.
32. Ibid., 3:249–53, 18:14, 107:568; Moore, *Rebellion Record,* 3:56; *Journal of the Southern Historical Society,* 3:195–96.

20: Family Ties

1. OR, 33:482–88; Civil War, 6:423–24.
2. Warner, Generals in Blue, 147; DeGregorio, Presidents, 508; America's Civil War, January 1990, 50; Civil War, January 1992, 22.
3. OR, 2:253, 286; 5:186; 59:69; MOLLUS, 7:445–46; Sifakis, Who Was Who, 695.
4. Sifakis, Who Was Who, 530f; Blue & Gray, October 1992, 41; Warner, Generals in Gray, 252.
5. Warner, Generals in Gray, 98–99; Faust, Encyclopedia, 299.
6. Dictionary of American Biography; National Cyclopedia of American Biography, 8:351; Sifakis, Who Was Who, 2; Faust, Encyclopedia, 1–4.
7. Boatner, Dictionary, 378; Sifakis, Who Was Who, 286; Dictionary of American Biography; National Cyclopedia of American Biography, 1:133.
8. Warner, Generals in Gray, 299–300; Boatner, Dictionary, 827; Dictionary of American Biography; National Cyclopedia of American Biography, 4:331; Commager, Blue and the Gray, 150f.
9. Journal of the Southern Historical Society, 15:76; Confederate Veteran, 5:469.
10. Sifakis, Who Was Who, 728; Civil War Times Illustrated, May 1976, 30f; May 1970, 4f; Dictionary of American Biography; National Cyclopedia of American Biography, 12:428; NOR, 2:3, 5, 7–12, 15, 28–30.
11. OR, 16:337, 378.
12. Ibid., 16:342; 122:269, 271, 287, 341–42; Civil War, 4:336, 405; Sifakis, Who Was Who, 700.
13. Confederate Veteran, 2:282; OR, 8:313; 24:257, 388, 390; 38:705.
14. MOLLUS, 13:299.
15. Boatner, Dictionary, 173.
16. Dictionary of American Biography; Davis, Great Battles, 34; National Cyclopedia of American Biography, 2:312, 4:272.
17. OR, 1:414, 415; 5:23, 752, 757; 108:39; 122:249; Boatner, Dictionary, 28; Dictionary of American Biography; National Cyclopedia of American Biography, 8:102, 104, 106; 9:11.
18. Allardice, More Generals in Gray, 61–62.
19. Sifakis, Who Was Who, 315; Civil War, 13:74f; Blue & Gray, March 1984, 47f; January 1987, 4f.
20. McHenry, Liberty's Women, 231–32; Nevins, War, 2:132; Civil War, 4:331–33.
21. McHenry, Liberty's Women, 240; Moore, Rebellion Record (p), 5:11.
22. Warner, Generals in Gray, 216–17; McHenry, Liberty's Women, 280; Sifakis, Who Was Who, 444.
23. Boatner, Dictionary, 692–92; Sifakis, Who Was Who, 538.

24. McHenry, *Liberty's Women*, 485; Warner, *Generals in Gray*, 340–41; *Dictionary of American Biography; National Cyclopedia of American Biography*, 9:298, 10:487.

25. Sifakis, *Who Was Who*, 515; McHenry, *Liberty's Women*, 328, 329; *NOR*, 1:3, 4, 5–13, 16–19, 22–24, 27–28; *OR*, 1:6, 7, 9, 19, 21, 20, 22–24, 60, 42, 111, 117–19, 128.

26. *OR*, 44:364; *Dictionary of American Biography; National Cyclopedia of American Biography*, 18:72, *Civil War Times Illustrated*, October 1965, 41f; May 1992, 39.

27. Warner, *Generals in Gray*, 111; *Dictionary of American Biography; National Cyclopedia of American Biography*, 12:295, 32:4.

28. *America's Civil War*, July 1995, 6; *Dictionary or American Biography*.

29. *Dictionary of American Biography*; McHenry, *Liberty's Women*, 286.

30. Faust, *Encyclopedia*, 485; McHenry, *Liberty's Women*, 355.

31. McHenry, *Liberty's Women*, 177; *Confederate Veteran*, 7:415; *Journal of the Southern Historical Society*, 17:34–46; 22:127–46; 35:274–75, 277–78; 36:233.

32. *Civil War Times Illustrated*, June 1961, 18; October 1995, 37f; McHenry, *Liberty's Women*, 312–13.

33. *OR*, 8:286, 787; 21:14–19; 25:835; 102:1273; 111:796; McHenry, *Liberty's Women*, 217.

Bibliography

Abbott, John S. *History of the Civil War in America.* 2 vols. N.p., 1863–66.
Abbott, Willis J. *The Naval History of the United States.* 2 vols. New York: n.p., 1886.
Allardice, Bruce S. *More Generals in Gray.* Baton Rouge: Louisiana State University Press, 1995.
The American Annual Cyclopedia and Register, 1861–65. 5 vols. New York: Appleton, 1870–74.
American Heritage.
American History Illustrated.
America's Civil War.
Andrews, Wayne, ed. *Concise Dictionary of American History.* New York: Scribner's, 1961.
Beatly, John. *Memoirs of a Volunteer.* Edited by Harvey S. Ford. 1879. Reprint, New York: Norton, 1946.
Bernard, George S. *War Talks of Confederate Veterans.* Petersburg: N.p., 1892.
Blue & Gray.
Boatner, Mark M., III. *The Civil War Dictionary.* Rev. ed. New York: McKay, 1988.
Botkin, Benjamin A., ed. *A Civil War Treasury of Tales, Legends, and Folklore.* New York: Random House, 1960.
Braden, Waldo W. *Abraham Lincoln, Public Speaker.* Baton Rouge: Louisiana State University Press, 1988.
Britton, Wiley. *Memoirs of the Rebellion on the Border, 1863.* Chicago: Cushing, Thomas & Co., 1882. Reprint, Lincoln: University of Nebraska Press, 1993.
Buell, Clarence C., and Robert V. Johnson, eds. *Battles and Leaders of the Civil War.* 4 vols. New York: Century, 1884–88. Reprint, Secaucus, N.J.: Castle, 1985.
Carpenter, Francis B. *Six Months at the White House with Abraham Lincoln.* New York: Hurd and Houghton, 1866.
Castel, Albert. *Decision in the West: The Atlanta Campaign of 1864.* Lawrence: University Press of Kansas, 1992.
Catton, Bruce. *The American Heritage Picture History of the Civil War.* New York: American Heritage Publishing Co., 1960.
———. *The Civil War.* New York: American Heritage Press, 1971.
The Charleston Courier.
The Charleston Mercury.
Chesnut, Mary Boykin. *A Diary from Dixie.* New York: Appleton, 1905.
Civil War.

Civil War Chronicles.

Civil War Times and *Civil War Times Illustrated.*

Clark, Walter A. *Under the Stars and Bars.* Augusta, Ga.: Chronicle Printing Co., 1900. Reprint, Jamesboro, Ga.: Freedom Hill Press, 1987.

Columbiad.

Commager, Henry Steele, ed. *The Blue and the Gray.* 2 vols. Indianapolis: Bobbs Merrill, 1950. Reprint, New York: Meridian, 1994.

The Confederate Veteran, 1893–1932.

Cooling, Benjamin F. *Jubal Early's Raid on Washington 1864.* Baltimore: Nautical & Aviation Publishing Co., 1989.

Dana, Charles A. *Recollections of the Civil War.* New York: Appleton, 1898. Reprint, Lincoln: University of Nebraska Press, 1996.

Davis, Jefferson. *The Rise and Fall of the Confederate Government.* 2 vols. Richmond: Garrett and Massie, 1881. Reprint, New York: Da Capo Press, 1990.

Davis, William C. *Battle at Bull Run.* Garden City, N.Y.: Doubleday, 1977. Reprint, Mechanicsburg, Pa.: Stackpole, 1995.

———, ed. *Great Battles of the Civil War.* New York: Gallery, 1989.

———. *Jefferson Davis: The Man and His Hour.* New York: Harper-Collins, 1991.

DeGregario, William. *The Complete Book of U.S. Presidents.* Fourth ed. New York: Wings, 1993.

Devens, Richard M. *The Pictorial Book of Anecdotes and Incidents of the War of the Rebellion.* Hartford: Hartford, 1866.

Dunaway, Wayland F. *Reminiscences of a Rebel.* New York: Neale, 1913.

Dyer, Frederick H. *A Compendium of the War of the Rebellion.* 3 vols. Reprint, New York: Yoseloff 1959.

Evans, Clement A., ed. *Confederate Military History.* 17 vols. 1899. Reprint, Wilmington, N.C.: Broadfoot, 1987–89.

Faust, Patricia L., ed. *Historical Times Illustrated Encyclopedia of the Civil War.* New York: Harper and Row, 1986.

Foote, Shelby. *The Civil War: A Narrative.* 3 vols. New York: Random House, 1958–74.

Forbes, Edwin. *Civil War Etchings.* 1876. Reprint, New York: Dover, 1994.

———. *Thirty Years After: An Artist's Memoir of the Civil War.* New York: Fords, Howard & Hulbert, 1890. Reprint, Baton Rouge: Louisiana State University Press, 1993.

Frank Leslie's Illustrated History of the Civil War. New York: Leslie's, 1895.

Frank Leslie's Illustrated Weekly.

Freeman, Douglas Southall. *R. E. Lee.* 4 vols. New York: Scribner's, 1949–51.

Fuller, Charles A. *Personal Recollections.* Shirburne, N.Y.: News, 1906.

Furness, Henry B. *Prisoners of War and Military Prisons.* Cincinnati: Lyman and Cushing, 1890.

Gordon, John B. *Reminiscences of the Civil War.* New York: Scribner's, 1903. Reprint, Baton Rouge: Louisiana State University Press, 1993.

Gragg, Rod. *The Civil War Quiz and Fact Book.* New York: Harper & Row, 1985.

Gutman, Richard J. S., and Kellie O. Gutman. *John Wilkes Booth Himself.* Dover, Mass.: Hired Hand, 1979.

Harper's Pictorial History of the Civil War. New York: Harper's, 1866.

Harper's Weekly.

Hay, John. *Lincoln and the Civil War.* New York: Dodd, Meade, 1939. Reprint, New York: Da Capo Press, 1988.

Herbert, George B. *The Model History of the War.* Springfield, Ohio: Mast, 1889.

Hewett, Janet B. et al., eds. *Supplement to the Official Records of the Union and Confederate Armies.* 10 vols. Wilmington, N.C.: Broadfoot, 1994–97.

Higginson, Thomas W. *Army Life in a Black Regiment.* Boston: Fields, Osgood, 1870. Reprint, New York: Penguin Books, 1997.

———. *Letters and Journals.* Boston: Harvard University Press, 1921. Reprint, New York: Negro Universities Press, 1969.

Jeffcoat, Francis R. *Confederate Records, Lancaster District, South Carolina.* Columbia, S.C.: Jeffcoat, 1986.

Joint Committee on the Conduct of the War. *Report.* 3 vols. Washington, D.C.: Government Printing Office, 1863.

Kane, Joseph Nathan. *Facts About the Presidents.* New York: Wilson, 1989.

Keesy, William A. *War as Viewed from the Ranks.* Norwalk, Ohio: Experiment and News, 1898.

La Bree, Benjamin. *The Pictorial Battles of the Civil War.* 2 vols. New York: Sherman, 1885.

Leech, Margaret. *Reveille in Washington.* New York: Harper and Row, 1941. Reprint, Alexandria, Va.: Time-Life Books, 1980.

Lincoln, Abraham. *The Collected Works of Abraham Lincoln.* Edited by Roy P. Basler and Christian O. Basler. 9 vols. New Brunswick, N.J.: Rutgers University Press, 1953–55.

Long, E. B., and Barbara Long. *The Civil War Day by Day.* Garden City, N.Y.: Doubleday, 1971. Reprint, New York: Da Capo Press, 1985.

Longacre, Edward G. *Pickett.* Shippensburg, Pa.: White Mane, 1995.

Lord, Francis A. *They Fought for the Union.* Harrisburg, Pa.: Stackpole, 1960. Reprint, New York: Bonanza, 1988.

Lossing, Benson J., ed. *Harper's Encyclopaedia of U.S. History.* 19 vols. New York: Harper, 1901. Reprint, Detroit: Gale Research Co., 1974.

———. *Pictorial Field Book of the Civil War.* 3 vols. Hartford: T. Belknap, 1870–76. Reprint, Baltimore: Johns Hopkins University Press, 1997.

Mathews, Mitford M., ed. *A Dictionary of Americanisms on Historical Principles.* 2 vols. Chicago: University of Chicago Press, 1951.

Marrin, Albert. *Unconditional Surrender: U. S. Grant and the Civil War.* New York: Atheneum, 1994.

Marszalek, John F. *Sherman: A Soldier's Passion for Order.* New York: Free Press, 1993.

McHenry, Robert, ed. *Liberty's Women.* Springfield: Merriam, 1980.

McPherson, James M. *Battle Cry of Freedom.* New York: Oxford University Press, 1988.

Mearns, David C., ed. *The Lincoln Papers.* 2 vols. Garden City, N.Y.: Doubleday, 1948.

Miers, Earl S., ed. *Lincoln Day by Day.* 3 vols. Washington, D.C.: Lincoln Sesquicentennical Commission, 1960.

Mitgang, Herbert. *Lincoln as They Saw Him.* New York: Rinehart, 1956. Reprint, New York: Octagon Books, 1980.

Mosocco, Ronald A. *The Chronological Tracking of the American Civil War per the Official Records.* Williamsburg, Va.: James River Publications, 1994.

Mottelay, Paul F., ed. *The Soldier in Our Civil War.* New York: J. H. Brown, 1884–85. Reprint, Jackson: University Press of Mississippi, 1992.

The National Cyclopedia of American Biography. 63 vols. New York: J. T. White, 1898– . Reprint, Ann Arbor: University Microfilms, 1967.

Neely, Mark E., Jr., ed. *The Abraham Lincoln Encyclopedia.* New York: McGraw-Hill, 1982. Reprint, New York: Da Capo Press, 1984.

———. *The Fate of Liberty.* New York: Oxford University Press, 1991.

New York Illustrated News.

Nicolay, John G., and John Hay. *Abraham Lincoln: A History.* 10 vols. New York: Century, 1890. Reprint, Chicago: University of Chicago Press, 1966.

Nofi, Albert A. *The Civil War Notebook.* Conshohocken, Pa.: Combined, 1993.

Page, Thomas Nelson. *Works.* 18 vols. New York: Scribner, 1906. Reprint, Grosse Point, Mich.: Scholarly Press, 1968.

Perkins, Howard C., ed. *Northern Editorials on Secession.* 2 vols. New York: Appleton, 1942.

Phisterer, Frederick. *Statistical Record of the Armies of the United States.* New York: Scribner's, 1883.

Pratt, Fletcher. *Stanton.* New York: Norton, 1953. Reprint, Westport, Conn.: Greenwood Press, 1970.

Priest, John M. *Antietam.* Shippensburg, Pa: White Mane, 1989.

———. *Before Antietam: South Mountain.* Shippensburg, Pa: White Mane, 1992.

Randall, James G. *Lincoln the President.* 4 vols. New York: Dodd, 1945–55.

Ray, Frederick E. *Our Special Artist: Alfred R. Waud's Civil War*. New York: Viking, 1974. Reprint, Mechanicsburg, Pa.: Stackpole, 1994.

Robertson, James I. *Soldiers Blue and Gray*. Columbia: University of South Carolina Press, 1988. Reprint, New York: Viking, 1991.

Roller, David C., and Robert W. Twyman, eds. *The Encyclopedia of Southern History*. Baton Rouge: Louisiana State University Press, 1979.

Sandburg, Carl, *Abraham Lincoln: The War Years*. 4 vols. New York: Harcourt, 1939.

Scharf, John T. *History of the Confederate States Navy*. 2 vols. New York: Rogers & Sherwood, 1887. Reprint, Freeport, N.Y.: Books for Libraries Press, 1969.

Schwab, John C. *The Confederate States of America*. New York: Scribner's, 1901. Reprint, New York: Burt Franklin, 1968.

Shane, Norman. *The Atlanta Century*. Atlanta: Capricorn, 1981.

Sherman, William T. *Memoirs*. 2 vols. New York: Appleton, 1875. Reprint, New York: Library of America, 1990.

Sifakis, Stewart. *Who Was Who in the Civil War*. New York: Facts on File, 1988.

Speed, Thomas. *Who Fought the Battle*. Louisville: Nunemacher, 1904.

Thompson, Holland. *The Photographic History of the Civil War*. 10 vols. New York: Review of Reviews, 1912.

Tucker, Glenn. *Chickamauga*. Indianapolis: Bobbs-Merrill, 1961.

———. *High Tide at Gettysburg*. Indianapolis: Bobbs-Merrill, 1958.

Turner, George E. *Victory Rode the Rails*. Indianapolis: Bobbs-Merrill, 1953. Reprint, Lincoln: University of Nebraska Press, 1992.

The Union Army, 1861–66. 8 vols. Madison, Wis.: Federal, 1908.

U.S. Navy Department. *Official Records of the Union and Confederate Navies in the War of the Rebellion*. 31 vols. Washington, D.C.: Government Printing Office, 1894–1927.

U.S. War Department. *The War of the Rebellion: A Compilation of the Official Records of the Union and Confederate Armies*. 128 vols. Washington, D.C.: Government Printing Office, 1880–1901.

Warner, Ezra J. *Generals in Blue*. Baton Rouge: Louisiana State University Press, 1964

———. *Generals in Gray*. Baton Rouge: Louisiana State University Press, 1959.

Wheeler, Richard. *Voices of the Civil War*. New York: Crowell, 1976.

Wilcox, Arthur M., and Warren Ripley. *The Civil War at Charleston*. Charleston: News and Courier, 1966.

Wiley, Bell I. *The Common Soldier in the Civil War*. New York: Grossett & Dunlap, 1958.

Williams, T. Harry. *The History of American Wars*. New York: Knopf, 1981.

————. *Lincoln and His Generals.* New York: Knopf, 1952.

Wills, Mary Alice. *The Confederate Blockade of Washington, D.C.* Parsons, W.V.: McClain Printing Co., 1975. Reprint, Shippensburg, Pa.: Burd Street Press, 1998.

Index

Illustrations are noted by **boldface.**

273

Webb Garrison is a veteran writer who lives in Lake Junaluska, North Carolina. Formerly associate dean of Emory University and president of McKendree College, he has written more than forty books, including *A Treasury of Civil War Tales, Civil War Curiosities, Lincoln's Little War,* and *Atlanta and the War.*